"Che is not only an intellectual, he was the most complete human being of our age."
JEAN-PAUL SARTRE

"In these present times, when for many ethics and other profound moral values are seen to be so easily bought and sold, the example of Che Guevara takes on an even greater dimension."
RIGOBERTA MENCHU

"The powerful of the earth should take heed: deep inside that T-shirt where we have tried to trap him the eyes of Che Guevara are still burning with impatience."
ARIEL DORFMAN

"There are people who carry inside them the dignity of the world, and one of those is Che."
FIDEL CASTRO

"Che symbolizes not selling out, staying true to what you believe in."
BENICIO DEL TORO

e agotadoras jornadas noc

pectivas inmediatas de acelerar la marcha

la tropa montada a medias y sin monturas.

aqui, en la arrocera Bartles, pero no llegó.

o se ha visto ni un casquito y los aviones

scuchada con muchas dificultades a travez d

Todo indeca que los guardias no quiere

ngo miedo a una retirada con 150 inexpertos

rrilla armada de 30 hombres puede hacer ma

o deje las bases de un sindicato arrocero

on al suelo. No es que haya claudicado fren

excesiva, les dije que eso se podría convers

o con conciencia social puede hacer maravil

nderse. De mis planes futuros no te puedo d

yo mismo no lo se; depende más bien de cir

e estamos esperando unos camiones para ver

los tiempos ana

I embrace you with all my revolutionary fervor

Letters 1947–1967

I embrace you with all my revolutionary fervor

Letters 1947–1967

ERNESTO CHE GUEVARA

*Edited and introduced by María del Carmen Ariet García
and Disamis Arcia Muñoz*

Foreword by Aleida Guevara

Centro de Estudios
CHE GUEVARA

SEVEN STORIES PRESS
New York • Oakland

First trade paperback edition June 2023.

Published by Seven Stories Press on behalf of Ocean Press, Melbourne,
Australia, and the Che Guevara Studies Center, Havana. Direct all rights inquiries
and permissions questions to rights@sevenstories.com.

Library of Congress Cataloging-in-Publication Data is on file.
ISBN: 978-1-64421-095-6 (hardcover)
ISBN: 978-1-64421-244-8 (paperback)
ISBN 978-1-64421-096-3 (e-book)

Printed in the USA

Published in Spanish by Ocean Sur as
Te abraza con todo fervor revolucionario, ISBN 978-1-925756-39-5 (paper);
ISBN 978-1-64421-123-6 (e-book)

9 8 7 6 5 4 3 2 1

Contents

**LETTERS FROM THE GUERRILLA WAR
IN CUBA (1956–1959)**

LETTERS AS A LEADER OF THE REVOLUTIONARY GOVERNMENT (1959–1965)

Reading my father's letters

Aleida Guevara[1]

This book is a real gem in the collaborative publishing project between the Che Guevara Studies Center (Havana) and Ocean Press and Ocean Sur. As a selection of his letters, it reveals the intimate side of the man my father was. We often might not know a person very well, but when we read their letters we learn who they really are. And this is what makes this book very special for me because they are letters from different periods of his life and show the development of a real person, the evolution of a human being.

In preparing a speech, Che would carefully weigh his words and plan what he was going to say. He was usually quite animated when giving a speech, clearly presenting his thoughts. In his letters to family and friends, however, he reveals himself candidly, spontaneously. So reading my father's letters is a fascinating way to really get to know him. The Cuban writer Miguel Barnet recently commented what a shame it is that we no longer write letters. And it's true. All you receive these days is an e-mail or a message on your cell phone. Hand-written letters are a lost art, which is a pity because, as you read this book, you can witness how a young person changes over time.

The initial selection of letters are from his youth, when Ernesto leaves Argentina for the first time. In a letter to his mother, whom he playfully calls *Vieja* or Old Lady, he writes:

---

1   Excerpts from Aleida Guevara's remarks at the Havana launch of the Spanish edition of this book in 2019.

I am certain of two things: first is that if I reach my truly creative phase at about 35, my exclusive, or at least main, concern will be nuclear physics, or genetics, or some other field that brings together the most interesting aspects of knowledge. The second is that the Americas will be the theater of my adventures in a way that is much more significant than I could have imagined. I think I have really come to understand it and I feel [Latin] American, which means having a character distinct from all other peoples on the earth. Naturally, I'll visit the rest of the world.

Starting out as a carefree traveler and ambitious scientific researcher, he writes to his mother that his worldview is becoming much "sharper" after witnessing first hand the 1954 US-backed overthrow of the democratically elected government of Guatemala:

The way that the gringos treat Latin America (remember that the gringos are Yankees) was making me feel increasingly indignant, but at the same time I studied the reasons for their actions and found a scientific explanation. Then came Guatemala and everything that is difficult to describe.

On the birth of his first child, Hilda, in February 1956, he writes addressing his mother as *Abuelita* [Granny]:

Both of us are a bit older, or if you consider yourself a fruit, a bit more mature. The baby is rather ugly, but you only have to look at her to realize that she is different from all other children of her age. Although she cries when she is hungry, pees herself frequently, light bothers her and she sleeps most of the time, there is something that immediately differentiates her from every other baby: her papa is called Ernesto Guevara.

That's my father!

Another of the most interesting letters in this book is one Che wrote as a leader of the revolutionary government to the director of the Cuban magazine *Bohemia* in May 1959, responding to personal criticisms made against him as a foreigner and outsider in Cuba:

It is not my intention to defend myself against the fallacious imputations and the insidious reference to my Argentine citizenship. I am Argentine and I shall never renounce my country of origin (if you will excuse my audacity in the comparison, neither did [Cuban independence hero] Máximo Gómez renounce his Dominican homeland). But I feel Cuban, independently of whether the laws certify it or not: as a Cuban, I shared the sacrifices of the people throughout the armed struggle and today I share their hopes of bringing them to fruition.[2]

There are many letters here that I am sure the reader will enjoy, including some sent to my mother during his travels abroad representing the Cuban revolutionary government, such as this one written only weeks after my parents were married in 1959:

They decorated me with the Order of the Republic [in Egypt]. A very big medal that looks great on me, and not just because I say so. I went to the silver market to buy you a bracelet but I didn't see anything resembling what I wanted for you, although I am bringing you a few other little things. So far the trip has gone very fast; we haven't had much of a chance to see anything, and it was the same in the UAR [United Arab Republic]. I'm sleeping very little and my eyelids are starting to stick together.

The following day the Cuban delegation visited Gaza and they were horrified at the conditions endured by the Palestinians living there.

---

2   Ernesto Che Guevara was granted Cuban citizenship on February 9, 1959.

I went to visit the Brazilian officials who are looking after those areas. I established new diplomatic norms of confraternity between peoples by falling asleep on the shoulder of the Egyptian official who was accompanying me.

He wrote some other delightful letters to my mother. I love this little fragment:

I can't write much because time is short. I only want to tell you that I bought you a beautiful kimono that has a special enchantment for me because of the enchanting geisha who modeled it.

You see, my mother is the jealous type.

There is a special letter written to Ernesto Sábato, an Argentine writer, in which Che explains the process of the Cuban revolution and how he saw Fidel's role. Che describes Fidel as steadfast, always on the frontline and someone who was always honest about what he was going to do. The United States government, Che comments to his fellow Argentine, had its own expectations of Latin American political leaders and Fidel's honesty confused them. To them, what the Cuban government said about the agrarian reform, for example, meant that it would not carry out the agrarian reform if they gave Cuba sufficient money. So when the revolutionary government did what it said it would do, the US government genuinely believed the Cubans had lied. It could never understand that the revolutionary leaders were being truthful.

My father's sense of humor is evident in many letters, such as the one written to Dr. Eduardo Ordaz, who was responsible for publishing 6,300 copies of a journal on psychiatry in Cuba. Che writes he is on "the verge of neuro-economic psychosis" because he thinks that 3,000 too many copies have been printed, given that there were only about 3,000 doctors in Cuba at the time:

Are the rats using the magazine to deepen their knowledge of psychiatry or to fill their stomachs? Or perhaps every patient gets a copy of the publication?

Che applauds the quality of the magazine but remarks, "the number of copies is intolerable. Believe me, because crazy people always tell the truth."

Che's previously unpublished letter to Fidel of March 26, 1965, is one of the most important in the book. It is a truly fascinating analysis of the situation in Cuba. He shares his thoughts about errors in the approach to political economy, the budgetary finance system, the internal functioning of the newly formed Communist Party and a range of other issues. He outlines his views about the importance of political consciousness in the challenge of creating a new society, explaining that the new human being will emerge in the process of transforming Cuba's economy.

The book ends with several letters of farewell, which I cannot read without crying. When I was about to turn six, he wrote to us, his children, from Bolivia.

I write to you from far away and in great haste, which means I can't tell you about my latest adventures. It's a pity, because they've been very interesting [....]

Right now I want to tell you that I love you all very much and I think about you all the time, along with mama, although I really only know the littlest ones through photos, as you were very tiny when I left. I'm going to get a photo taken soon so that you can see what I look like these days — a little older and uglier.

My father instructs me, as the oldest child, to "study hard and help [my] mother in every way [I] can." He reminds Camilo not to swear at school and learn "what is appropriate." His youngest child, Ernesto, he hopes will grow up and, as a man, be ready to fight imperialism. And if imperialism has already been defeated, he promises to take him and Camilo on a vacation to the moon.

I was annoyed when I read this letter as a child. Why wasn't I going to the moon with my brothers, while my sister Celia and I were advised to be good little girls and help out at home? Later I came to forgive him when I saw that he had so many photographs of me in his office. I realized that, although he would never take me to the moon, he always carried me in his heart.

Ernesto Che Guevara: Biographical note

One of *Time* magazine's "icons of the century," Ernesto Guevara de la Serna was born in Rosario, Argentina, on June 14, 1928. He made several trips around Latin America during and immediately after his studies at medical school in Buenos Aires, including his 1952 journey with Alberto Granado, on the unreliable Norton motorcycle described in his early journal, *The Motorcycle Diaries*.

He became involved in political activity while living in Guatemala in 1954, before the elected government of Jacobo Árbenz was overthrown in a CIA-organized military operation. Ernesto escaped to Mexico, profoundly radicalized.

Following up on a contact made in Guatemala, Guevara sought out the group of exiled Cuban revolutionaries in Mexico City. In July 1955, he met Fidel Castro and immediately enlisted in the guerrilla expedition to overthrow Cuban dictator Fulgencio Batista. The Cubans nicknamed him "Che," a popular form of address in Argentina.

On November 25, 1956, Guevara set sail for Cuba aboard the cabin cruiser *Granma* as the doctor to the guerrilla group that began the revolutionary armed struggle in Cuba's Sierra Maestra mountains. Within several months, he was appointed by Fidel Castro as the first Rebel Army commander, although he continued ministering medically to wounded guerrilla fighters and captured soldiers from Batista's army.

In September 1958, Guevara played a decisive role in the military defeat of Batista after he and Camilo Cienfuegos led separate guerrilla columns westward from the Sierra Maestra to the center of the island.

After Batista fled on January 1, 1959, Guevara became a key leader of the new revolutionary government, first as head of the Department of Industrialization of the National Institute of Agrarian Reform (INRA), and then as president of the National Bank. In February 1961, he was appointed minister of industry. He was also a central leader of the political organization that in 1965 became the Cuban Communist Party.

Apart from these responsibilities, Guevara represented the Cuban revolutionary government around the world, heading numerous delegations and speaking at the United Nations and other international forums in Asia, Africa, Latin America and the socialist bloc countries. He earned a reputation as a passionate and articulate spokesperson for Third World peoples, most famously at the 1961 conference at Punta del Este in Uruguay, where he denounced US President Kennedy's Alliance for Progress.

As had been his stated intention since joining the Cuban revolutionary movement, Guevara left Cuba in April 1965, first to lead a Cuban-organized guerrilla mission to support the revolutionary struggle in the Congo, Africa. He returned to Cuba secretly in December 1965, to prepare another Cuban-organized guerrilla force for Bolivia. Arriving in Bolivia in November 1966, Guevara's plan was to challenge that country's military dictatorship and eventually to instigate a revolutionary movement that would extend throughout the continent of Latin America. The journal he kept during the Bolivian campaign became known as *The Bolivian Diary*. Che was wounded and captured by US-trained and run Bolivian counterinsurgency troops on October 8, 1967. The following day he was murdered in cold blood and his body hidden.

Che Guevara's remains were finally discovered in 1997 and returned to Cuba. A memorial was built at Santa Clara in central Cuba, where he had won a major military battle during the war against the Batista dictatorship.

CHRONOLOGY

June 14, 1928 Ernesto Guevara is born in Rosario, Argentina to parents Ernesto Guevara Lynch and Celia de la Serna; he will be the eldest of five children (Roberto, Celia, Ana María and Juan Martín).

January 1, 1950 Young Ernesto sets out on a 4,000-kilometer trip on a motorized bicycle through the northern provinces of Argentina.

January–July 1952 He travels around Latin America with his friend Alberto Granado, starting out on a vintage Norton motorcycle.

March 10, 1952 General Fulgencio Batista carries out a coup d'état in Cuba.

July 6, 1953 After graduating as a doctor on June 12, Ernesto sets off again to travel through Latin America. He visits Bolivia, observing the aftermath of the 1952 revolution.

July 26, 1953 Fidel Castro leads an unsuccessful armed attack on the Moncada army garrison in Santiago de Cuba, launching the revolutionary struggle to overthrow the Batista regime.

December 1953 Ernesto meets a group of Cuban survivors of the Moncada attack in San José, Costa Rica. He travels on to Guatemala, where the land reform program of the popularly elected government of Jacobo Árbenz is challenging the control of the United Fruit Company.

September 21, 1954 Ernesto flees Guatemala, after a CIA-backed military coup topples President Árbenz and brutally suppresses his supporters. In Mexico City, he gets a job at the Central Hospital.

July 1955 Ernesto Guevara meets Fidel Castro soon after the latter arrives in Mexico City following his release from prison. Now nicknamed "Che" (an Argentine term of greeting) by his Cuban friends, he immediately agrees to join the planned guerrilla expedition back to Cuba.

August 18, 1955 Che marries Peruvian revolutionary Hilda Gadea in Mexico. Their daughter Hildita is born the following year.

June 24, 1956 Che is arrested as part of a roundup by Mexican police of exiled Cuban revolutionaries.

November 25, 1956 Eighty-two combatants, including Che Guevara as troop doctor, sail for Cuba from Tuxpan, Mexico, aboard the small cabin cruiser *Granma*.

December 2, 1956 The *Granma* reaches Cuba at Las Coloradas beach in the eastern province of Oriente, but the rebels are surprised by Batista's troops at Alegría de Pío and dispersed. A small group successfully reunites and moves deeper into the Sierra Maestra mountains and begins to recruit local peasants. Within a month they are able to score a significant victory over Batista's forces.

July 21, 1957 Having stood out among the guerrilla combatants in recent battles, Che is selected to lead the newly established second column of the Rebel Army and is promoted to the rank of commander.

July 11–21, 1958 The rebels inflict a decisive defeat on Batista's army and are able to significantly expand their operational zone in the Sierra Maestra.

August 31, 1958 Che Guevara and Camilo Cienfuegos lead "invasion" columns west from the Sierra Maestra mountains toward central Cuba, opening new battle fronts in Las Villas province.

December 28, 1958 Che Guevara's guerrilla column initiates the battle of Santa Clara and succeeds in taking control of that city within a few days.

January 1, 1959 Batista flees Cuba. Fidel enters Santiago de Cuba in the east of the island as the military regime collapses. Rebel Army columns led by Che Guevara and Camilo Cienfuegos reach Havana the next day.

February 9, 1959 Che Guevara is declared a Cuban citizen.

June 2, 1959 Che marries Aleida March, who had been an urban underground activist and guerrilla fighter during the revolutionary war.

June 12–September 8, 1959 Che Guevara travels through Europe, Africa, and Asia; he signs various commercial, technical, and cultural agreements on behalf of the revolutionary government.

October 7, 1959 Che Guevara is designated head of the Department of Industrialization of the National Institute of Agrarian Reform (INRA).

November 26, 1959 Che Guevara is appointed president of the National Bank of Cuba.

March 5, 1960 At the funeral for the victims of a terrorist bombing of the French ship *La Coubre* in Havana's harbor, Cuban photographer Alberto Korda snaps his famous photograph of Che Guevara.

March 17, 1960 President Eisenhower approves a CIA plan to overthrow the revolutionary government and to train a Cuban exile army to invade Cuba.

October 23–December 23, 1960 Che Guevara makes an extended visit to the Soviet Union, the German Democratic Republic (East Germany), Czechoslovakia, China, and North Korea.

November 24, 1960 Aleida March gives birth to her and Che's first child, Aleidita ("Aliucha").

January 3, 1961 Washington breaks diplomatic relations with Havana.

February 23, 1961 The revolutionary government establishes the Ministry of Industry and Che Guevara is appointed minister.

April 15, 1961 As a prelude to the planned invasion by US-organized forces, planes attack Santiago de Cuba and Havana. The following day, at a mass rally, Fidel Castro proclaims the socialist character of the Cuban Revolution.

April 17–19, 1961 One thousand five hundred Cuban-born and other mercenaries, organized and backed by the United States, invade Cuba at the Bay of Pigs but are defeated within 72 hours. Che Guevara is sent to command troops in Pinar del Río province in the west.

August 8, 1961 As head of Cuba's delegation, Che Guevara condemns US President Kennedy's "Alliance for Progress" in a fiery speech to the Organization of American States (OAS) Economic and Social Conference in Punta del Este, Uruguay. Cuba is subsequently expelled from the OAS.

February 3, 1962 President Kennedy orders a total trade embargo against Cuba.

May 20, 1962 Camilo Guevara March, Che and Aleida's first son, is born.

August 27–September 7, 1962 Che Guevara makes his second visit to the Soviet Union.

October 1962 An international crisis breaks out after US spy planes discover Soviet missile installations in Cuba. Cuba responds by mobilizing its population for defense. Che Guevara is assigned to lead forces in Pinar del Río province in preparation for an imminent US invasion.

June 14, 1963 Aleida March gives birth to a second daughter, Celia Guevara March.

July 3–17, 1963 Che Guevara visits Algeria, recently independent under the government of Ahmed Ben Bella.

March 25, 1964 Representing the Cuban government, Che Guevara addresses the UN Conference on Trade and Development in Geneva, Switzerland.

November 4–9, 1964 Che Guevara visits the Soviet Union.

December 11, 1964 Che Guevara addresses the UN General Assembly meeting in New York, condemning the US war in Vietnam and supporting independence movements from Puerto Rico to the Congo.

December 17, 1964 Che Guevara leaves New York for Africa, where he visits Algeria, Mali, Congo (Brazzaville), Guinea, Ghana, Tanzania, and Egypt.

February 24, 1965 Ernestito ("Tatico"), Che and Aleida's fourth child, is born in Havana. The same day, Che Guevara addresses the second Economic Seminar of the Organization of Afro-Asian Solidarity in Algiers, controversially urging the socialist countries to do more to support Third World struggles for independence.

March 14, 1965 Che Guevara returns to Cuba and shortly afterwards drops from public view.

April 1, 1965 Che Guevara delivers a farewell letter to Fidel Castro. He then leaves Cuba on a Cuban-sponsored internationalist mission in the Congo, Africa, entering through Tanzania with a passport in the name of Ramón Benítez.

April 18, 1965 In answer to questions about Che Guevara's whereabouts, Fidel Castro informs foreign reporters that Che "will always be where he is most useful to the revolution."

June 16, 1965 Fidel Castro announces Che Guevara's location will be revealed "when Commander Guevara wants it known."

October 3, 1965 Fidel Castro publicly reads Che Guevara's letter of farewell at a meeting announcing the central committee of the newly formed Cuban Communist Party.

November 21, 1965 Che Guevara leaves the Congo and begins writing up his account of the African mission, which he describes as a "failure."

December 1965 Fidel Castro arranges for Che Guevara to return to Cuba in secret in order to begin preparations for a Cuban-sponsored guerrilla expedition to Bolivia.

January 3–14, 1966 The Tricontinental Conference of Solidarity of the Peoples of Asia, Africa, and Latin America is held in Havana.

March 1966 Che Guevara returns clandestinely to Cuba and meets with Cuban volunteers selected for the mission to Bolivia at a training camp in Cuba's Pinar del Río province. Meanwhile, the first Cuban combatants arrive in Bolivia to begin advance preparations for a guerrilla movement. Fellow Argentine Tamara Bunke ("Tania") has already been working there since 1964.

November 4, 1966 Che Guevara arrives in La Paz, Bolivia, in disguise, using a Uruguayan passport in the name of Adolfo Mena González.

November 7, 1966 Che Guevara and several others arrive at a farm on the Ñacahuazú River where the guerrilla group will be based. Che makes the first entry in his diary of the Bolivia campaign.

December 31, 1966 Che Guevara meets with the secretary of the Bolivian Communist Party, Mario Monje. There is disagreement over perspectives for the planned guerrilla movement.

March 1967 The first guerrilla military action takes place in a successful ambush of Bolivian army troops and the formation of the National Liberation Army (ELN) of Bolivia is publicly announced.

April 16, 1967 Publication of Che Guevara's "Message to the Tricontinental," which calls for the creation of "two, three, many Vietnams."

April 17, 1967 The guerrilla detachment led by Joaquín (Vilo Acuña) is separated from the rest of the unit. The separation is supposed to last only a few days, but the two groups are never able to reunite.

April 20, 1967 French intellectual Regís Debray and Ciro Bustos are arrested after having spent several weeks with the guerrilla unit in Bolivia. They are subsequently tried and sentenced to 30 years' imprisonment.

May–June 1967 US Special Forces arrive in Bolivia to train the counterinsurgency troops of the Bolivian army, which carries out a massacre of miners and their families at the Siglo XX mines.

July 1, 1967 President Barrientos publicly announces that Che Guevara's presence in Bolivia has been discovered.

July 31–August 10, 1967 The Organization of Latin American Solidarity (OLAS) conference is held in Havana in support of the guerrilla movements throughout Latin America. Che Guevara is elected honorary chair.

August 1967 A deserter leads the Bolivian army to the guerrilla's main supply cache. Documents discovered lead to the arrest of key urban contacts.

October 8, 1967 After an entire guerrilla detachment is ambushed and annihilated several weeks earlier, the remaining group of 17 guerrillas is trapped by the Bolivian army and fight a desperate battle in El Yuro ravine. Che Guevara is seriously wounded and captured.

October 9, 1967 Che Guevara and two other captured guerrillas (Willy and Chino) are murdered by Bolivian soldiers following instructions from the Bolivian government and Washington. The remains of Che Guevara and the other guerrillas are secretly buried in Bolivia.

October 15, 1967 On Cuban television, Fidel Castro confirms news of Che Guevara's death and declares three days of official mourning in Cuba. October 8 is designated the Day of the Heroic Guerrilla. Three days later, Fidel delivers a memorial speech for Che Guevara in Havana's Revolution Plaza before an audience of almost one million people.

Mid-March 1968 Microfilm of the pages of Che's Bolivian diary arrives in Cuba.

July 1968 Che Guevara's *Bolivian Diary* is published in Cuba and distributed free of charge to the Cuban people. It is simultaneously published in many countries to counter the CIA campaign to discredit the revolutionary movement in Latin America. With an introduction by Fidel Castro, it becomes an instant international bestseller.

July 1997 Almost 30 years after his murder, Che Guevara's remains and those of other guerrilla fighters are finally located in Bolivia and returned to Cuba to be buried together in a new memorial built in the central Cuban city of Santa Clara, where Che led a famous military victory in the revolutionary war.

INTRODUCTION

"Let me say, at the risk of seeming ridiculous, that the true revolutionary is guided by great feelings of love."
Ernesto Che Guevara

Letters often reveal the innermost thoughts and emotions of a writer, an intellectual or artist, or, in this case, a revolutionary, who had both an outstanding intellect and a brilliant pen. Ernesto Guevara de la Serna — or "Che" as the world came to know him — was an inveterate letter writer and diarist throughout his short but extraordinary life. His letters and diaries are those of a master narrator, characterized by a brutal honesty, a remarkable lack of ego, a razor-sharp wit, an iron will and a great capacity to express his love and affection for his closest friends and family.

More than 80 percent of the letters in this selection of Che Guevara's correspondence have never previously been translated and published in English. Beginning with the letters young Ernesto penned in his early travels around Latin America as a medical student, the reader can observe how he polished his unique style over the years. And as Ernesto is transformed into "Che" (a common way Argentines refer to themselves and are referred to by others), a dedicated revolutionary and original political thinker emerges from the wide-eyed young Argentine who set out to discover Latin America. "Each one of us is the architect of a new type of human being," wrote Che years later, "for the new society we seek to create," and it is that process of becoming or transformation that the reader can witness here in his letters.

Although he was never a student radical during his time at university, by 1954 he is writing to his mother from Guatemala, saying: "the Americas will be the theater of my adventures in a way that is much more significant than I could have imagined. I think I have really come to understand it and I feel [Latin] American, which means having a character distinct from all other peoples on the earth."

Always an uncompromising seeker of the truth, committed only to what he described as "the sacred cause of the liberation of humanity," in one of his last letters to his young children, Che advised them to "always be capable of feeling deeply any injustice committed against anyone, anywhere in the world. This is the most beautiful quality in a revolutionary."

His final letters to his partner Aleida, his children and Fidel Castro are both nostalgic and wistful, while also reiterating his unwavering commitment to his ideals. "Many will call me an adventurer," Che wrote to his parents before leaving Cuba in 1966 on his fateful mission in Bolivia, "and that I am, only one of a different sort: one who risks his neck to prove his truths."

As Che's daughter Aleida comments: "When you write a speech, you pay attention to the language, the punctuation and so on. But in a letter to a friend or a member of your family, you don't worry about those things. It is you speaking, in your authentic voice. That's what I like about these letters; they show who Che really was. This is the true political testimony of my father."

A few of these letters are well known, but most have only now been released from Che Guevara's personal archive held at the Che Guevara Studies Center in Havana, directed by his widow Aleida March, and are published in English for the first time. This selection, compiled chronologically, presents letters from different moments of Che's life, offering a new and intimate insight into the motivation, emotions and actions of an extraordinary human being. Living only 39 years, Che had an impact on our lives and dreams as few have had in all of human history.

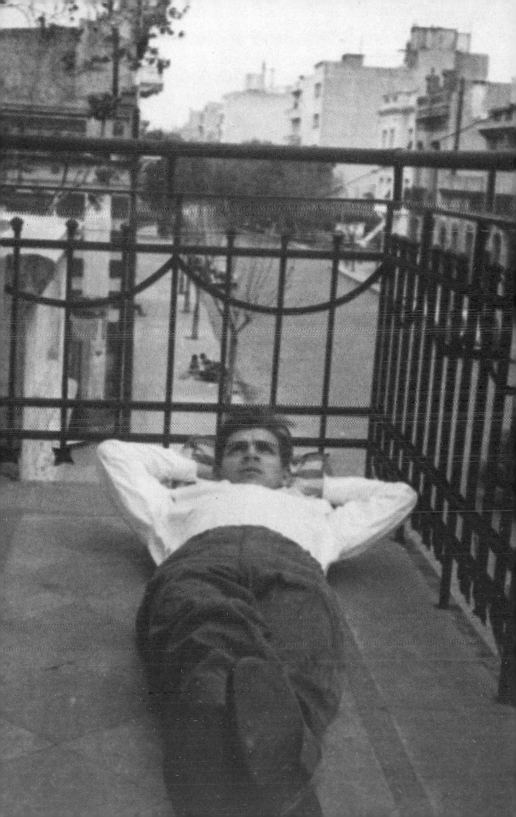

LETTERS FROM YOUTH
(1947-1956)

Introduction

A dedicated diarist from his youth, Ernesto candidly recorded his thoughts and experiences in letters to friends and family and took prodigious notes on the extensive reading program he set himself. The first letters in this volume were written at the age of 18 when Ernesto first leaves his family home in Buenos Aires. Having graduated from high school at the end of 1946, he trains as a soil technician and then goes to work with his school friend Tomás Granado at the Department of Highways in the city of Villa María.

In January 1950, Ernesto uses the summer break in his medical studies to explore 12 provinces of his native Argentina on a motorized bicycle. He keeps a travel diary, in which he describes much of the territory he travels through as arid and inhospitable, where the population lives in poverty and isolation, in stark contrast to the prosperity enjoyed by middle-class Argentine families like his in the urban centers.

Before completing his medical degree, in December 1951, Ernesto and his compañero Alberto Granado (Tomas' brother) undertake an extended trip through the continent of Latin America, setting out on a vintage Norton motorcycle, "El Poderoso, II" (Mighty One, the Second), which only makes it as far as Chile. The travelers continued by hitchhiking to Peru, Colombia and Venezuela, spending some time in a leper colony in the Amazon.

After spending a month in Miami, Ernesto returns to Buenos Aires on a cargo plane loaded with horses. These adventures are portrayed in a posthumously published book and popular movie, *The Motorcycle Diaries*.[1]

As a newly graduated doctor in 1953, Ernesto heads off on yet another journey that takes him back through the Andes and on to Central America, where he witnesses the aftermath of the 1952 Bolivian revolution and the 1954 CIA-backed overthrow of the popularly elected government of Jacobo Árbenz in Guatemala. These experiences profoundly influence the young Argentine's political world view.[2]

Up until the moment he is first introduced to Fidel Castro in Mexico in 1955 by Cuban friends he had made in Guatemala, Ernesto is still aiming for a successful career as a medical researcher and dreaming of traveling to Europe where he plans to meet up with his mother in Paris. His letters home still give the impression that these are his goals, but in reality he has begun training with the Cubans for the guerrilla expedition back to Cuba to combat a military dictatorship that emerged from a coup in March 1952.

His correspondence during these years already displays an inimitable style, an astute wit and wry sense of humor, a loyalty to friends and a deep affection for his family, especially his mother and maternal aunt Beatriz. What is most notable, however, is young Ernesto's intense quest to understand the world and a readiness to call out injustice or barbarity whenever and wherever he encounters it, foreshadowing his future revolutionary trajectory.

---

1   See Ernesto Che Guevara, *The Motorcycle Diaries: Notes on a Latin American Journey* (Seven Stories Press, 2021).
2   See Ernesto Che Guevara, *Latin America Diaries: The Sequel to* The Motorcycle Diaries (Seven Stories Press, 2021).

To Father[3]

Villa María, January 21, 1947

My dearest *Viejo* [old man],[4]

I received the money you sent the other day and, without a doubt, it arrived at just the right time. I didn't respond to you before because my situation was still up in the air.

They have silenced me and sent me to Villa María. What I like about this is that I'll have to behave like a supervisor and I'll be able to use the time to try to improve myself. For now, I have to work hard because the previous laboratory technician was a first-rate bum. I'll have to carry out trials that have accumulated and are equivalent to 10 kilometers of the project. However, after 10 days of work I hope the situation will have improved a bit and that I'll have time to study.

I am waiting for news from Osvaldo Payer, who went to Uruguay to ask about the programs. If I can do them free of charge I'll stay all winter, as I have worked out that I can save between 80 and 100 pesos a month. My wage is 200 plus board, which means that my costs are simply food and buying some books to distract myself. My address is Vélez Sarsfield… Villa María.

I'm about 10 blocks from the center.

Chau and love from

Ernesto

---

3   Ernesto Guevara completed his secondary education in 1946 at the age of 18. He then trained as a soil technician and worked for a while with his friend from high school, Tomás Granado, in the Department of Highways in the city of Villa María, from where he wrote the following two letters.

4   This was the affectionate way Che addressed his parents.

To Father
Villa María, [late] 1947

My dearest *Viejo*,

I can see that you are very worried about the issue with the truck. The company wasn't doing me any "favor," I was doing them a favor because it is their obligation to provide me with a vehicle and peons that are up to the task, and I don't think the workforce is even remotely up to it.

As of now my main concern is food, because the company had previously paid for this, and it seems to me a bit like a "bribe." The only thing left for me to do is to consult with the boss (who is a first-rate bribe taker) and do what he says.

This famous Department of Highways has turned out to be little more than a club of bribe takers.

The person in charge told me that, in 20 years, I have been the only laboratory technician he had known who has not accepted the food, and one of only two or three who didn't take bribes.

You were worried that I would be too lenient on them, but in fact I have made them dig up and compact a good chunk of the road, and am now carrying out some of the postponed trials. If these fail, they will have to dig 80 centimeters (deep) and compact the road in three layers, meaning they will have a terrible job ahead of them. (It seems to me that there is something suspicious going on.)

Well, *Viejo*, hugs,

Ernesto

To AMERIMEX[5]

Buenos Aires, February 28, 1950
"Year of the Liberator General San Martín"

Manager
AMERÍMEX S.R.L.
Calle Reconquista. 575.
Cap. Fed. [Buenos Aires]

Dear Sirs,

I am sending you a "Micron" motor, which you represent, with which I have traveled 4,000 kilometers through 12 Argentine provinces. The motor worked perfectly during my extensive trip and it was only at the end that I realized it had lost pressure, which is why I am sending it to you for repairs.

Yours sincerely,

Ernesto Guevara Serna

---

5   This letter was written after Ernesto's extensive trip around Argentina in the summer of 1950 on a motorized bicycle. It was published in the magazine *El Gráfico*, as publicity for the Argentine company AMERIMEX, which sold Micron motors.

To Mother[6]

San Martin de los Andes [Argentina], January 1952

Dear *Vieja* [old lady],

I know that you haven't received news from me, but at the same time I have had no news from you, and this has left me concerned. It is not possible for me to recount everything that has happened to us in these few lines. The only thing I'll say is that shortly after leaving Bahia Blanca, I had a fever of 40 degrees for two days, which left me in bed for a whole day. The next day I was able to stand up and went to the Choele Choel Regional Hospital, where I was cured within four days after being administered a not very well-known drug: penicillin.

After this, amid the thousands of difficulties we were able to overcome with our usual skill, we arrived at San Martin de los Andes, a beautiful place, in the middle of virgin forest with a very pretty lake. In short, it is well worth coming to see it yourself. Our faces are acquiring the consistency of silicon carbide. We are already asking for shelter, food and anything else we can get our

---

6   In December 1951, before completing his medical studies, Ernesto joined his friend Alberto Granado (the brother of Tomás) in a trip around Latin America on a vintage Norton motorbike, called La Poderosa II ("Mighty One, the Second") that only made it to Chile. The travelers continued by hitchhiking to Peru, Colombia and Venezuela, spending some time in a leper colony on the Amazon. After spending a month in Miami, Ernesto returned to Buenos Aires on a cargo plane loaded with horses. Ernesto later edited his diary of this trip as a series of chronicles that was posthumously published as *The Motorcycle Diaries* and was the basis of Walter Salles' popular movie of the same name, starring Gael García Bernal as Ernesto and Rodrigo de la Serna as Alberto Granado.

hands on at any house we see along the way. By chance, we ended up at the estate of the Von Puthamers, who were friends of Jorge, especially one of them who is a Peronist, a drunk and the best of the three. I also had a test done for an occipital area tumor of probable hydatid etiology. Let's see what eventuates. Within two or three days we'll head off in the direction of Bariloche. Without rushing, if you think your letter can reach us by about February 10, write to me at the post office there.

Well *Vieja*, my next piece of paper is destined for Chichina.[7] Please give a big *hug* to everyone and let me know if the old man is in the south or not.

An affectionate embrace from your son who loves you,

Ernesto

---

7   Ernesto's girlfriend at the time.

To Aunt Beatriz[8]

Iquitos [Peru], June 1, 1952

[...] In passing, I am going to make a confession. What I wrote you about the headhunters, etc. was a lie. Unfortunately, it turns out that the Amazon is as safe as Paraná, and Putumayo as safe as Paraguay. This means I won't be able to bring you a shrunken head as a gift as I intended. In short, I hope you will be able to forgive your loving nephew who, victim of the impetuosity of his young age, came up with such a hare-brained scheme. I had also hoped to show off my qualities as a martyr, hanging around in the midst of malaria and yellow fever, but it turns out that they, too, no longer exist here. The situation is exasperating.

Tomorrow I'm leaving on a boat that will take three days to reach Sao Paulo. We will stay there for a week at a leprosarium. From there to Leticia it's a day's travel, which means that if I don't immediately find transport to continue on my trip, you might be able to send me a letter there.

Regarding your offer of money: I am enough of a man to deal with matters myself without having to plead in letters to any family member, particularly knowing that pesos are in short supply. I still have the dollars Ercilia gave me, and they have helped us out a bit in Lima.[9] This means we are not facing any immediate economic concerns, although we may have to work in Colombia later on if things continue the way they are. I don't think

---

8   Aunt Beatriz was Ernesto's mother's sister.
9   Ercilia Guevara Lynch was Ernesto's aunt on his father's side.

this will be the case, as we are leaving Peru with a few more pesos than we arrived with. What I do need is a favor from you: that you send to the below address the following (if you are willing to help, that is): a Yanal vaporizer [for asthma] and vials. It is important to remember: I don't have asthma [right now], but this product does not exist in Peru nor, most likely, in Colombia, and it is much better than what is available here.

The trip down to Putumayo (you will see on a map) takes about a month. This will be about the amount of time that you will be without news from me, unless somehow we are able to jump on a plane to Bogotá or at least to Leguisamo port, which would save us traveling down this somewhat tedious river.

If I am lucky, I'll return by the end of July or beginning of August; if not, I can't tell you how much you will admire the great beard I have grown in six months of travel [...].

[Unsigned]

To Father
Iquitos, June 4, 1952

[...] The banks of the great rivers have been completely colonized; to find savage tribes one needs to travel deep into the tributary — the tributary in this zone — a trip that, at least this time, we are not planning to make. Infectious diseases have completely disappeared; despite this we are vaccinating people against typhoid and yellow fever and distributing a good amount of atebrina and quinine.

There are a great number of diseases here that are due to metabolic disorders arising from the limited nutritional resources available in the jungle. This is not something we are personally concerned about because these diseases are not the result of going a week without sufficient vitamins, which, in the worst of cases, is the longest time we would be without food if we decide to go down the river. We are still not sure about this, as we are hoping to travel by plane to Bogotá or at least Leguisamo, and there are roadways here. This is not because of the dangerous nature of the trip but rather because we want to save a few bucks that could turn out to be precious later on.

The further away we travel from scientific centers that could provide us with some help, the more our trip acquires importance for the people working in the leprosarium here, who treat us with a respect worthy of two researchers visiting them. The desire to practice leprology has hit me with some intensity and I don't know how long this sentiment will last. It's just that farewells like the one that the patients from the leprosarium in Lima gave us are what motivate us to continue. They gave us a *Primus* heater; together they raised 100 soles, which for them, given their economic situation, is a huge amount. Many of them said goodbye with tears in their eyes. All of their love for us was due to the fact that we spent time with them without wearing masks or gloves, shaking hands with them as we would any neighbor, sitting among them just chatting about this and that and playing football with them Perhaps this doesn't seem like much to you, but the psychological impact of this is incalculable for patients who are normally treated like savage animals, that is, just being treated as normal human beings, while the risk [for us] is extremely remote. For now, only one nurse from Indochina, who lived with his patients, has caught the disease and a jealous friar for whose story I wouldn't put my hands in the fire.

Since entering foreign territory I have not taken out my revolver even to clean it and, if the Colombian guerrillas don't attack us, I can't see any reason why I would need it. Rather than coming here to follow our tracks, I would suggest you dash off to Venezuela as quickly as possible. You aren't the type of person who saves money, but any dollar that you forget about in your pocket is 30 pesos here, which is always something.

If I were you, I would rush as quickly as possible; in general, most people agree that Colombia and Venezuela are the two ideal countries on the continent to make money today. In terms of money, don't worry about us; we will be leaving Peru with more than we came here with, after living here for two months and traveling throughout the country, from point to point. In general, we have found that we can find work anywhere. Alberto, for example, has already received two job offers in Lima.

We'll be in this town for as little time as possible, which means you will have to write soon. Just recently, for the first time, I felt homesick, but it quickly passed; I genuinely have a traveling spirit and it would not be at all strange if, after this trip, I decide to make a trip to India and another one to Europe. With Alberto we have a thousand projects in the pipeline, but we will decide what to do after seeing what there is in Venezuela. In general our plan is for him to stay in Venezuela and save some dollars, and for me to travel [home] to graduate, but there are many possible variants to this plan. What I roughly outlined to the *Vieja* was the following: if I can, I'll return at the beginning of August so that I can graduate this year, or at the beginning of next year; if for whatever reason I can't make it at that time, I'll continue traveling until March, after which I would go back to studying, naturally having lost a year. Given the success of this trip, the only thing that I would be concerned about would be the economic side of things, because, being able to practice in these countries, it is easy to live as an allergist as no one knows anything about it. It seems ridiculous that my little experience working with Pisani would put me so many kilometers ahead of the average allergist [...][10]

I'll write from Leticia to let you know where I'll be going next. Well, *Viejo*, I hope that things improve for you and that you can go to Caracas soon. Until we see each other there, a big hug for you and the *Vieja* and another one for the kids.

Ernesto

---

10 Dr. Salvador Pisani was an allergy specialist with whom Ernesto worked and with whom he published his first articles as a medical student. This experience was later useful to Ernesto during his time working as a doctor in Mexico, where he continued some of his research into allergies.

To Mother
Bogotá, July 6, 1952

Dear *Vieja*,

Here I am, a few kilometers further away and a few pesos poorer, getting ready to continue on our journey towards Venezuela. First of all, I have to wish you a happy birthday. I hope you had a great day with the family. Now, I want to tell you about my great adventures since leaving Iquitos: our departure occurred roughly within the timeframe I had set. We spent two nights in the loving company of mosquitos and reached the leprosarium in San Pablo in the early morning, where they provided us with board. The medical director, a great guy, immediately got on well with us and in general we got on well with the whole leprosarium, with the exception of the nuns who asked us why we didn't go to mass. It turned out that the nuns are the administrators and that whoever does not go to mass has their rations cut as much as possible (we were left without [...], but the guys helped us out and found something for us every day). Apart from this small cold war, life continues to be a pleasure.

On the 14th [Ernesto's birthday] they organized a party for us with a lot of pisco, a type of gin that goes down really nice. The medical director made a toast to us and I, inspired by what I had already drunk, responded with a very Pan-American speech that was received with great applause from the qualified and somewhat drunk public.[11] We stayed there longer than planned, but finally left

---

11   For an account of this event, see the chapter "Saint Guevara's Day" in *The Motorcycle Diaries*, op.cit..

for Colombia. The night before, a group of the patients came from their part of the leprosarium on a big canoe, as this was the only way to reach us, and at the pier they bid us farewell by serenading us and giving some very moving speeches. Alberto, who is already shaping up to be Perón's successor, gave a demagogic speech that was so effective it moved those who had come to pay homage to us. It was one of the most interesting spectacles we had witnessed until now: an accordionist with no fingers on his right hand who had tied a few sticks to his hand to be able to play, the singer was blind, and all of them had monstrous disfigurements, provoked by the nature of their illness, which is very common in the area; to all this we must add the lighting provided by the lanterns and torches above the river. It was a cinematic spectacle.

This place is beautiful, surrounded by jungle with indigenous tribes just a short distance away whom we, of course, visited. There is an abundance of fish and animals to hunt and eat every-where, and an incalculable amount of potential resources. All of this inspired in us a beautiful dream of traveling through the plateau of Matto Grosso by water, beginning on the Paraguay River to reach the Amazon as doctors and and so on. It's a dream much like having one's own home... we'll see... the fact is that we felt ourselves to be a bit more like explorers and went down the river on a raft that they had built especially for us. The first day was really good, but at night, instead of taking turns to keep watch, we both fell asleep, protected by a mosquito net they had given us, and woke up the next day stranded on the riverbank.

We ate like sharks. We spent the whole of the next day happy and decided to take hourly turns keeping guard to avoid any problems, given that the current was pushing us towards the riverbank and some submerged tree branches almost tore a hole in our raft.

[...] We continued keeping watch until the morning, when

we approached the riverbank where we could both get under the mosquito net, as there were a great deal of them about. After sleeping well, Alberto, who prefers chicken to fish, discovered that two of our fishing hooks had disappeared during the night, which only made him angry. As there was a house nearby, we decided to go and find out how much further it was to Leticia When the owner of the house responded to us, in Portuguese, that Leticia was seven hours upstream and that we were in Brazil, we began a heated discussion, attempting to apportion blame on each other. No resolution was found. We gave away the fish and a four-kilo pineapple that the patients had given us, and we stayed at the house until the following day, when they could take us back upstream.

[…] What saved us was the fact that we were hired as coaches for a football team while we waited for the plane, which comes every two weeks. At first we thought about training the players so that they would at least avoid making fools of themselves, but as they were very bad, we decided to play ourselves, achieving the brilliant result of taking a team considered to be the worst in the competition to the final where we only lost on penalties. Alberto, because of his physique which shares certain similarities with Pedernera and his millimeter perfect passes, was given the nickname of *Pedernerita*, and I saved a penalty that will forever be remembered in Leticia. The celebration would have been even better if they had not decided to play the Colombian anthem at the end. I bent over to clean a bit of blood off my knees as they played it, provoking a violent reaction from the colonel, who verbally attacked me. I gave him a mouthful but remembered our trip and other stuff so I let it drop.

After a nice flight on a plane that shook like a cocktail shaker we arrived in Bogotá. […] The first day in Bogotá was okay. We found some food at the University but no board, because it was full of students on scholarships who were doing a course organized by the U.N. Of course, there were no Argentines. It was not until 1:00 in the morning that we were finally given somewhere to stay at a hospital, simply chairs on which we passed the night. It's not that we are completely broke, but travelers like us prefer to die rather than pay for the bourgeois comforts of a boarding house. After this, the service looking after lepers took us into consideration after having read the letter of recommendation that we brought with us from Peru, signed by Dr. Pesce, who fulfills the same role as Lusteau. Alberto gave various speeches, and as soon as he stopped to breathe I would hit them with my allergy talk and leave them flabbergasted. The result: offers of contracts for both of us. I was not planning to accept it, but Alberto was, for obvious reasons, when due to Roberto's knife — which I had taken out in the street to use to draw on the ground — we got into big trouble with the police who treated us in a humiliating manner. We decided instead to leave as soon as possible for Venezuela, meaning that probably by the time you receive this letter we will have left […].

Of everywhere we have traveled, this is the country where individual rights are most trampled upon. The police patrol the streets with rifles in their hands and demand to see everyone's passport. There is a tense atmosphere, which leads us to imagine there will be a revolt here within a short period of time. The towns are in open revolt and the army is unable to repress them. The conservatives fight among themselves, unable to agree with each other, and the memory of April 9, 1948, weighs heavily on everyone.[12] In short, it is an asphyxiating atmosphere, so while the Colombians may be okay with putting up with this, we want to get

---

12   A mass protest arose in Bogotá on April 9, 1948, in the wake of the assassination of the popular political leader Jorge Eliécer Gaitán.

out of here as soon as possible. It seems Alberto has a good chance of finding a job in Caracas […].

An embrace from your son who misses you in his elbows, heels and backside. […]

Chau

Ernesto

To Father[13]
La Paz [Bolivia], July 24 [1953]

Dear *Viejo,*

You didn't hear from me because I had to wait a month for a job in a tin mine as a doctor, with Calica as my aid. In the end, we didn't take it because the supposed doctor (the one who was going to give us work), never appeared and we cannot afford to hang around waiting for money. I am somewhat disillusioned that I was unable to stay because this is a very interesting country and it is experiencing a particularly effervescent moment. On August 2, agrarian reform was enacted and parades and parties were announced across the country. We have seen some incredible parades with people armed with Mausers and *piripipí*[14] that they fired at will. Every day we hear gunshots and there are injuries and deaths as a result of firearms.

The government seems to be almost completely unable to halt or lead the masses of peasants and miners, but they respond to them in certain measure and there is no doubt that if there were

---

13   Having graduated as a doctor, Ernesto set out again on July 7, 1953, for a second trip through Latin America. This time he left by train with his childhood friend Carlos Ferrer ("Calica"). They traveled to Bolivia, Peru and Ecuador, and then the plan had been to meet up with Alberto Granado in Venezuela. Ernesto continued instead to Guatemala in the company of Eduardo García ("Gualo"), passing through Panama, Costa Rica, Nicaragua and El Salvador. They were interested to observe the revolutionary process taking place in Guatemala under the government of Jacobo Árbenz.

14   Term used by Paraguayans and Bolivians for machine guns, due to the sound they make.

to be a revolt by the Falange (the opposition party), these masses would be on the side of the Nationalist Revolutionary Movement.

Human life has little value here and is given or taken with little regard; all of this means that, for a neutral observer, the situation is really interesting, despite the fact that, on one pretext or another, everyone who can takes it pretty easy.

[...] Here the people have received us magnificently, and there has not been a single Bolivian or Argentine who has not, in one way or another, taken an interest in our trip. We are doing the paperwork to get a visa for Venezuela, but nothing is certain yet. If you remember anyone who you might know in Ecuador, send me their addresses via the Argentine consulate in Lima. My health is formidably good, despite not doing the exercises I should be doing. Write to me to see if I have fresh news in Lima. A hug for all the family. Until next time. I cannot continue the conversation because they have come to get me to take me to a *milonga* [Argentine-style dance party].

[Unsigned]

To Mother

Cuzco [Peru, August] 22 [1953]

Look closely at the letterhead *mami*,[15]

I have treated myself for a second time and now in style, but the effect is different. Alberto would have done anything to marry Inca princesses and recover [lost] empires.[16] Calica swears at all the dirt and each time he steps on one of the numerous turds in the streets, instead of looking up to the sky or at some cathedral he looks at his filthy shoes. He fails to breathe in the intangible evocative atmosphere of Cuzco but instead only the stench of stew and sewerage — I guess it's a question of temperament.

All this apparent incoherence of I'm going, I've gone, I haven't gone yet, etc. was because we needed to make sure no one outside of Bolivia knew what we were doing, as a revolt was expected at any moment and we had the healthy intention of staying to see it up close. Unfortunately for us, it didn't occur and we only saw demonstrations of strength from the government that, despite everything people have told us, appears to me to be solid.

I was going to go to work in some mine but I was not willing to stay for more than a month and they offered me three as a minimum, so I didn't take the job.

We then went to the shores of Lake Titicaca, to Copacabana, and spent a day on Isla del Sol, a famous sanctuary from the Inca

---

15   The letter was most likely written on paper from some upmarket hotel.

16   Alberto Granado was Ernesto's companion on his first visit to Cuzco in 1952.

times, where I fulfilled one of my most heart-felt desires as an explorer: I found, in an indigenous cemetery, a small statue of a woman, the size of a little finger, but an idol nevertheless, made from the famous *chompi*, the alloy of the Incas.

On reaching the border [between Bolivia and Peru] we had to travel two kilometers without getting a lift, and for one of those kilometers I had to carry my bag full of books. The two of us and our two little peons, arrived with our tongues hanging out.

Our battle with customs began in Puno. They took a Bolivian book from me, saying that it was "commie" [literature]. There was no way of convincing them that these were scientific publications.

I have told you nothing about my future because I don't know anything yet, not even how things will go in Venezuela, but we now have a visa that we obtained through [...]. Regarding the more distant future, I should say that I'm continuing to pursue my goal of US$10,000, and that we will perhaps embark on a new trip around Latin America, but this time in a north-south direction with Alberto, and perhaps via helicopter. Then Europe and then who knows.

[Unsigned]

To Tita Infante[17]
Lima [Peru], September 3, 1953

Dear Tita,

Sadly, I have to write to you in my beautiful handwriting, as I haven't been able to get hold of a typewriter to remedy the situation. At any rate, I hope you have a day free to dedicate to reading this letter.

Let's get to the point. Thank your friend Ferreira for the letter of introduction to the Bolivian college. Dr. Molina was very kind to me and seemed enchanted with both me and my traveling companion, the one you met at home. He subsequently offered me a job as a doctor and Calica work as a nurse in a mine; we accepted but wanted to reduce the three months he wanted us to stay to one. Everything was settled and amicable and we were to report the next day to finalize details. Imagine our surprise when the next day we found out Dr. Molina had left to inspect the mines and wouldn't be back for two or three days. So we presented ourselves then, and still no Molina, although they believed he would be back in another couple of days. It would take too long to recount the number of times we went looking for him; the fact is that he returned 20 days later, and by then we could no longer agree to a month — the lost time would have made it two — so he gave us some introductory letters for the director of a tungsten mine, where we went for two or three days. Very interesting, especially

---

17   Berta Gilda Infante ("Tita") was a fellow medical student at the University of Buenos Aires and a close friend. She died December 14, 1976.

because the mine is in a magnificent location. Overall the trip was worthwhile.

I should tell you that in La Paz I ignored my diet and all that nonsense, but nevertheless felt wonderful for the month and a half I spent there. We traveled quite a bit into the surrounding area — to Las Yungas, for example, where there are some very pretty tropical valleys — but one of the most interesting things we did was to observe the fascinating political situation. Bolivia has been a particularly important example for the Americas. We saw exactly where struggles have taken place, the holes left by bullets and even the remains of a man killed in the revolution and only recently discovered in the cornice of a building — the lower part of his body had been blown away by one of those dynamite belts the miners wear around their waists. In the end, they fought heroically. The revolutions here are not like those in Buenos Aires — two or three thousand (no one knows for sure how many) were left dead on the battlefield.

Even now the fighting continues, and almost every night people are wounded by gunfire from one side or the other. But the government is supported by an armed people, and there is no possibility of liquidating such an armed movement from outside. It might, however, succumb to internal conflicts.

The [Bolivian] MNR [Nationalist Revolutionary Movement] is a coalition with three more or less definite tendencies: the right, represented by Siles Suazo, vice president and hero of the revolution; the center, represented by Paz Estenssoro, shiftier and probably as rightwing as the first; and the left, represented by Lechín, the visible head of a serious protest movement, but who himself is an unknown given to partying and chasing women. Power is likely to remain in the hands of Lechín's group, which counts on the powerful support of the armed miners, but resistance from their colleagues in government may prove serious, particularly as the army is going to be reorganized.

Well, I've told you something about the Bolivian situation. I'll tell you about Peru later, when I've been here for a little longer, but in general I think that Yankee domination in Peru has not even created the fiction of economic wellbeing that can be seen in Venezuela, for example.

Of my future life, I know little about where I am headed and even less when. We have been thinking of going to Quito and from there to Bogotá and Caracas, but of the intermediary steps we haven't got much of an idea. I've only recently arrived here in Lima from Cuzco.

I won't tire of urging you to visit there if possible, especially Machu-Picchu. I promise you won't regret it.

I guess that since I left, you must have taken at least five subjects, and I imagine you still go fishing for worms in the muck heap. There's little or nothing to write you about vocations, but if one day you change your tune and want to see the world,

remember this friend
who would risk his skin
to help you however he could
when the occasion arises

A hug, and until that happens and we're in the same place when it does,

Ernesto

To Mother
Guayaquil [Ecuador], [October 21, 1953]

I'm writing you this letter (who knows when you'll read it) about my new position as a 100 percent adventurer. A lot of water has flowed under the bridge since the news in my last epistle.

The gist is as follows: As Calica [Carlos Ferrer], [Eduardo "Gualo"] García (one of our new acquisitions) and I were traveling along for a while, we felt homesick for our beloved homeland. We talked about how good it was for the two members of the group who had managed to leave for Panama, and commented on the fantastic interview with X.X., that guardian angel you gave me, which I'll tell you about later. The thing is, García — almost in passing — invited us to go to Guatemala, and I was disposed to accept. Calica promised to give his answer the next day, and it was affirmative, so there were four new candidates for Yankee opprobrium.

But then our trials and tribulations in the consulates began, with our daily pleas for the Panamanian visas that we required and, after several psychological ups and downs, Calica seemed to decide not to go. Your suit — your masterpiece, the pearl of your dreams — died heroically in a pawnshop, as did all the other unnecessary things in my luggage, which has been greatly reduced for the benefit of the trio's financial stability — now achieved (whew!).[18]

---

18   The trio now consisted of Gualo García, Andrew Herrera and Ernesto. Calica left for Venezuela, as had been his and Ernesto's original plan.

What this means is that if a captain, who is a sort of friend, agrees to use an old trick, García and I can travel to Panama, and then the combined efforts of those who want to reach Guatemala, plus those from there, will drag along the straggler left behind as security for the remaining debts. If the captain I mentioned messes it up, the same two partners in crime will go on to Colombia, again leaving the security here, and will head for Guatemala by whatever means Almighty God unwarily places within their reach.

[Continued from] Guayaquil, [October] 24

After a lot of coming and going and many calls, plus a discreet bribe, we have the visa for Panama. We'll leave tomorrow, Sunday, and will get there by the 29th or 30th. I have written this quick note at the consulate.

Ernesto

To Aunt Beatriz

San José de Costa Rica, [December 10, 1953]

Aunty, aunty mine,

My life had been a sea of contradictory resolutions until I valiantly abandoned all my luggage and, with a backpack on my shoulders, set out with compañero García down the winding path that has led us to where we are today. In El Paso, I had the opportunity to pass through the realms of United Fruit [Company], which once again convinced me of how terrible these capitalist octopuses are. I swore before a picture of the old and lately lamented compañero, Stalin, not to rest until I see these capitalist octopuses annihilated. In Guatemala, I'll perfect myself and do what is necessary to become a true revolutionary.

I should let you know that besides being a doctor, I am a journalist and conference speaker, things that will enable me to obtain US dollars (although not many).[19]

Along with all the rest, I send you hugs and kisses from a nephew who loves you, he of the iron constitution, empty stomach and shining faith in a socialist future.

Chau,

Chancho[20]

---

19   Ernesto's article, "A view from the banks of the giant of rivers," was published in *Panamá-América* on November 22, 1953, and his article on Machu-Picchu was published in the weekly supplement of *Siete*, in Panama, on December 12, 1953.

20   Argentine for pig.

To Mother
Guatemala City, December 28 [1953]

Dear *Vieja*,

I have finally reached my destination and face a tough choice, given that the Argentines around here have not received everything they expected and there are many who are not happy. I think I'll stay two more years, if things turn out right, and six months, more or less, if I see there is little chance of that happening.

After leaving San José [Costa Rica] we hitched as far as we could. From there we walked some fifty kilometers to reach the Nicaraguan border, as the Pan American highway is but a beautiful illusion in these parts. My heel was in a bad state as a result of the accident I told you about in a previous letter, which meant I had a terrible time.[21] But after wading through a river some 10 times and getting soaked in the constant rain, we reached the border. There we waited a day until a truck, or anything that could transport us, came by traveling north, because in Nicaragua there are good roads. We had already lost hope and had decided to continue on foot (my ankle had improved thanks to the help of an old woman; I would not have been able to cure it even by accident) when a car with a tremendous number plate from Boston University appeared. Although we were distrustful, we decided to grab a ride with the "gringos," when all of a sudden we saw the huge moustache of big Rojo, the exiled radical, who

---

21   On the way to Guatemala, the truck in which Ernesto and his friend Gualo García were traveling tipped over and Ernesto dislocated an ankle.

was attempting to reach Costa Rica via land together with the Beberaggi Allende brothers, whom papa would have heard of because the name of one of them became well known when Perón took away his citizenship. Of course, we immediately gave up on the trip, which was impracticable due to the state of the road, and instead celebrated with an *asado* and more which made us all feel patriotic.[22]

We reached Managua, where I found the stupid telegram that papa sent; he always does this.[23] I would have thought that by now he would know that even if I was dying I would not ask him for money, and that if one day you don't receive a letter from me you should be patient and wait as sometimes I don't have a stamp, but know that I am perfectly well and that I always find a way. When you are feeling uncertain, use the money that you plan to spend on the telegram and get drunk or do whatever, but I'll not respond to these telegrams from now on.

From Managua we immediately continued in the Beberaggi brothers' car, which they brought to sell in Guatemala. But we were running out of money and in the end had to sell the jack, torches, tires, eventually anything that could be sold.

I'm having conversations to see if I can get a job in a leprosarium here for 250 quetzales and the afternoon off, but so far there is nothing concrete. However, I'll inevitably find a way because the people here are more than willing to give me a hand and there is a shortage of doctors. If I'm not able to do this, I'll perhaps join a campaign, for the same wage, but in some place with ancient ruins of the type that you know interest me.

The only country in all of Central America that is worth visiting

---

22   *Mate* is a traditional Argentine herbal tea and *asado* is an Argentine-style barbeque.

23   Ernesto's father had sent a telegram asking his son for news and if he needed any money.

is this one, even if its capital is no bigger than Bahia Blanca,[24] and is just as sleepy. Naturally, all regimes lose their shine when you look at them up close, and arbitrary abuses and robberies occur here, ensuring that it is no exception to the rule. But here there is a climate of authentic democracy and of collaboration toward all foreigners who, for various reasons, come to visit. I get the impression that I could even exercise my profession here without any problems, and they tell me that there is not a single allergist in the whole country. But I'm not sure about doing this as it can be very stupefying and, moreover, accustoms one to a bourgeois lifestyle.

Well, *Vieja*, a big hug for everyone, a special one for the birthday girl, and until next time.

[Unsigned]

---

24   Bahia Blanca is the main port city in the area south of Buenos Aires.

To Father
January 15, 1954

[...] I have been exchanging ideas with a gringo[25] who doesn't speak a word of Spanish. We now have our own language and understand each other perfectly. They say that this gringo went into exile in Guatemala because the FBI was pursuing him; others say he is from the FBI. The point is that he writes extremely anti-Yankee articles and reads Hegel, but I don't know which side he bats for. The truth of the matter seems to be always out of reach. Here I end, wishing [his sister] Ana María[26] a happy birthday...

[...] I went to see the minister of public health and asked him for a job, but I requested a categorical response from him, either a yes or no. The man was very gracious in meeting me, took down all my details and told me to come back in two or three days. The days were up yesterday and the minister didn't let me down, because he gave me a categorical response: NO.

Nevertheless, I have in mind a good idea for passing my initial time here and settling in, because to practice one needs to join a very closed and oligarchical medical circle. (I'll throw spears at them.)

For now, I'm selling on the streets a precious image of the Señor de Esquipulas, a Black Christ who produces marvelous miracles.[27]

---

25   This was Professor Harold White from the University of Utah. As Minister of Industry, Che invited White to visit Cuba where he stayed until his death a few years later. They became great friends, sharing a passionate interest in Marxism.
26   His sister Ana María's birthday was on January 28.
27   A popular figurine in Mexico.

The one I am selling is illuminated by a system similar to that which Adolfo used, but much worse.[28] I already have a long list of miracles this Christ has done, one that is constantly growing. Funnily enough, someone with bad luck sent it to me, if you can believe that. The weather is magnificent and that's it.

[...] The only thing I can tell you is that I don't want to leave here without visiting Mexico. For me, in all of the Americas, and I know a bit about this, there is no country as democratic as this one [Guatemala]; both extremes [of the political spectrum] and everyone in between say what they want without fear.

My personal viewpoint is that this will have to come to an end at some point, as United Fruit (a company that cultivates bananas but has piles of money) is able to spend a lot of cash on this type of propaganda. Each day, the opposition newspapers carry entire transcripts of speeches by democrats sent by the company or statements from the United States government, and the "stew" appears to be being concocted in conferences in Caracas, where the Yankees are pulling on all their strings to try to impose sanctions on Guatemala. It is true that all the governments have bowed before them, and that Pérez Jiménez, Odría, Trujillo, Batista, Somoza are their foot soldiers.[29] They are the most fascist and anti-popular of the reactionary governments. Bolivia was an interesting country, but Guatemala is even more so because it has stood up to everyone, despite not having an ounce of economic independence and having had to endure armed insurrections of all types (President Arévalo had to overcome about forty of them), and without attacking freedom of expression in any way. [...]

[Unsigned]

---

28 Adolfo was one of Ernesto's friends, a photographer who did something similar in Buenos Aires.

29 The heads of state of Venezuela, Peru, Dominican Republic, Cuba and Nicaragua, respectively.

To Aunt Beatriz
February 12, 1954

My very dear, always adored and never sufficiently praised aunt,

I was very happy to receive your last letter, the culmination and a complement to the two previous ones, of which only one reached me, meaning that the democratic employee at the post office must have carried out a just redistribution of wealth. Don't send me more money, it costs you an arm and a leg to do so and I find dollars just lying on the street here, so much so that at first I got back pains from bending down so often to pick them up. Now I only pick up one out of every ten dollars lying around, more than anything to maintain public hygiene, because having so much paper flying around and on the ground is dangerous.

My plan for the next few years: at least six months in Guatemala, as long as I don't find something that can pay me well enough to allow me to stay for two years. If the first occurs, I'll go to work in another country for a year. That country could be, in descending order of probability: Venezuela, Mexico, Cuba, United States. If the two-year plan comes to fruition, after visiting the last three countries I mentioned and Haiti and the Dominican Republic, I'll go to Western Europe, probably with my mother, where I'll remain until I have used up my last dollar. If time and money permit, I'll visit sometime, using some cheap means such as a free plane or boat ride, working as a doctor, etc.

Of all these plans there are two constantly changing variables that could go either way. The first is money, which for me is not fundamentally important, but it has the ability to shorten stays or modify itineraries. The second and most important is the political situation. My position is in no way that of a dilettante who is all talk and no action. I have taken a firm position in support of the Guatemalan government and, within it, of the PGT, which is communist.[30] Moreover, I have established relations with intellectuals from this tendency who publish a magazine here and I have been working with the unions as a doctor, which has placed me at odds with the medical college, which is totally reactionary. I can imagine everything you are going to say and comment on right now, but at least you cannot complain that I did not make myself clear.

[...] In the area of social medicine, and on the basis of my limited personal experience, I am preparing a very pretentious book, which I believe will take me two years to write. Its title is *The Role of the Doctor in Latin America*. I have only written a general outline and the first two chapters. I believe that with patience and a plan I can write something good.

An embrace of steel from your proletarian nephew.

An important PS: Let me know what you intend to do with your apartment and whether I can send some books for you to keep for me. Don't worry, they're not compromising.

[Unsigned]

---

30   Guatemalan Workers Party.

To Tita Infante
Guatemala City, March 1954

Despite everything, my dearest Tita, we grow old.

It has been nearly a year since my departure and I have not made much progress in anything; but I suppose you like exotic adventures, which is why I'll tell you about my projects, travels and misfortunes.

First, an apology for not having responded earlier; various things have happened which prevented me, as I wanted to send you a decent chronicle of my time in Guatemala, but I didn't have the time to write it. I then went in search of an indigenous writer who could write it for me to publish over there, but I also failed in this because it seems that the person who invented work here died several years ago. Then I was asked to write a report on Guatemala for a magazine here, whose name I don't recall, and I thought about sending you a copy, but I haven't done it and I don't think I'll finish it any time soon, as I want to do a good job of it.

I say all this because I believe that Guatemala is a country worthy of being known and understood. I believe that your fears are not unjustified, given the belligerent and, until now, victorious situation of this republic. On the first of March, in his annual message to Congress, President Árbenz spoke in unequivocal terms about the cooperation between the Communist Party and the government and the need for the government to defend the rights of those involved in this political group against any type of sanction. In general, communists have taken a cautious position, and if it were not for the national media outcry over "the interference of exotic doctrines," its presence would have gone largely unnoticed. But it is the only political group in Guatemala that joined the government in order to implement a program in which individual interests are not the priority (perhaps there is an element of demagogy in its leadership). This is in frank contrast to the other three groups of parties that are a complete mess, to the point that each of them has split into at least two antagonistic wings and have made deals with the opposition to obtain the presidency of the Congress (which needs to be approved by both chambers). For your information, that is if you don't know more than me about the situation, I would say that the influence of the PGT over the other three parties is quite strong, mainly due to internal elements that are pushing them to the left and willing to help with the total socialization of Guatemala, an extremely difficult task, among other reasons, because the revolution suffers from a lack of human resources (I am referring here, above all, to the intellectual sense of the word).

This is a country with a typical agricultural economy that has only recently broken free from the handicap of an almost "orthodox" feudalism. The only card it has up its sleeve is a monoculture that has an important position in the world market: coffee. Without being too much of a pessimist, I am convinced that a large fall in production of this commodity would bring down the government unless it took emergency measures, which would only be possible in the face of an international boycott pushed by the gringos. I believe that Guatemala's most difficult moment will come in about three years time, when a new president has to be elected. The names put forward so far are those who cannot be trusted in terms of maintaining the magnificent way that the revolution has been carried out up to now. If you are interested, and not afraid that you might be harassed over there, I can send you some interesting publications. But I won't do so until I hear from you.

I thought about only writing on one sheet of paper, as my economic situation is very precarious and a new sheet will cost another 10 cents, but I want to hear about things:

First, how is student life going in this month of March (and any month that may have passed between now and when you write)? What are your plans or lack thereof? I ask because your letter indicated that you were in a desperate, very romantic, but dangerous situation. By way of advice, if one wants to be a fatalist, I recommend that one should be a fatalist in the positive sense of the word and not worry so much about wasted time and potential failure. The most difficult thing you can do is to try to stop time moving forward and it seems that you are trying to do just that by lamenting the days as they pass. If you look back in one or two years, you will see how much progress you have made. Sorry for adopting the tone of a doctor.

Second, what has happened with your group of intellectuals and the magazine — something extra difficult to bring together? What can you tell me about the life of Paz and her health?

Third, what about Montenegro. I wrote him a letter but he didn't reply. Then I wrote to Dicstein and he also didn't respond. So I know nothing about the lives of the tiny group of people I knew back there in the dives the doctors frequented. When you decide to write to me again, read these questions and answer them.

Turning now to talk about myself, I would say that my efforts to find work as a doctor here have been a complete failure due to the hermetic spirit of the law, which was written to satisfy the prerogatives of a group of oligarchs. They're all the heirs of those who wanted the revolution — typically bourgeois — of [19]44 but who now won't let go of their loot, under any circumstance.

Among my occasional occupations, I have looked into some of your research [into parasites] and discovered some worrying statistics: 98 percent of children are infected with roundworms or hookworms. I dedicated myself to breaking open the backside of a *vinchuca* (which they call triatomines here) to find *cruxi* and *rangelis* trypanosomes, which are also present in abundance. That's it as far as medicine is concerned, other than that I have done whatever job I can to avoid dying of hunger, only to have finally struck it lucky: it seems I'm going to Petén, in the Guatemalan jungle, having been hired as a nurse on a meager wage, but I'll be deep in the bush working with rubber and timber workers in an ancient Mayan area — the Yucatán is a more modernized version of this culture lost in the jungle — and have the opportunity to study all kinds of tropical diseases. The only thing I'm waiting for — because here you always have to wait for something — is for the union to approve my appointment, as it is an important position in terms of the boss-union relationship. I hope to convince them that I am not as bad a guy as they think I am just because the boss recommended me. If all goes well, within a fortnight mosquitos will be feasting on my body and once again I'll be communing with Mother Nature. The only thing I am a bit sad about is that in Venezuela I could have being doing the same thing for $800 instead of $125. Damn the money!

Tita, fraternal vibes, I hope to receive news via the same consular route and encourage you to overcome your *via crucis*. Until we meet again.

Ernesto

To Mother

[Guatemala, late] April 1954

Vieja, my own *Vieja*,

You won't believe that I can begin to make papa happy, but there are signs that things are improving for me and my economic prospects are not looking so dire. I have no problem telling you when tragedy strikes only because it happens to be true and I assumed that the old man would regard me as being macho enough to take whatever came along. But if you prefer fairytales, I can tell some very beautiful ones. Since I've been silent, my life has been as follows: I headed off with a backpack and a briefcase, half walking, half hitching, only sometimes (shame!) paying my way, thanks to the $10 the government itself had given me. I reached El Salvador and the police confiscated some books I was bringing from Guatemala, but I got through and managed to obtain the visa to reenter Guatemala (and this time the correct one). I went to visit the ruins of the *Pipiles*, an [indigenous] race of Tlaxcaltecas that set out to conquer the south (their center was in Mexico), and they remained here until the Spaniards arrived. The ruins are nothing like the Mayan constructions, and even less like those of the Incas.

Then I went and spent a few days at the beach while waiting for my visa to come through. I had asked for it in order to visit some splendid Honduran ruins. I slept on the seashore in a sleeping bag I have acquired and, although my diet was not entirely strict, I was in fine shape from this healthy lifestyle, except for some sunburn. I befriended some guys who, like everyone in Central America, are good drinkers, and taking advantage of the extroversion arising from the imbibing of alcohol, I hit them a with a bit of Guatemalan propaganda and recited some little verses in deep Red. The result: we all ended up in the slammer, but they let us out after a word of advice from a commander, a fine fellow, who suggested I sing to the evening roses and other things of beauty. I preferred to vanish like a sonnet into the smoke. The Hondurans denied me a visa for the simple fact of my living in Guatemala although, I should say, it was my healthy intention to check out the strike that has taken broken out there that has the support of 25 percent of the entire working population, an impressive figure anywhere but extraordinary in a country where there is no right to strike and the unions must organize clandestinely. The fruit company is furious and, of course, Dulles and the CIA want to intervene in Guatemala because of its terrible crime of buying arms on whatever market it can, since the United States hasn't sold them as much as a single cartridge for a long time [...].

Naturally, I didn't consider the possibility of staying on there. On the way back, I headed off on semi-deserted roads with my wallet in a terrible state because here a dollar is worth about one *mango* [peso], so even 20 don't go very far. One day I walked about 50 kilometers (maybe that's a bit of an exaggeration, but a lot anyway) and, after many days, I arrived at the fruit company's hospital where there is a complex of small but very beautiful ruins. There I became totally convinced of what my Latin American blood didn't want to acknowledge: that our forebears are Asian (tell the old man that they will soon be claiming paternal authority). There are figures in basrelief that represent Buddha himself, all the details show they are exactly the same as those of the ancient Hindu civilizations. The place is really beautiful, so much so that I committed Silvestre Bonnard's[31] crime against my stomach and

---

31   A character in a novel by the famous French writer Anatole France.

spent a dollar and a bit to buy film and hire myself a camera. Then I begged a bite to eat at the hospital but didn't even manage to get the tank half full. I had no money to get back to Guatemala City by train, so I headed off to Puerto Barrios where I found work as a laborer unloading barrels of tar, earning $2.63 an hour for 12 hours, working as hard as hell in a place where there are lascivious mosquitoes diving at you in astonishing numbers. My hands finished up in a terrible state and my back worse, but I confess that I was quite happy. I worked from 6:00 in the afternoon until 6:00 in the morning and slept in an abandoned house by the sea. Then I left for Guatemala and here I am with better prospects […].

(This writing isn't really my own scattered thoughts but because four Cubans[32] are arguing right next to me.)

Next time, when things are a bit quieter, I'll send you any news I have… A hug for everyone.

[Unsigned]

---

32   Ñico López, Mario Dalmau and Armando Arencibia were some of the Cuban friends Ernesto refers to.

To Zoraida Boluarte[33]

Guatemala, sixth month of being skinny

Woman, you dumped me at the prime of my life,

I didn't respond earlier to your loving, energetic missive due to the simple fact that I just had no way of doing so. These have been six months of tightening the belt, meaning the complete abandonment of anything that is superfluous, such as fats and certain proteins, to focus on what is genuinely important: carbohydrates, skin and bones. I should say that this has heightened my faculties and I now have an extraordinary agility. The other day they timed me over 90 meters, placing a steak at the finish line, and the timer was still on zero by the time I got there. I was almost on the verge of leaving for Mexico, leaving behind all the stuff I've collected in six months. Although my honor didn't hold me back, because I did everything I could to leave, on the border they demanded that I show one hundred dollars, a sum twice my most optimistic dream. In the end, they gently turned me away, and my honor won out. Those photographs that you continue to ask for still haven't been processed, I guess I'll develop them one day. [...]

My economic prospects appear to be somewhat clearer as there are indications that the government will take me on as a nurse in a remote area where no one else is willing to go. I am not paying

---

33   Che's relationship with Dr. Pesce and his assistant Zoraida Boluarte dates back to his first trip through Latin America with his friend Alberto Granado. Both of them provided him with support and friendship, which is why Ernesto visited them again on his return visit to Peru.

too much attention to my medical studies, as all my books are in Panama and here I have nowhere to go to read. [...]

Please pass on my greetings to all the patients, to all the hospital employees, and especially to Ms. Peirano and to your family and yourself and Blanquita, a loving embrace from the poor

Che[34]

---

34   In signing this letter as "Che," Ernesto is identifying himself as an Argentine.

To Mother
[Guatemala] April 1954

Vieja,

As you can see, I didn't go to El Petén. The son of a bitch who was supposed to hire me made me wait for a month, only to tell me it wasn't on. […]

I'd already given him a list of medicines, instruments and everything else, and had studied up hard on the region's most common tropical diseases. Of course, the knowledge will serve me well anyway, and more so now that I have an opportunity to work in a banana growing region for the [United] Fruit Company.

What I don't want to miss is a visit to the ruins of El Petén. There's a city there, Tikal, which is a wonder, and another, Piedras Negras, much less important but where Mayan art nevertheless reached extraordinary heights. The museum here has a lintel, which, although completely wrecked, is a true work of art by anyone's standard.

My old Peruvian friends lacked this tropical sensibility and weren't able to create such high-quality work, apart from the fact that they didn't have the limestone from around here that is so easy to sculpt. […]

I am increasingly happy to have left. My medical knowledge is not expanding, and at the same time I'm absorbing another kind of knowledge that engages me much more. […]

Yes, I want to visit those places, but don't know when or how. To discuss plans in my situation would be to hurry a dream. Anyway, if, but only if, I get the fruit company job, I think I'll try to settle my debts here, and the ones I left there, buy myself a camera, visit El Petén, and take myself north in Olympian style, that is, to Mexico […].

I'm happy you have such a high opinion of me. In any case, it is very unlikely that anthropology will be the exclusive focus of my mature years. It seems somewhat paradoxical to me that I should make my life's "guiding star" the study of what is definitively dead. I am certain of two things: first is that if I reach my truly creative phase at about 35, my exclusive, or at least main, concern will be nuclear physics, or genetics, or some other field that brings together the most interesting aspects of knowledge. The second is that the Americas will be the theater of my adventures in a way that is much more significant than I could have imagined. I think I have really come to understand it and I feel [Latin] American, which means having a character distinct from all other peoples on the earth. Naturally, I'll visit the rest of the world. [...]

There's little to say my about daily life that would interest you. In the mornings I go to the health department and work in the laboratory for a few hours; in the afternoons I visit libraries or museums to study a bit about the region; in the evenings I read medicine or whatever else, write letters and do domestic chores. I drink *mate* if we have any, and engage in endless discussions with compañera Hilda Gadea, an *aprista*,[35] whom I try to persuade gently to leave that shit party. She has a heart of platinum, at least. She helps me in every aspect of my daily life (in particular at the boarding house).

[Unsigned]

---

35   Hilda Gadea was a member of APRA (American Popular Revolutionary Alliance) in Peru. Hilda and Che married the following year in Mexico.

To Mother
[Guatemala], June 20, 1954

Dear *Vieja,*

This letter will reach you a little after your birthday, which might pass a little uneasily on my account. Let me say there's nothing to fear at the moment, but the same cannot be said of the future, although personally I have the feeling that I'm inviolable (inviolable is not the word, perhaps my subconscious is playing a bad joke on me).

To paint a picture of the situation: For the first time, five or six days ago, a pirate light plane from Honduras flew over Guatemala for the first time but did nothing. The next day and on successive days they bombed several Guatemalan military installations, and two days ago a plane machine-gunned the lower neighborhoods of the city, killing a two-year-old girl. The incident has served to unite all Guatemalans behind their government, and others who, like myself, have been drawn to the country.

Simultaneously, mercenary troops led by an ex-army colonel (dismissed from the army some time ago for treason) left Tegucigalpa, the capital of Honduras, crossed the border, and have now penetrated quite deeply into Guatemalan territory. The government, proceeding with great caution to ensure that the United States cannot declare Guatemala the aggressor, has limited itself to protesting to Tegucigalpa and sending a full report of events to the UN Security Council, allowing the attacking forces to advance far enough that there would be no so-called border incidents. Colonel Árbenz certainly has guts; he's prepared to die at his post if necessary. His latest speech only reaffirmed this fact, which everyone already knew, bringing a measure of calm. The danger does not come from the number of troops that have entered the country so far, as this is minimal, or from the planes that have done no more than bomb civilian homes and machinegun people; the danger lies in how the gringos (in this case, the Yankees) manipulate their stooges at the United Nations, since even the vaguest of declarations would greatly benefit the attackers.

The Yankees have finally dropped the good guy mask Roosevelt had adopted, and now commit atrocities everywhere. If things reach the point where it's necessary to fight the planes and modern troops sent by the [United] Fruit Company or the United States, then a fight it will be. The people's spirits are very high, and the shameful attacks, along with the lies in the international press, have united even those who are indifferent to the government. There is a real climate of struggle. I have been assigned to the emergency medical services and have also joined the youth brigades to receive military instruction for whatever comes next. I don't think the tide will reach us, although we'll see what happens after the [UN] Security Council meets, which I think is tomorrow. At any rate, by the time this letter reaches you, you'll know what to expect in this regard.

For the rest, there's nothing much new. As the Argentine embassy is currently not functioning, I've received no fresh news since a letter from Beatriz and another of yours last week.

I'm told that at any minute I'll get the job at the health department, but the offices have been so busy with the commotion that it seems a little imprudent to hassle them about my little job when they're busy with much more important things.

Well, *Vieja*, I hope you had the happiest birthday possible after this troubled year. I'll send news as soon as I can.

Chau,

[Unsigned]

To Mother
[Guatemala], July 4, 1954

Vieja,

Things have happened as in a beautiful dream from which you don't want to wake. Reality is knocking on many doors and the gunfire rewarding the most fervent devotees of the old regime is beginning to be heard. Treason continues to be the birthright of the army, and once again we have proof of the aphorism that the liquidation of the army is a fundamental principle of democracy (even if that aphorism doesn't exist, I believe it to be true). [...]

The cold, hard truth is that Árbenz didn't know how to rise to the occasion.

This is how it all happened: After the attacks from Honduras began, without a declaration of war or anything, in fact, all the while protesting against alleged border violations, planes began to bomb the city. We were completely defenseless, without planes, antiaircraft guns, or shelters. There were some deaths, not many. But panic took hold, especially among the "brave and loyal army" of Guatemala. A US military mission met the president and threatened a bombing campaign that would reduce Guatemala to ruins, and then there was declaration of war from Nicaragua and Honduras, which the United States would have to join under the terms of its mutual-aid pacts. The military stood up and gave Árbenz an ultimatum.

Árbenz didn't consider the fact that the city was full of reactionaries, and that the homes being destroyed would belong to them rather than the people, who have nothing and who were defending the government. He didn't consider that an armed people is invincible, despite the recent examples of Korea and Indochina. He could have armed the people, but he chose not to, and this is the result.

I already had my little job but lost it immediately, so I'm now back to where I started, although without debts, having canceled them for reasons of *force majeure*. I live comfortably thanks to a good friend who is returning some favors, and I don't want for anything. I know nothing about my future, except that it's likely I'll go to Mexico. I'm somewhat ashamed to say that I've thoroughly enjoyed these recent days. That magical sensation of invulnerability I mentioned in another letter really got me going when I saw people running like crazy as the planes appeared or, at night, when blackouts meant the city was lit up with gunfire.

By the way, the bombers are impressive. I watched one heading for a target relatively close to me. It grew larger by the second as little tongues of fire flicked intermittently from its wings, the noise of shrapnel exploding and machine-gun fire was so loud. For a moment it was suspended in the air, horizontal, before diving sharply and quickly — you felt the impact of the bombs shaking the earth. Now all this is over, and you only hear the rockets of the reactionaries who have emerged like ants from under the ground to celebrate victory and hunt down communists to lynch, as they call anyone from the previous government. The embassies are full to the brim, especially ours, along with that of Mexico. You could make a sport of all of this, but it's obvious now that the few fat cats can be easily conned.

If you want some idea of what this government is about, I'll mention a few things: One of the first villages to fall belonged to the [United] Fruit company, whose workers were on strike. The invaders immediately declared the strike over, took the leaders to the cemetery and killed them there by throwing hand grenades at their chests.

One night a flare fired from the cathedral lit up the darkened city just as a plane was flying overhead. The first act of thanksgiving was given by the bishop; the second, by [John] Foster Dulles, the fruit company's lawyer.[36] Today, July 4, there's a solemn mass with all the trappings, and all the papers congratulate the US government in ridiculous terms on its national day.

Vieja, I'll see how I can get these letters to you. If I put them in the mail it will ruin my nerves (the president said — whether you believe this is up to you — that this was a country with strong nerves). A big hug for everyone.

[Unsigned]

---

36   John Foster Dulles later became US Secretary of State under President Eisenhower.

To Tita Infante
Mexico, September 29, 1954

Dear Tita,

Today, far from Guatemala — materially and spiritually — I am rereading your letter in order to reply, and it came across as strange to me. I felt a special warmth in it, full of desperation for not being able to do anything, which really moved me. I would like to believe that much of this was directed toward me but I imagine it was provoked more by [events in] Guatemala. Inside and out, we felt the same thing: betrayed from within and from outside, just like the Spanish Republic, but we didn't fall (allow me to plough in a little deeper) with the same nobility. It was a different time, and I have heard all the explanations that the compañeros have given and which I was able to pass on to you, but something was nonetheless missing. From here, I look at events with a totally different perspective and have begun to realize that Mexico played a role in this comedy, the same sad role that France played in the other one [Spain]. The atmosphere here is completely different from what it was like in Guatemala. Here you can also say what you want, but on the condition that you can pay for it; that is, you can smell the scent of the democracy of the dollar. Frankly, I would prefer to spend time in the ruins rather than hear one of Mexico's best poets say that it was crazy for Guatemala to have "flirted with Russia." Guatemala's enemy was the communists: they have already forgotten who paid for the planes and who put the puppet that is now in power there, and everything else.

Argentina unites, among its enormous number of castrates, a

force that allows it to maintain a much more coherent policy than that of this country, where individual bravery is an axiomatic requirement.

My aspirations are unchanged and my immediate goal continues to be to go to Europe and then Asia; how, is another question. Regarding Mexico, beyond this general impression, I can tell you nothing definitive, nor about myself. I hope you have finished or are about to finish that shitty course you are doing and are getting your wings ready to fly somewhere, that is if no one has clipped them with the prosaic scissors of marriage.

Tita, as always a hug, and thanks for writing such a nice letter as the one about Guatemala.

Ernesto

To Zoraida Boluarte
México, October 22 [1954]

Dear friend,

As you can see, I'm still alive and I have added a new country to my collection, which means I now have the full set of Latin American countries, and am only missing the [Caribbean] islands to complete it. I like Mexico a lot, for a variety of reasons that I don't have time to outline in detail, but I didn't come here because I wanted to but rather because the (spurious, to put it politely) Guatemalan government expelled me from my beloved post, one that I had obtained, after seven months of arduous battle in the halls of ministries, just two days before Árbenz's resignation.

My experience in Guatemala (putting aside my time as a doctor) was very enriching. It taught me about all the fallacies the Yankees are capable of and their marvelous propaganda machine. I know you are not interested in politics, but I consider it my duty to tell you the truth about all the lies that the newspapers in your country, and in the continent as a whole, are spreading. There were no murders or anything like that. A number of executions, however, should have been carried in a timely manner, which is a different thing; if those executions had been carried out, the government may have had a fighting chance. Colonel Monsón was a minister without portfolio in the Árbenz government and was in that post precisely because he knew how to conspire. Castillo Armas is a wimp who didn't even know what he wanted and whose lack of politics led him to wage a fight against the church, one of the factors behind their triumph; naturally, in this he was influenced by the northern grandparents, but nevertheless he is an imbecile.

Talking about me, I would say that my hunger, which I mentioned in the attached letter, has subsided a fair bit, as I am now working with a camera in the city's parks and they feed me well. In the mornings I go to the hospital to work a bit on whatever they need to make sure that I don't completely forget that I'm a doctor. I cannot dedicate myself full-time to medicine because they don't pay me, but I hope that this situation will change in the coming months. My future projects continue to be nebulous; if I get a chance I'll "visit the belly of the beast," and from there go to Europe. If this doesn't work out, I'll go directly to Europe (how, I don't know) or perhaps to Cuba. The future will tell. The same hugs to the same people and remind them that I live in Etchegoyen. As always, my address is the Argentine Consulate, Mexico D.F.

Chau,

Che

To Mother
[Mexico], November 1954

Vieja, my *Vieja,*

(I confused you with the date)

[...] Even Beatriz is engaging in reprisals, and those telegrams she used to send no longer arrive.

To tell you about my life is to repeat myself because I'm doing nothing new. Photography is bringing in enough to live on and there is really no basis for believing I might be able to give it up anytime soon, although I'm working every morning as a researcher in two local hospitals. I think the best thing for me would be to slip into an unofficial job as a country doctor, somewhere near the capital. This would make it easier to devote my time to medicine for a few months. I'm doing this because I'm perfectly aware of how much I learned about allergies with Pisani. I have now compared notes with people who have studied in the United States, and who are no fools with regard to orthodox knowledge, and I think that Pisani's method is light years ahead. I want to get practical experience with the nuts and bolts of his systems so that I can land on my feet wherever that might be [...].

I'm slaving away here, busy every morning in the hospital and in the afternoons and Sundays I work as a photographer, while at night I study a bit. I think I mentioned I'm in a good apartment, I cook my own food and do everything myself, as well as bathe every day thanks to the unlimited supply of hot water.

As you can see, I'm changing in this aspect, but otherwise I'm the same because I don't wash my clothes very often, and wash them badly when I do, and I still don't earn enough to pay a washerwoman.

The scholarship is a dream I've given up on, as I had thought that in such a large country all you had to do was ask for something and it happened. You know that I have always been inclined to make drastic decisions, and here the pay is great. Everyone is lazy, but they don't get in the way when other people [want to] get things done, so I've got a free rein either here or in the countryside where I might go next. Naturally, this doesn't make me lose sight of my goal, which is Europe, where I'm planning to go no matter what happens. As for the United States, I haven't lost an ounce of hostility, but I do want to check out New York, at least. I'm not in the least worried about what might happen and know that I'll leave just as anti-Yankee as when I arrive (that's if I do get in).

I'm happy that people are waking up a bit, although I don't know what direction they are moving in. Anyway, the truth is that Argentina is as insular as you can get, even though in general terms the picture we get from here seems to suggest that they are taking important steps forward and that the country will be perfectly able to defend itself from the crisis the Yankees are about to set off by dumping their surplus food [...].

Communists don't have your sense of friendship but, among themselves, it is the same or better than yours. I have seen this very clearly and, in the chaos of Guatemala after the government was overthrown when it was every man for himself, the communists maintained their faith and comradeship and they constitute the only group that continued to work there.

I think they deserve respect and sooner or later I'll join the party. What mainly holds me back from doing so right now is that

I'm desperate to travel around Europe and I couldn't do this if I had to submit to a rigid discipline.

Vieja, till Paris.

[Unsigned]

To Tita Infante
Mexico, November 29, 1954

Dearest Tita,

I didn't immediately reply to you because my economic woes continue to be very dire and by the time that the end of the month comes around, I have to do a balancing act (and fast) to make it through. The information [about the situation in Argentina] you have given me is of great interest and will also be of much use to the people here who have had no news. [...]

Speaking about you, I see that your little disaster is clouding your thoughts and stopping you from doing anything right. Although by nature I am full of life — unlike you — I too have had my moments of abandonment and great pessimism. [...] Giving advice is something new to me, and giving it to you, who has always felt like my mother, seems even stranger, but I'll say something more generally: first, graduate as soon as possible; make it happen and do whatever it takes. Second, as soon as you have your degree, get the hell out of there, at least for a while.

I would sincerely like to inject you with some of the materialist love that I have for life, of which I consciously enjoy every moment. But for that I need more than a letter and my poor ability to convince you. Moreover, I would be a hypocrite if I put myself forward as an example, as the only thing I have done is run away from everything that bothered me; and even today, when I think that I am ready to go into battle (above all in the social aspect), I go peacefully on my pilgrimage wherever events take me, while never giving a thought to returning to Argentina to fight there. [...]

To finish, this business of thanking me for the confidence I have in you sounds hollow to me or false modesty. You know fully well that I trust you completely, not because of some isolated factor but because I am thoroughly aware of all your qualities, and playing the shrinking violet is not right. I do not thank you for any demonstration of your capabilities, I demand it, which is very different.

I have already carried on long enough, so to finish I'll tell you that I am making a living taking photos in the plaza and writing reports on the "*ches*" [i.e. Argentines] that pass through here for Agencia Latina de Noticias [Latin News Agency], a Peronist outfit. As I said at the start, this does not always give me enough to live on, above all to satisfy my wolf-like hunger, but there are signs that my situation will improve, and if it doesn't, at least it can't get worse, which is some kind of consolation. My economic problems become immaterial because they are somewhat chronic, while on the other hand, the scientific accolade I've had in Mexico has made me optimistic in terms of my medical studies and encouraged me to work like crazy on allergies, for free, in a hospital. Nevertheless, the results will certainly be good because Pisani is leagues ahead of any allergist, at least in the Western world, even though you have your doubts. All this leads me to believe that my economic luck will improve because, as they say here, success is converted into money in these blessed lands of God, as long as one is not a total fool.

Well, I'll stop here because otherwise I'll end up writing an encyclopedia in one sitting.

'Bye Tita. Receive as always an affectionate embrace from your friend along with the hope of materializing it soon, somewhere in the world, and as "doctor to doctor." Write if you see one.

[Unsigned]

To Mother
[Mexico, late 1954]

Vieja, my own *Vieja*,

It's true, I've been too lazy, but the real guilty party, as always, is Don Dinero [Mr. Money]. Anyway, the end of this wretched financial year of 1954 — part of which has treated me beautifully (like your face) — coincides with the end of my chronic hunger. I'm working as an editor at the Agencia Latina for 700 Mexican pesos a month (equivalent to 700 Argentine pesos), which provides a basic level of subsistence with the added bonus that I work for only three hours, three days a week. I can therefore spend the entire morning at the hospital, where I am stirring things up using Pisani's method. [...]

I'm still working as a photographer, but also spending time on more important things, like "studying," and some other little things that pop up. [...]

My immediate plans involve staying some six months or so in Mexico, which I find interesting and like a lot, and in this time apply, by the way, for a visa to visit "the sons of a great power,"[37] as [Guatemalan President] Arévalo calls them. If I get it, I'll go. If not, I'll see what other concrete plans I can make. I haven't abandoned the idea of slipping behind the Iron Curtain to see what's happening there. As you see, there's nothing new since my previous letter.

I'm very enthusiastic about the scientific research, which I'm

---

37   A reference to the United States.

capitalizing on because it won't last. I have two research projects on the run and may start on a third — all related to allergies — and very slowly I'm collecting material for a little book that will see the light of day (if ever) in a couple of years with the pretentious title, *The Role of the Doctor in Latin America*. I can speak with some authority on the subject, considering that, although I don't know much about medicine, I do have Latin America sized up. Of course, apart from a general outline and three or four chapters, I've written nothing, but time is on my side.

Regarding the change in my thinking, which is becoming sharper, I promise you that it will not be for much longer. What you are so afraid of can be reached in two ways: the positive one, when you are totally convinced, or the negative one, through a disillusionment with everything. I came along the second path, only to be immediately convinced that it is essential to follow the first. The way that the gringos treat Latin America (remember that the gringos are Yankees) was making me feel increasingly indignant, but at the same time I studied the reasons for their actions and found a scientific explanation.

Then came Guatemala and everything that is difficult to describe. I saw how the object of one's enthusiasm was diluted by what those gentlemen decided, how a new tale of Red guilt and criminality was concocted, and how the same treacherous Guatemalans set about propagating the story to beg a few crumbs from the table of the new order. I can't tell you, even approximately, when it was that I put reasoning aside and acquired something akin to faith, because the road was long and full of setbacks. [...]

[Unsigned]

To Father

[Mexico, February or March] 10, 1955

Dear *Viejo*,

As always, I am late in writing to you to congratulate you
for your 55th birthday, a memorable age in which you begin
to "settle down" and all that. I imagine you had a terrible time
trying hard to forget it was your birthday, and that you have
finally accepted that you are another year older. I am always
waiting for my financial situation to improve to be able to send a
present to someone in the family, but there seems no way at the
moment for me to convert debts into credits. For now I am just
managing hand to mouth. When I can, I'll send you the present
I have promised in the form of a funny book, such as *The Hidden
Truth of the Korean War* or *Guatemala, Democracy and the Empire*; in
other words, something that you'd enjoy and learn from at the
same time.

So that you stop bothering me about plans for my life, I'll tell
you what I have in mind: do what I can to get to Europe. This is
a bit vague, but it is all that I can give you at the moment. My
intentions: get a French scholarship, stay there for a year, and
then go to the [Soviet Union], any way I can and then, as always,
visiting compañero Mao as the final goal, but India is also on my
itinerary. We'll see about the scholarship, but there are serious
indications that I'll be lucky. I have submitted three or four
scientific projects that (with the modesty of a Guevara) I think are
very good. One of these in particular I hope will open doors for

me in any European university and allow me to improve myself
at my leisure.

[...] Regarding what you said about Mexico, this is completely
ridiculous, and I'll never tire of repeating what I told Ani [his
sister Ana María]: upheavals are taking place everywhere in the
world and now even more so with the change of government in
Russia. Mexico has been completely handed over to the Yankees,
to the point that when Nixon came they rounded up all the Puerto
Rican nationalists and others like them, and are holding them
hostage without anyone knowing where they are. The media says
nothing about this and talking to the media is banned, at the risk
of them being shut down. The FBI is much more dangerous than
the Mexican police; here they act as they please and arrest anyone
without any pretext. This is the political scenario.

The economic situation is terrible, prices are rising at an
alarming rate and the rot is so great that union leaders have been
bought off and are signing detrimental agreements with various
Yankee companies in which they give up the right to strike for one
or two years. There is practically no independent industry, much
less free trade. Without exaggerating, this is all heading towards a
giant shitstorm, and the only way you can make any money here is
by becoming a direct lackey of the gringo, something that I would
not recommend for a variety of reasons. Argentina is the oasis of
the Americas, we need to support Perón as much as possible to
avoid a terrible war. Like it or not, this is the situation we face.
Nixon is already touring each country to establish the quota
of labor and cheap primary materials (paid for with expensive
and out-dated machinery) which each of the poor states of the
Americas will contribute to the new Koreas.

[...] I am tired of writing nonsense, and you of reading it,
especially because our letters have crossed. So I'll bid you farewell,
wishing you everything one wishes when one's old man has a

birthday, and sending a big hug for you and all the gang. This one doesn't have stamps because I am writing and sending it to you without going home, but the next one will.

Chau,

[Unsigned]

To Aunt Beatriz
[Mexico] April 9, [1955]

Little Aunty,

I know I am ungrateful, a bad nephew, a hypocrite, a Red, etc. What has happened is the following: just as I reached a peak of enthusiasm about responding to my backlog of correspondence, the hurricane that was the Second Pan American Games hit, and I dedicated myself to the task of informing the Latin American public in detail about the games, along with providing them with beautiful photographs, which combined immediacy and beauty.[38] Once the great event was over and the personnel that covered the games had all been congratulated, a laconic cable from Agencia Latina informed us that they were ceasing transmission and that each correspondent should do what they thought best in terms of the personnel in their change (of wages, not a word). Hearing this news, and dedicating myself heart and soul to the task of biting my ass, all became mixed into one. Yesterday I finally achieved the feat, and from now on I belong to the race of the single-cheeked.

[...] Regarding the famous job you have offered me in consecutive letters, the only thing I can say — to add a pinch of seriousness — is that despite my wandering spirit, my repeated fecklessness and my other defects, I have deep and well-defined convictions. These convictions hold me back from accepting a job of the kind you have described as it would mean working in the

---

38   A selection of Ernesto's photos taken at the Pan American games are published in *Latin America Diaries: A Second Look at Latin America*, op. cit.

dungeons of the worst kind of thieves, those who traffic in human health, of which I consider myself a protector, when this work really should be done by qualified hands. I didn't reply earlier due to the work I had with the games, but nevertheless my answer is the same: I am poor but I have honor, as the thieves say.

A big and loving embrace for you, the recently married timid one, Baldy and Hercilita.[39]

Always affectionately,

Stalin II

---

39   The "recently married timid one" is referring to his aunt Ercilia (a widow who remarried). "Baldy" is Ercilia's new husband and Hercilita is her daughter.

To Tita Infante
Mexico, April 10, 1955

Dear Tita,

As always, I was very happy to receive your letter and, like almost always, it has taken me a long time to reply.

Apologies aren't important and I have had to dispense them in abundance, as my silence has been almost absolute in this past period, so that I won't bother to send you any. I'll only say, by way of informing you, that I held the prestigious role of sports writer for Agencia Latina, which is funded by the Top Guy in the Pink House [the president of Argentina]. My work during the Pan American Games was exhausting in every sense of the word, as I had to compile news, take photographs and chaperone the journalists who arrived from South America. I got no more than an average of four hours sleep a night during the games, as I was also responsible for developing and printing the photographs. I should have received monetary compensation for all this in the form of some $4,000, but the unexpected happened when Agencia Latina closed down without notice, from one day to the next, and without paying out a cent. I suspect that this was all due to some secret deal between the heads of state (in the Pink House and the White House). Or maybe the one in the Pink House just simply bent over. You would know more about this than I, as I'm so far away here and no one knows what information to believe […].

My projects are fluid and conditional, for a change. If I get the money I am owed (difficult but not impossible) I'll travel through Mexico to get to know this country better, and then I'll go to Cuba to complete my map of Latin America. Perhaps at the end of the year I'll get back to Caracas, to meet up with my great friend Granado, who is constantly insisting that I join him so that we continue [traveling] together. The only thing preventing me is the fact that Alberto is making a lot of money and this is always a brake on one's desire to roam. Nevertheless, we did a long trip together through the Americas and I have never been able to find a compañero like him, in every sense of the word. During our protracted materialistic debates, we always talked about the best place to set up shop together and he recently wrote to me from Italy where he is doing a course (which is not true), reiterating that we should meet up there around the 19th...

Scientifically speaking, I am a first-rate failure; all my big research projects have been blown away by the same wind that swept the Agencia and I find myself limited to presenting a modest paper in Mexico, in which I basically repeat Pisani's findings on semi-digested foods. This project will be presented at the Mexican Allergies Congress, on the 23rd of this month, and if it is published I'll send it to you, for no other reason than curiosity, as there is nothing new in it but simply a repetition of theories.

[...] Tita, I hope that we will soon bump into each other on some corner of some old European city, I with a satisfactorily full stomach and you with your degree in hand. For now this is the most we can aspire to, but we can confidently hope that the future belongs to the people. While we wait for that distant future or that chance meeting in Europe, receive a warm and tight embrace from your eternal friend.

[Unsigned]

To Mother
[Mexico] May 9, 1955

Oldest *Vieja*,

Your first-born son, who was on the verge of appearing in police records as a death from starvation, will now go down in history as a prominent allergist due, firstly, to the help of some friends and, secondly, to my own great scientific merits, both of which have helped me obtain a scholarship at the General Hospital of Mexico. The scholarship includes board, food, laundry, and nothing else, which means I'll have to find a way of obtaining cash elsewhere, according to those who have promised to help me. I don't necessarily believe this but it makes no difference as money is an interesting luxury, nothing more. The project I presented was not as successful as it appeared in the publication of the little article I have included, but it was well received and resulted in congratulations from the main head of allergies in Mexico[40] and the scholarship I mentioned. [...] I was about to go to the United States, or at least to Nueva Laredo, on the border, to work there on allergies, but I decided to take this job, which will provide me with some facilities and the opportunity to compile (over four to six months) some three or four specialist projects to publish in a magazine here [...].

[...] Regarding the 10 years, two have already passed, but I don't think our total separation will last for more than another two years, in the most extreme of cases, as my standing as a doctor is

---

40   Dr. Mario Salazar Mallén.

rising and I think that at my next stop, I'll be able to obtain a living more in accord with my status. The next step could be the United States (very difficult), Venezuela (feasible) or Cuba (probable). But my irrevocable goal continues to be Paris, and I'll get there, even if I have to swim across the Atlantic.

Big kisses for everyone and until next time.

[Unsigned]

To Zoraida Boluarte
Mexico, May 16, 1955

My dearest Zoraida,

I am responding to you after 10,000 years and, lo and behold, I am writing to you from the same place. I am still in Mexico and will be for a few more months, as I am now a researcher and intern in a hospital; I am dedicating myself solely to allergies. Leprosy has gone with the wind, although I haven't lost hope of being able to dedicate myself to it, if only to repay all the benefits I received from the patients and the healthy when it comes to Hansen's disease. [...]

I would usually now mention my plans, which regularly change every three days. The latest one, which has matured over the past two days, is to stay at the hospital for four to six months to work on three research projects on allergies, travel for two months through this wonderful country, and then fly with the fresh wind to Europe. Perhaps I'll make a brief stopover in Cuba, to add it to my collection, and Caracas, to hug the unfaithful one, or better said, unfaithful ones. Speaking of them, Calica is pursuing his marvelous vocation as a vagabond in Caracas, although minus the beard and making US dollars, and Alberto has gone on a short four-month trip to Old Europe to spend some of his pesos (he has plenty). As you can see, I am the only poverty-stricken one.

There is little left for me to say about this beautiful part of the planet, now it is up to you to tell me how things are going there: how are the people from Guía, especially the doctor? How is everyone at your place and where is your sister (in your previous letter she was tossing up between university or the kitchen)?

I sincerely believe that the kitchen is a beautiful place for her (whether in Peru or Mexico, her marmalades have arrived in perfect condition and are always eaten with great delight — this is not a suggestion but rather a statement of fact). The brochure you promised about the poor married New Yorker never arrived. The photos have been carried away by that same wind that halted my trek to the East and are probably somewhere in Panama. My inspiration is dying, and my asthma has almost completely died, in Mexico. My tentacles open up to send fraternal and material vibes from my gaucho soul to the lands of the titans (the Incas, Pizarro, Odría). The paper tore: a coincidence, or was it the anger of the spirits of the land for including Pizarro?

Enough of my stupidities, *arrivederchi*, or whatever. My address is always the Consulate, a tight embrace for the whole family.

Respond, *papusa*,

Chau,

Ernesto

To Father
⌊Mexico⌋ May 27, 1955

Dear *Viejo*,

The decreasing frequency of my replies (see how important I am?) means that today it's your turn. Once again, I don't know what to say, as I've told almost everything to at least one of the other family members who are always so concerned about my health. Given my position in the hospital, I seem to be fulfilling your aspirations, as I spend 24 hours a day speaking about illnesses and how to cure them (I don't cure anything, of course). After presenting my project, and finally getting them to approve my residency, I decided to try to demonstrate *in vitro* the presence of antibodies in allergy sufferers (I think I'll fail); to create so-called *propectanes*, a bit of food digested in such a way that if the patient eats a larger amount later it does not harm them (I think I'll fail); to demonstrate that hyaluronidase — let's see if you know as much as you say you do — is an important factor in the cause of allergies (my greatest hope); and two other collaborative projects, a big one with the head of allergies in Mexico, M. Salazar Mallén, and the other, with the best chemist here in Mexico, on a problem that I only have an intuition about but I believe something important will come of it. These are my scientific prospects. This outlook also means the possibility of a change in my aspiration to wander […].

[…] In general, my next adventures seem to look more promising, as I'll be able to present anywhere I go, not only as Pisani's collaborator (by far the most capable of the allergists I've met), but also now because of my own project and my limited, given how extremely focused it is, but very clear knowledge of the problem. If the next country I get to is Cuba, I won't work there but make a quick trip around the island, catching up with all the friends I made in exile (theirs), and then escape to Europe or wherever.

[...] I think I told you that Agencia Latina had promised me a trip to Melbourne next year [for the Olympic Games], something that is now out of the question, as they haven't even paid me, but I really liked the idea and would have loved to see kangaroos.[41]

Of my current daily life I can't tell you much, as it is simply a succession of ward, laboratory and library, enlivened by some English translations.

Viejo, until the candles go out, an embrace.

[Unsigned]

---

41   The 1956 Olympic Games were held in Melbourne, Australia.

To Mother
[Mexico] June 17, 1955

Dear *Vieja*,

I am writing this message of congratulation in the midst of the uncertainty provoked by the series of events and contradictory news received from there.[42]

[…] I hope that things are not as bad as they say they are, and that no one we know is mixed up in a mess that can't be resolved.

[…] According to the news we have here, the death toll is high, almost terrifyingly so for Argentina. And the impression is that the majority of the dead are civilians, which only deepens the sensation of anxiety and uncertainty I get from reading the news, despite the fact that I don't believe anything I read because everything is censored, distorted or simply made up just so that they can publish something because people here read any news from Buenos Aires avidly. I hope there have not been any bombings or anything of the sort for your [special] day, as you deserve to be starting the new year peacefully after all the upheavals you've had since I left. Please continue to write often, to give me the news from around the world, and to tell me how the doctor[43] is doing and when he is getting married.

Regarding my future, there was a chance that things were going to change, but in the end nothing happened: I don't know if I told

---

42   His mother's birthday was on June 23. The Argentine navy had recently launched an attack on the government of Juan Perón and there were rumors of a coup.

43   Roberto Guevara, Ernesto's brother.

you that Agencia Latina screwed me out of a sum of about 6,000 pesos. They have now paid me, but only 3,000, of which I have to deduct 500 to pay some debts. They gave me 10 days' notice that they were going to pay me, so I immediately went to buy a ticket for a boat to Spain, as they told me they were going to pay me the full amount, which was just enough. With what I have now, there is no chance that I can travel in the same style (as a paying passenger). So I have decided to follow my old, regular routine of staying here until September 1; spend two months getting to know Mexico; and then head to Veracruz to get a boat to wherever it takes me. After all, this tough and inhospitable Mexico has treated me well and I'll leave here with more money than when I arrived, my respectable name on a number of more or less useful articles and, most importantly, having consolidated many ideas and aspirations that had been swirling around in my head. My main goal continues to be to become a physician one day, but this remains an ideal aspiration that from the start was destined to be recorded as an unfulfilled aspiration […].

Thinking about you today I felt, like in the tangos, a melancholic need to yearn for those times when I had no work: the main thing is that I'm in a tango mood, or rather, feeling like an Argentine, a feeling I've usually ignored. I think this indicates that I'm aging (which is essentially characterized by weariness) or perhaps I'm missing my sweet and peaceful home, where lulled by the gentle tones of family arguments I spent my childhood and youth. Nevertheless, you must get your aunt's inheritance, even if you have to kill for it, and you must go to Paris, where we will meet up.[44] I think you will like it, but for me, it is a biological need, something I feel is feasible and is continually maturing. I don't know if it's the right term, but I view it as an entelechy. My non-

---

44   The inheritance that his mother should have received was from her aunt
      Sara de la Serna.

medical life continues to move along at a monotonous, Sunday rhythm, marked by feats such as climbing Popocatépetl (I finally got to see the Pacha Mama's tonsils), the highest volcano in Mexico at 5,400 meters.[45] Honestly, it was easy and thrilling, and now I know that I have the minimum conditions required, I plan to repeat the exploit of Orizaba, the tallest peak in Mexico and the second tallest in North America, but I have to wait a bit as it is an expensive endeavor.

[…] Anyway, I have to tell you, there is a group of little children from sixth grade whom I have enchanted with my adventures and who are interested in learning about the teachings of Saint Karl [Karl Marx]. I have decided to dedicate what little spare time I have to this.

[…] I'm telling you all this so that you don't feel as though you have grown another year older in vain, because together with the bureaucratic specie you gave birth to, you brought into this world a little wandering prophet who, in a loud voice, goes around announcing the coming of the final judgment day .

Vieja, I can only keep boring you for so long because a sheet of paper costs 80 cents and, as the boss[46] says, the internal organ that pains Argentines the most is the pocket. I hope you pass every winter happily and that you are able to get the cash together to meet me in Paris before you turn 50 (I say this not as a superstition but so that I see you soon), a kiss and big embrace from your wandering first born.

[Unsigned]

45　Pacha Mama is the mythical Incan goddess representing Mother Earth.
46　A reference to General Juan Perón, who was president of Argentina three times: 1946–1952, 1952–1955 and 1973–1974.

To Mother
Buenos Aires,[47] July 20, 1955

Dear *Vieja*,

I had no excuse for not writing for several days, which I can't explain, given that even at work I am better organized and have a few hours to myself. One of the reasons I took my time was your analysis of what has happened in Argentina because I totally disagree with you, a little *a posteriori* and a little *a priori* regarding the dates that you mentioned. Things from here are as unclear as they are there, but there are some things we know based on current information and previous experience. The "monstrous" rallies by the Catholics are something I can't get my head around; I remember the monstrous rallies of the UD[48] that came to nothing in clean elections.

[...] The others, for whom there is no way of escaping their fate, are those shits from the air force who, after slaughtering people indiscriminately, flew on to Montevideo saying they were simply acting according to their faith in God. It is remarkable to see people, who cried when their church was burnt down, turning around and viewing the deaths of so many "blacks" as the most natural thing in the world.[49] Don't forget that many of them went to die for a cause, because the idea that they were forced to go is only partly

---

47   Ernesto wrote Buenos Aires in error. This letter was sent from Mexico to his mother in Buenos Aires.

48   The Unión Democrática, a coalition of political parties in Argentina that opposed Perón.

49   President Perón affectionately (and somewhat patronizingly) called his supporters "*cabecitas negras*" {black heads] due to the predominance of dark-skinned, indigenous or mixed-race Argentines among them.

true, in any case. Every "black" person has a family to maintain and the people who have left those families on the street are the same ones who went to Uruguay to beat their chests about their macho prowess. Another important thing is the number of "good people" who died, putting aside those fortuitous cases; this also gives us an indication of the character of the people who wanted to overthrow Perón and the future of an Argentina governed by an Olivieri or a Pastor, which is the same thing anyway.[50] The army only remains in its barracks when the government serves its class interest; the only thing that changes is a certain democratic veneer, as we see in Mexico, where pseudo-democratic acts obscure what is really going on. Olivieri or Pastor or whoever they put forward, as this is still not clear, will turn on the people as soon as the first serious strike occurs, and then it will not be any kids like Inchauspi who die; they will kill hundreds of "blacks" for the crime of attempting to defend social gains.[51] And *La Prensa* will say, in a dignified tone, that there could be no doubting just how dangerous it would have been to allow workers from a vital industry in the country to go on strike and, moreover, to use violence to win their demands, as occurred in the case in point, where they shot at police officers.[52] Whether you agree or disagree with such actions, this only occurred sporadically under Perón, and for me this is more important than the well-publicized deaths of people from our social class who had the misfortune of being hit by a bomb or shrapnel.

Moreover, I don't know how it's possible to believe that the navy is made up of pure little angels while the army is a pack of devils; the only appreciable difference is that in the navy there are

---

50   Olivieri was an Argentine marine who was a minister under Perón and
        Pastor was a key figure in a conservative Argentine party.
51   Inchauspi was a young man from an elite family who was shot during the
        coup against Perón.
52   *La Prensa* was a reactionary newspaper in Argentina.

more kids from very wealthy backgrounds who resent the loss of some of the class privileges they had previously, losses that Perón is not responsible for because he is little more than an interpreter of a preexisting situation in Argentina. And besides, no matter how many rumors there are to the contrary, the Church had a lot to do with the coup of [19]16, as did our dear friends whose methods I was able to see up close in Guatemala.[53] Don't forget that Olivieri was in the United States not long ago, on the one hand, and that, on the other, the Vatican is one of the principal capitals in Europe and that when it comes to international politics it marches side by side with the United States. The way in which the Mexican media dealt with the issue leaves no room for doubt, despite a commentator closely aligned to the White House insinuating that Perón's error (error in the minds of the free world) was his tendency to remain neutral and his propensity to trade with countries behind the Iron Curtain. Anyway, enough of politics.

[…] On the contrary, there was no better school for my scientific development nor will there be for some years. Everything I am working on here, stumbling along without help, I would have been able to perfect with [Pisani's] help; not to mention how his laboratory was perfectly set up. Here I work in a laboratory for bacteriology that is one of the best in Mexico and yet far inferior to [Pisani's], as well as a physiology lab that is not worth mentioning, as it doesn't even have a simple gas burner.

My article was published in an allergy journal, very glossy. I'll send you a copy when they give me one.

There is little to tell you about me apart from the news that I tackled the Popo[54] — as they call it here — we were truly heroic but failed to reach the peak. I was prepared to leave my bones

---

53   A reference to the role of the United States in the overthrow of President Árbenz in Guatemala in 1954.
54   Popocatépetl (or Popo) is an extinct volcano near Mexico City.

there but we got a fright when both feet of my Cuban climbing compañero became frozen and the five of us had to go back down. After climbing down some 100 meters (which at that height is a lot) the storm died down briefly and the mist lifted; it was then that we realized that we were nearly at the edge of the crater, but it was too late to turn back. We had been battling for six hours with snow up to the groin with every step and our feet soaking wet due to the poor quality of our equipment (I'm still using Roberto's boots).

Our guide got us lost in the snow trying to avoid crevasses, which can be very dangerous, and all of us were exhausted from the effort of walking through such soft, deep snow. We descended like toboggans, throwing ourselves down the slope like we used to do in the pools in the Sierra, and with the same result, as I reached the bottom without my pants. The Cuban won't try the climb again but when I get together the few dollars I need, I'll go back to Popo, not to mention that I have Orizaba to tackle in September as well.

My trotters finally thawed when we came down, but my face and neck are as burnt as if I had been an entire day in the sun in Mar del Plata. My face at the moment looks like Frankenstein's, because of the vaseline I've applied and the puss oozing from the blisters that have formed. Moreover, my tongue is in a similar condition because I binged on snow. It was a wonderful experience, my only concern is that an old man of 59 who climbed with us showed he was in much better shape than the rest of us. He looked exactly like *Cara de Ángel* [Angel Face], and at the start said that his mama had told him he was crazy for coming along, but when he began climbing our hearts sank as we watched him climb like a mountain goat. [...]

[Unsigned]

To Mother
[Mexico] September 24, 1955

Dear *Vieja*,

This time it seems my fears have come true and that your despised enemy of so many years has fallen. Here the reaction was immediate: all the newspapers in the country and foreign journalists announced with great joy that the terrible dictator had fallen. The North Americans breathed a sigh of relief for the $425 million they will now be able to extract from the country. The bishop of Mexico displayed his satisfaction with the fall of Perón, and all the Catholics and right-wingers I've met in this country have not hidden their happiness. My friends and I, on the other hand, are not so happy. We are following with natural anguish the fate of the Peronist government and the threats made by the fleet that they would shell Buenos Aires. Perón fell like the people of his ilk do, with neither the posthumous dignity of [Brazilian President] Vargas[55] nor the energetic denunciations of Árbenz, who named those responsible for the aggression against him. Here, progressive people have defined the Argentine process as "another triumph of the dollar, the sword and the cross."

I know that you are happy today, breathing the air of freedom. [...]

Not long ago, in another letter, I pointed out that the military never hands over power to civilians unless those civilians

---

55   Getulio Vargas was president of Brazil who preferred to commit suicide in 1954 rather than be overthrown by the military.

guarantee that they will protect their class domination [...]. I confess with complete sincerity that the fall of Perón has made me very bitter, not for him, but for what it means for all of the Americas, because as much as you don't like this, and despite the forced retreats of recent times, Argentina was the champion for all of those who believe the enemy lies to the north. For me, who lived through bitter times in Guatemala, this was but a poor replica. When, together with the loyal news outlets (it's strange to call them that) we heard the voice of Córdoba,[56] which theoretically was occupied, I began to sense trouble. Afterwards, everything followed the same script: the president resigned; a junta began negotiations but from a position of resistance; then this came to an end, and a military man stood up with a little marine by his side — the only new ingredient with respect to Guatemala. Then Cardinal Copello spoke to the people, full of pride, as he made mental calculations how his business would go under the new junta. As usual, newspapers from around the world — from this side of the world — began to howl. The junta refused to give Perón a passport, but announced freedom for all. People like you think you are witnessing the dawn of a new day. I can assure you that [Arturo] Frondizi[57] will not see it like that, because assuming the Radicals take power, it won't be him who takes the reigns, but Yadarola, Santander[58] or someone else who serves the interests of the Yankees, the clergy and, of course, the military. Maybe you won't see the violence because it won't be inflicted on your circle [...]. The Communist Party, over time, will be wiped out, and perhaps the day will come when even papa is convinced he made

---

56   Córdoba was a bastion of anti-Perón mobilizations.

57   Arturo Frondizi became president of Argentina in 1958 as the leader of the Unión Cívica Radical Intransigente (Intransigent Radical Civic Union) but was overthrown by fascist soldiers in 1962.

58   Yadarola and Santander were two Radical politicians who supported the coup against Perón.

a mistake. Who knows what will happen between now and then to your wandering son. Perhaps he might have decided to settle in his homeland (a genuine possibility) or initiate a real struggle. [...][59]

Perhaps a bullet, one of those so common in the Caribbean, will put an end to my existence (this is not a brag, nor is it a concrete possibility, it's just that lots of bullets are flying about in these parts). Perhaps, I'll simply continue as a vagabond long enough to complete a solid education and and do all those things I want to do before seriously dedicating myself to pursuing my goals. Things are moving at a rapid pace and no one can tell where I'll be, or what cause I'll be pursuing, next year

I don't know if you have heard the news of my marriage and the impending arrival of an heir. From Beatriz's letter it would appear not. So, if this is the case, I am hereby making the official announcement so that you can tell others: I have married [Hilda] Gadea and we are expecting a child sometime soon. I received Beatriz's newspapers; they have been of great interest. I would like to receive those published recently, and especially *Nuestra Palabra* [the paper of the Argentine Communist Party] every week.

Chau,

A kiss for all the family, Hilda sends her regards.

[Unsigned]

---

59   Ernesto had recently met Fidel Castro in Mexico and agreed to join the struggle to overthrow the Batista dictatorship in Cuba. Events in Argentina and the coup against President Perón obviously firmed up his commitment.

To Tita Infante

Mexico, September 24, 1955

Dear Tita,

I am once again writing full of anguish because of what has occurred in Argentina; this time doubly so because apart from the deaths we now have to add a series of inauspicious events for our country. From here it is hard to say anything with great certainty, but the unanimous jubilation of the United States and the Catholics, together with the statements coming from the new junta, and the fact that they are all from the military, is a demonstration of what this new liberation will look like. With all the respect due to Árbenz (who was completely different from Perón ideologically), the fall of the Argentine government has eerily followed the same track as Guatemala. You'll soon see how the total handover of the country and a political and diplomatic rupture with the popular democracies will be the sad but expected consequence of all this. It's wrong for me, however, to start pronouncing my political views when what should be happening, and what I want, is for you to give me your opinion on recent events and tell me what is really going on. Would it be too much to ask for you to send me a package with newspapers from the last few days [of Perón] and the first few days of the new regime? You could send them by boat, I'm not worried about how long it takes, I just want to get an idea of what it was like.

Regarding my cancelled trip to Europe, I can say that my phrase was indeed pompous and that the author of the letter was actually the president of the Council of Ministers of Poland. I was thinking of going to the Festival of Youth, but I wanted my own references from Argentina. But because things were in such a state, I didn't dare call them directly, and I thought that my friend Isalí would be able to help. Nevertheless, this didn't matter, as Agencia Latina only ended up paying me only part of what they owed me, and it was not enough for me to be able to get there.

Regarding other things, my financial situation has improved enough for me to be able to meet my basic needs, and my scientific situation is generally good. I have three projects that are slowly moving forward, although I don't think they will be completed before the end of the year.

I hope to receive good news from you soon in terms of your degree and that your problem with personal conflicts is improving. I am not sending you the journal with my little article, which has now been published, because they didn't give me any copies and anyway it's not worth the effort. Receive an embrace from your eternal friend Ernesto and reply soon.

[Unsigned]

To Zoraida Boluarte
Mexico, October 8, 1955

My dearest Zoraida,

You can imagine my interest and delight in receiving your letter, or better said your postcard, from Puerto Rico. Given it's impossible for me to go, I would love to see you do a little trip through these lands, which are really worth getting to know and where you'll find many similarities with where you come from. Among other things, you'll find beside me a large woman, a representative of your noble Quechua race, whom I married a few months ago. Hilda, the name of your compatriot and my wife, sends her regards, even though you haven't had the pleasure of meeting her yet. She is an APRA supporter and is living in exile here.

I'd love you to tell me what you're up to, specifically on that island that I'm told is very beautiful, and if it's easy to get there or if it's as hard as entering the United States. I'm asking because I'm planning a visit to Cuba next year, around March, and if you're still there, I'd like to give you a passionate Argentine embrace.

I would also like to know something about all my Peruvian friends, who spring to mind from time to time.

My life here is pleasant enough, although I have a lot of work (this time scientific) which is poorly remunerated. Nevertheless, we've saved a few pesos and on the first of November, I'm doing a little trip to the south of Mexico with my wife. There are some magnificent archeological sites in that region, such as Chichén-Itzá, which we hope to visit.

Well Zoraida, the only thing left is for me to tell you that my new address is Nápoles 40, Apartment 16, Colonia Juárez, Mexico D.F., which is is also your home — not a euphemism. Sending you the required farewell embrace, this time from somewhat closer proximity. Regards to your family from me, and pass on my fraternal hug to the *papusita*.

Gurbai [goodbye], as they say here.

Ernesto

To Mother
Mexico, day 25 of the new era[60]

Abuelita [Granny],

Both of us are a bit older, or if you consider yourself a fruit, a bit more mature. The baby is rather ugly, but you only have to look at her to realize that she is different from all other children of her age. Although she cries when she is hungry, pees herself frequently, light bothers her and she sleeps most of the time, there is something that immediately differentiates her from every other baby: her papa is called Ernesto Guevara.

I'm unhappy because I missed out on an opportunity: if we had married under Argentine law, I would not be afraid of Hilda leaving me for someone else and divorcing me. These Mexicans are libertarians; they allow divorce here. Moreover, I hear that they're going to ban the party of the Reds [in Argentina]. This has dispelled any doubt I had that this new government is one of national liberation, which will save us from the Red plague. Moreover, we will have nuclear energy, because I saw that *So and So and Power* [sic] are willing to build reactors in Argentina; they are just waiting for the government to redress an injustice and pay them for what was expropriated under the tyrant. Naturally, they are also going to sign a nuclear [non-proliferation] pact, as the United States cannot take the risk of the cow growing horns. But these are beneficial agreements: here, they are going to sign one,

---

60   This letter was written soon after the birth of Che's daughter Hilda Beatriz Guevara Gadea on February 15, 1956.

and it seems that the gringos are most generous with their friends. Mexico only has to grant the United States complete control over the extraction of uranium; exploration will be overseen by Mexico, but with US personnel to make it easier for them here. The uranium will only be able to be sold to the United States, but in return they will sell one or two reactors in the near future, although it is not clear when.

Not to Mexico, naturally, but to a subsidiary of Bon and Whare that operates here, which will be in charge of distributing the fluid (a very delicate job for the Mexicans who are a bit too passionate; it's enough to mention that they are chased by dogs on the border to make sure they don't disturb anyone up north).

You can't know how much I want to see you, more so there than here, but that is unlikely at the moment. But the inverse doesn't seem practical either as by the time you receive [your aunt's] inheritance, the Argentine peso will perhaps be in a similar shape to the boliviano. I am working to make sure that this is my last year in Mexico (at least the last ending in 6). My scientific endeavors are so-so, but if I tell you about them I'll have nothing left to tell papa, and I want to write to him today or tomorrow, making use of my day off (Sunday).

Vieja, I hope to see you within the next millennium in some part of this little piece of shit left to us by God called Earth.

Kisses from Hilda Beatriz and me. We will leave old Hilda to one side as she has no business involving herself in young people's stuff.

Arrivederchi mia javie[61]

[Unsigned]

---

61   Javie is the word *vieja* (old lady) jumbled.

To Tita Infante

México, March 1, 1956

Dear Tita,

Now it has been my turn to abandon our epistolary friendship for some time. Even if it's the most stale of excuses, I genuinely have a crazy job (and, what's worse, one that is futile in both scientific and monetary terms). The heir, who turned out to be an heiress, has been born and bears the name Hilda Beatriz. She is 15 days old and for me is cause for a double happiness. [...] she might even convert me into a boring father [...]. I know that won't happen and that I'll continue my bohemian lifestyle for who knows how long, and that one day I'll return to Argentina, where I'll do my duty of abandoning my knight-errant cape and take up some kind of weapon for combat [...].

It's difficult for me to talk about my scientific work. After losing almost a year, I decided I was unable to complete a project on the chemical make up of histamines. Another, on the oral production of anaphylaxis through the eating of foods with hyaluronidase, which was at least original, was halted soon after some initial failures because I lost my financial support; I think something could still come of this. Two less important ones ended up with negative results and I decided not to publish them. I was never able to fully develop the one on electrophoresis due to a lack of means. Another, to discover some kind of relationship between histaminase and progesterone, is still ongoing and might turn up some results. (They assure me that, if the results are positive, I'll get a scholarship to work wherever I want: I don't believe them).

I have begun to study the histochemistry of histaminase, which is very complicated, as a complement to the other research. They have offered me a job as a physiologist at the university, but here it's much easier to offer you a job without actually employing you. I have another offer from a hospital to do research in the area of allergies. This would solve my most pressing financial problems and allow me to finish another project in Mexico, which would bring me closer to a much-desired scholarship in France (you, maliciously, suspect that study is not my sole purpose for pursuing this [...], and you're right).

I can't comment on the political situation; it's up to you to provide me with a view, even if it's just a general one, of what is happening, as you did in your previous letter, which I completely agreed with. We have to have a long, hard talk about you and ask when you're going to cure yourself of your perennial homesickness. Don't tell me that it's a product of circumstances, because that isn't true, nor is it due to your constitution. Anyway, today I'm not up to attempting a long-distance catechism, [...]. Here's a firm embrace from your eternal friend, and courage, don't give up. [...]

[Unsigned]

To Mother
[Mexico] April 13, 1956

Dear *Vieja*,

[...] I had lost the habit writing until I convinced myself that this is the only way to receive news from the upper echelons of Buenos Aires society [...].

So I'll now talk about *la chamaca* [the kid]. I am so happy with her; my communist soul is bursting with happiness because she looks just like Mao Tse Tung. You can already see the incipient receding hairline across the middle of her head, the kind-hearted eyes of a leader and a protuberant double chin. For now, she weighs less than the leader as she's only 5 kilos, but give her time. She is far more spoilt than other children and eats like I used to eat, according to grandmother's stories (her grandmother), sucking without breathing until the milk pours out her nose.

I'm going to be a professor of physiology at the National University of Mexico, on a meager wage of the kind universities here normally pay but with all the status that comes with such a position. [...]

I am working like crazy in order to finish a few projects that I'm sick and tired of so that I can completely dedicate myself to a new focus, which is conditioned reflexes. I've got it into my head to come up with an anti-asthma sedative on the basis of the thallus reflexes, but I don't know where all this will take me. They are covering all my costs but are not providing me with personnel, despite the fact that the poor patients in the hospital here don't care if you strangle or shoot them, as long as you pay them some attention.

I received a letter from Beatriz in which she tells me that the economic crisis was the result of the deficit Perón left behind, but that the North Americans, as they always do, have rushed in to help in a very selfless manner. It consoles me to think that my country is benefitting from the help of our big neighbors, just like they helped APRA, meaning that people will soon be able to return to Peru and that Hilda will be able to return without any concern. It's a great shame that her impulsive marriage to an ardent slave to that Red plague means that she will be denied her salary as a deputy in the next parliament [...]. I'm glad you liked big [Ricardo] Rojo. I hope to be able to continue being friends with him, but I fear that this won't be possible. Speaking to him, you will have noticed that he thinks I'm one of those nice crazies who is good at telling stories. I have no doubt that in time, I will be, but when it comes to political analysis, I heard him say all kinds of rubbish that shocked me.

I'm sending you an embrace the size of the monument to the *descamisados*,[62] not the one they were going to build but the one that can be found in the hearts of the Argentine people, alongside the image of our dear presidential couple, may God protect them, amen.

While I'm at it, a hug for the other members of the family.

[Unsigned]

---

62   *Descamisados* (shirtless ones) was a term used to refer to Perón's supporters, who generally came from a poor background. Shortly before being deposed in 1955, Perón proposed a gigantic monument to the *descamisados*. The term comes from an incident that occurred in the Argentine Chamber of Deputies, where an anti-Perónist deputy referred to a Perónist deputy, as a "*descamisado*," suggesting he could not even afford a shirt. The following day, speaking at a rally of thousands of supporters, Perón took off his coat and said that he, too, was a *descamisado* like his people. His ministers and personnel in the presidential palace did likewise. After that, Perón would often attend events without a jacket.

To my parents

Mexico, July 6, 1956
Carcel de la Gobernación [Miguel Schultz prison]

Dear *Viejos* [Old Folks],

I got your letter (papa) here at my new and delightful mansion known as Miguel Schultz, and had a visit from Petit who told me about your concerns. To give you some idea what has happened, I'll tell you the story.

Some time ago — quite a while ago now — I was invited by a young Cuban leader to join his movement, an armed movement to liberate his homeland, and I, of course, accepted.[63] Over the past few months, I have maintained the cover of saying I had a job as a professor, whereas in fact I have been dedicating myself to the physical training of the guys who must one day set foot again in Cuba. On June 21 (after being away from home in Mexico City for a month and living on a ranch on the outskirts of the city), Fidel was arrested along with a group of compañeros. At his house [the police] discovered the address where we were, which is why we were all caught in their dragnet. I had documents on me that identified me as a student in Russian, which was enough for them to consider me an important link in the organization, and the newsagencies that papa loves so much began to shriek all around the world.

---

63   A reference to meeting Fidel Castro and his revolutionary organization that took its name from the date they launched an assault on the military barracks in Bayamo and Santiago de Cuba on July 26, 1953.

That's a summary of what has happened. The future is now divided into two: the medium- and short-term. Regarding the medium-term, I see my future tied to the Cuban Revolution. I'll either triumph with it or die there. (This was the reason behind the somewhat enigmatic and romantic letter that I sent to Argentina some time ago.) Regarding my immediate future, I have little to say because I don't know what will happen to me. I am at the disposition of the judge and it would be easy for them to deport me to Argentina, unless I am given asylum in an intermediary country, something that I imagine would be good for my political health.

In any case, I'll have to leave for somewhere, whether I'm deported straight from jail or whether I'm released. Hilda will return to Peru because the new government there has decreed a political amnesty.

For obvious reasons I won't be able to write often. Moreover, the Mexican police have the charming practice of confiscating letters, which is why I suggest you only write about mundane matters like things at home. No one likes it when a son of a bitch is following your intimate problems, no matter how insignificant they are. Give Beatriz a kiss and explain to her why I am not writing, and tell her to not worry about sending newspapers for now.

We are about to go on an indefinite hunger strike over our unjustified detention and the torture of some of my compañeros. The group's morale remains high.

For now, keep sending letters to my home address.

If, for whatever reason, although I don't think it will happen, and I can't write any more and my number is up, consider these lines as my farewell, not very eloquent but at least sincere. During my life I've spent much time stumbling around looking for my truth and now, having found my way, and with a daughter to perpetuate me, I feel I have closed a cycle. From now on, I wouldn't consider my death to be a frustration, but simply as [Turkish poet Nazim] Hikmet put it: "I take to my grave only the sorrow of an unfinished song."

A kiss for everyone.

Ernesto

To Mother
Mexico [Miguel Schultz prison, July] 15, [1956]

Vieja,

I received your letter and it seems as though you have been experiencing a pretty bad bout of depression. It contains a lot of wisdom and many things I didn't know about you.

I'm neither Christ nor a philanthropist, *Vieja.* I'm exactly the opposite of a Christ and philanthropy looks [illegible] to me, but I fight for what I believe in with all the weapons at my disposal, trying to lay out the other guy instead of letting myself get nailed to a cross or whatever. As for the hunger strike, you're totally wrong. We started it twice and the first time they released 21 of the 24 detainees; the second time they announced that they would free Fidel Castro, the head of the Movement, and this will happen tomorrow; if they do what they say, only two of us will be left in prison. I don't want you to believe, as Hilda suggests, that the two of us who remain have been sacrificed. We are simply the ones whose papers aren't in order and so we can't access the resources that our compañeros can.

My plan is to leave for the nearest country that will grant me asylum, which might be difficult given the interAmerican notoriety I've now achieved. From there I'll get ready for whenever my services are required. I'm telling you yet again that it's possible I won't be able to write for a quite a while.

What really distresses me is your lack of understanding about all this and your advice about moderation, selfishness, etc. — in other words, the most execrable qualities an individual can have. Not only am I not moderate, but I shall try never to be so. And if I ever see in myself that the sacred flame has become a timid little votive flicker, the least I can do is to vomit on my own shit. As for your appeal to moderate selfishness, which means crass and spineless individualism (the virtues of X.X. — you know who), I have to say that I've tried hard to purge that from myself, not only of that unmentionable moderate being but the other one, the bohemian, unconcerned about his neighbor, filled with a sense of self-sufficiency because of a consciousness, mistaken or otherwise, of his own strength. During this time in prison, and during the period of training, I totally identified with my compañeros in the struggle. I recall a phrase that I once thought was ridiculous, or at least strange, referring to such a total identification among members of a group of combatants to the effect that the idea of "I" was completely subsumed in the concept of "we." It was a communist moral principle and naturally might look like doctrinaire exaggeration, but it was (and is) really beautiful to feel this sense of "we."

(The splotches aren't tears of blood but tomato juice.)

You are deeply mistaken to believe that moderation or "moderate selfishness" gives rise to great inventions or works of art. All great work requires passion and the Revolution needs large doses of passion and audacity, things we possess collectively as humankind. Another strange thing I noted was your repeated mention of God the Father. I really hope you're not reverting to the fold of your youth. I also warn you that the SOSs are to no avail: Petit shat himself, Lezica dodged the issue and gave Hilda (who went there against my orders) a sermon on the obligations of political asylum. Raúl Lynch behaved well from afar, and Padilla Nervo said they were different ministries. They would all help but only on the condition that I abjure my ideals. I don't think you would prefer a living son who was a Barabbás rather than a son who died somewhere doing what he considered his duty.

These attempts to help only put pressure on them and me.

But you have some clever ideas (at least to my way of thinking), and the best of them is the matter of the interplanetary rocket — a word I like. Besides, there's no doubt that, after righting the wrongs in Cuba, I'll be off somewhere else; and it's also certain that if I were to be locked up in some bureaucrat's office or some allergy clinic, I'd be stuffed. All in all, I think that this pain, the pain of an aging mother who wants her son alive, is a feeling to be respected, and I should heed it and, more than that, I want to attend to it. I would love to see you, not just to console you, but also to console myself in my sporadic and shameful homesickness.

Vieja, I kiss you and promise to be with you if nothing else develops.

Your son,

el Che[64]

---

64   Ernesto is now signing as "el Che" or "the Argentine," the name by which he will become known internationally.

To Mother

[August or September, 1956][65]

Dear *Vieja*,

I am writing from somewhere in Mexico, where I am waiting for a few things to be resolved. The air of freedom is, in reality, the air of clandestinity, but nevertheless, it adds an intriguing cinematic touch of mystery.

My health is very good and my optimism even better. With respect to your views about the liberators, I see that little by little, almost without realizing it, you are losing confidence in them.

What you said about being firm and confident is one of the most tragic things you have ever written, but don't worry I won't show it to anyone. Just have a look at what the newspapers in Egypt are saying, for example, and the "loss of confidence of the West." This is logical. They have a lot more confidence in a fiefdom that belongs to them than in a country, even one without an independence project. The oil won't belong to Argentina either. The bases they so feared Perón would hand over will be handed over by them; or they are at least making some concessions in this direction. Freedom of speech is the new myth; we previously had a Perónist myth, now we have the liberators' myth that is propagated in the newspapers. By the time the general elections come around, they will have made the Communist Party illegal and have tried everything to neutralize Frondizi, who is the best that Argentina can hope for. In conclusion, *Vieja*, the panorama that I see from

---

65   This letter was written after Che was released from prison.

here is bleak for the poor Argentine workers' movement, that is, the majority of the population.

Anyway, I have little time to write and I don't wish to waste it on such matters, although, in reality, I have little to say about my life here as I spend most of my time exercising and reading. I think I'll come out of this quite invincible in terms of understanding economics, even if I've forgotten by then how to take a pulse and use a stethoscope (I was never very good at that anyway).

My path seems to be slowly but surely diverging from that of clinical medicine, but not so far that I have lost my nostalgia for hospitals. What I told you about the professorship in physiology was a lie, but not a big one. It was a lie because I never planned to accept it, but the offer was real and there was a strong possibility that they were going to give it to me, as I had an interview and everything. Anyway, that's all history. Saint Carlos [Karl Marx] has made a new recruit.

I cannot tell you anything about the future. Write to me soon and tell me the family news which would be very refreshing in these latitudes.

Vieja, a big kiss from your clandestine son.

[Unsigned]

To Mother
[Mexico, October 1956]

Dear Mama,

Your lousy son, who, besides being the son of a bad mother, is not a good-for-nothing. He's like Paul Muni,[66] who says what he says in that tragic voice and then disappears into the lengthening shadows to the sound of evocative music. My current profession is that of a grasshopper, here today, there tomorrow, etc... [...]

By the way, within a month, Hilda will go to visit her family in Peru, taking advantage of the fact that she is no longer a political criminal but a somewhat misguided representative of the admirable and anticommunist party, the APRA. For my part, I'm in the process of changing the focus of my studies: whereas previously I devoted myself — for better or worse — to medicine, and spent my spare time informally studying Saint Carlos [Marx], this new stage of my life demands that I change the priorities. Now Saint Carlos is primordial; he is the axis and will remain so for however many years the spheroid has room for me on its outer mantle. Medicine is more or less a trivial and passing pursuit, except for one small area about which I'm thinking of writing more than one substantive study — the kind that causes bookstore basements to tremble beneath its weight.

As you'll recall, and if you don't remember I'll remind you now, I was working on a book on the role of the doctor, etc., of which I only finished a couple of chapters that whiffed of some newspaper

---

66   Paul Muni was the lead actor in the movie "Fugitive from a Chain Gang."

serial with a title like "Bodies and Souls."[67] It was nothing more than poorly written rubbish, displaying a thorough ignorance of the fundamental issues, so I decided to study. Besides, in order to write I realized I was kicking against my essentially adventurous nature, so I decided to deal with the main things first, to pit myself against the order of things, shield on my arm, the whole fantasy, and then, if the windmills don't crack my nut open, I'll get down to writing.

I owe Celia the congratulatory letter that I'll write after this if I have time. The others are in debt to me as the last word has been mine, even Beatriz. Tell her that the papers arrive like clockwork and that they give me a very good idea of all the government's wonderful deeds. I cut out the articles carefully, following the example of my *pater*, and now Hilda is emulating her *mater*. A kiss for everyone, with all the appropriate extras and a reply — negative or positive, but definitive — about the Guatemalan guy.[68]

All that remains now is the final part of the speech, which refers to the man, which could be titled: "And now what next?" Now comes the difficult part, *Vieja*, the part I've never shunned and always enjoyed. The sky has not darkened, the stars have not fallen out of the sky, nor have there been terrible floods or hurricanes. The signs are good. They augur victory. But if they're wrong — and in the end even the gods can make mistakes — I think I'll be able to say, like a poet you don't know: "I take to my grave only the sorrow of an unfinished song." To avoid *pre-mortem* pathos, this letter will be sent when things get really hot, and then you'll know that your son, in some sundrenched land in the Americas, is swearing at himself for not having studied enough surgery to help a wounded man, and cursing the Mexican government for

---

67   *Corps et âmes* [Bodies and Souls] by the French writer Maxence Van der Meersch.

68   One of Ernesto's friends had arrived in Argentina as a political exile.

not letting him perfect his already respectable marksmanship so he could knock over targets with better results. The struggle will be with our backs to the wall, as in the hymns, until victory or death.

Another kiss for you, with all the love of a farewell that refuses to be a final one.

Your son

To Mother[69]

Mexico City, 15 [probably November 1956]

Dear *Vieja*,

Still on Mexican soil, answering your last letters. I can give you very little news about my life. At the moment, all I do is some gymnastics and read like crazy — you can imagine what — and I see Hilda some weekends.

I've given up trying to get my case resolved through legal channels, so my stay in Mexico will only be temporary. Anyway, Hilda is taking the little girl to spend New Year with her family. She'll be there for a month and after that we'll see what happens. My longterm ambition is to see Europe and, if possible, to live there, but that's becoming increasingly difficult. When one contracts the kind of disease I have, it just keeps getting worse, and is cured only in the grave.

I did have a life plan involving 10 years as a vagabond, then some years studying medicine and then, with any remaining time, I would dive into the great adventure of physics.

All that is over. The only thing that is clear is that the 10 years of wandering will probably be longer (unless unforeseen circumstances put an end to my wandering altogether), but it will be very different from what I imagined. Now, when I land in a new country, it won't just be to have a look and visit museums or ruins,

---

69   Written shortly before Che embarked on the *Granma* expedition with Fidel Castro and other Cubans to initiate the revolutionary struggle against the Batista dictatorship.

but also (because the former will always interest me) to join the people's struggle.

I have read the latest news from Argentina about the refusal to legalize the three new parties and the remnants of the Communist Party. Predictable as this is, the measure is less symptomatic than everything else that has been happening in Argentina for some time. All these events display such a clear tendency — to favor one caste or class — that there can be no mistake or confusion. That class is the national landowning class, allied with foreign investors, as always,

If I say these rather harsh things to you, it's a case of "beating you because I love you." Now comes an embrace, one of my last from Mexico and, since I'm admonishing you, here is a final one: The only lament of the mother of the Maceo brothers was that she had no more sons to offer to Cuba.[70] I don't ask that much of you, only that the price of seeing me does not alter your convictions, or is something you'll regret some day.

Chau,

[Unsigned]

---

70 Mariana Grajales was the mother of General Antonio Maceo and his brother, who were leaders of Cuba's struggle for independence against Spain in the 19th century.

To Tita Infante
[Approximately November 1956]

Dear Tita,

It has been so long since I wrote that I have lost the confidence that comes with frequent communication. (I'm sure you won't understand much of what I write, I'll explain everything little by little.)

First, my little Indian girl is already nine months old, very cute and full of life, etc.

Second and most important: A while back some Cuban guys, revolutionaries, invited me to help the Movement with my medical "knowledge," and I accepted, because you probably know that this is the kind of work which *me piace* [I like]. I went to a ranch in the mountains to direct the training, vaccinate the troops, etc., but I got "mixed up in the salad" as they say in Cuba and the police nabbed us all. And because I was "*chueco*" [my papers were suspect] (a Mexicanism) I had to swallow two months in jail and, moreover, they stole my typewriter and some other stuff, hence this handwritten missive. Then the government committed the grave error of believing my word as a gentleman, and they released me on the proviso that I would leave the country within 10 days. Three months later I'm still hanging around, even though I'm underground and with no prospects in Mexico. I'm just waiting to see what happens with the Revolution: if it works out well, I'll head for Cuba; if not, I'll start to look for a country where I can set up camp. This year my life could change drastically, but this has already happened so many times that I'm not too worried or bothered by it.

Of course, all my scientific work went to hell and now I'm just an assiduous reader of Carlitos [Karl Marx] and Federiquito [Friedrich Engels] and the like. I forgot to tell you that when I was arrested, they found several little books in Russian and a card from the Institute for Mexican-Russian Exchange, where I was studying the language in connection with the problem of conditioned reflexes.

It might interest you to know that my marriage has almost completely broken down and will be definitively so next month. My wife is going to Peru to see her family, from whom she has been separated for eight years. There is a certain bitterness in the breakup, as she was a loyal compañera and her revolutionary conduct was irreproachable during my enforced vacation. Our spiritual discord was too great, however, and I live with this anarchic spirit that leads me to dream of new horizons the moment I feel "the cross of your arms and the earth of your soul," as Pablito [Neruda] said.[71]

I'll sign off now. Don't write to me until after the next letter, which will have more news or at least a fixed address.

With an ever-affectionate embrace from your friend,

Ernesto

---

71   A quotation from Pablo Neruda's poem *A Song of Despair*.

LETTERS FROM THE GUERRILLA WAR
IN CUBA
(1956-1959)

Introduction

Having decided to "follow his own road," Ernesto — now called "Che" by his new Cuban friends — commits himself to the Cuban guerrilla struggle to overthrow the US-backed dictatorship of General Fulgencio Batista. Signing on as troop doctor, the armed revolutionaries led by Fidel Castro arrive on a cabin cruiser from Mexico on the Cuban coast in Oriente province in December 1956. Che soon faces what he describes as his "baptism of fire" and the dilemma of having to choose between his backpack with medical supplies or a rifle and ammunition.[1]

Within months, Che shows himself to be not just a fearless guerrilla combatant, for which he earns the rank of commander, but also demonstrates his skill as an asute political leader. After the defeat of General Batista's military offensive in August 1958, the war turns in favor of the revolutionary forces. At this point, two new guerrilla columns are created, one led by Camilo Cienfuegos, and the other commanded by Che Guevara. On August 21, Fidel orders Che and Camilo to take their troops westward toward Las

---

1   See Ernesto Che Guevara, *Reminiscences of the Cuban Revolutionary War* (Seven Stories Press, 2021) and Ernesto Che Guevara, *Diary of a Combatant* (Ocean Press, 2013).

Villas province. Che leaves the Sierra Maestra on August 31 and heads for El Jíbaro on the plains of central Cuba.

Fidel Castro has entrusted Che with the politically delicate task of uniting the disparate revolutionary forces active in that region under the leadership of the July 26 Movement. The difficult nature of this assignment is evident in Che's correspondence with Fidel, which is published here for the first time and which reveals the extraordinary personal bond and political synergy already established between the two men.

As Batista's army begins to fall apart, in late December 1958 Che initiates a decisive battle in the city of Santa Clara. General Batista flees from Cuba early on January 1, 1959, and the next day the guerrilla columns led by Che and Camilo reach Havana. From Santiago de Cuba in the east, Fidel declares: "The revolution begins now."

LETTERS WRITTEN FROM
THE SIERRA MAESTRA

To *Daniel*[2]
[Sierra Maestra] October 1, 1957

Dear *Daniel*,

I am taking advantage of the messenger to write to you, although, it just so happens that today I have a meeting with Alejandro [Fidel Castro] and I'll be showing him your letter. I'll now respond to you in an orderly fashion: I don't know who is the executive of Palma, I naively believed in Márquez's word and wrote with the best of intentions — of course, putting my foot in it. I'll completely abstain from making new contacts in that area, *unless I have to operate there and don't receive the necessary help* [italics in the original] in which case I'll have no other option but to establish contact with the first "free" helper I come across. Once again you mention the problems that arose because I didn't make contact with Santiago [de Cuba]. In the previous letter I took all the blame because I was not interested in palming off some of the responsibility when I'm

---

2   Daniel was the *nom de guerre* of René Ramos Latour (1932-1958), the leader of the July 26 Movement's action and sabotage group in Oriente province after the death of Frank País on July 30, 1957. He later joined Column One and attained the rank of commander. He died in combat in July 1958.

the one who made the mistake. But I remind you that Santiago is the same distance away from the Sierra as the Sierra is from Santiago, and that you should have known where I was if you really were in contact with Carlos, because we are permanently in contact with him and they made contact with me because here is where they established contacts.[3]

You say that the letter you have is the one I gave Andrés Menés; unfortunately, it is only now that I have a copy of what I wrote in our little file, but, if I'm not mistaken, he was given the task of being the point of contact between this city and the Sierra, and he was only asked to carry out a task that he proposed and which I thought was correct. Attached is a note for him.

Regarding Bayamo, I think you are being a bit unfair to me, as I was not the one who invented [political] factions; they didn't come about after conversations with me. The only thing I'll say is that there are things I asked for two months ago that have never arrived, and a week after talking with Piferrer they did. I think it is a crime against the revolution to act like this. I won't do anything without an order from Fidel, who I'll be speaking to today and who I'll show the letters to and tell him my views on the problem. Whether I work with Carlos or not is an issue that Carlos must resolve, as I have always specified that he is the head of the Movement [in Bayamo]. The order to detain Lara arrived late; you can ask Carlos for the letter I sent with the same emissary. When he asked me if he could join the column, I refused to allow it because I understood that those who had committed an act like this could not join us, but Pepín Lupíañez is here and you will soon know about the problems this has caused. Moreover, I wouldn't allow him to join this column, even if the Movement had sent him. Also, I hope that I have unconditionally dedicated my modest effort for

---

3   Che had been promoted to the rank of commander on July 21, 1957, and given command of a newly established guerrilla column.

the good of the cause and that Bayamo will be able to help us more in the future.

I believe I'm innocent of the crime of not sending news. You have pressured me to report every event, even if we failed to capture a single rifle during any supposed "feat" [action]. I'm sending news of the deaths at Peladero in a separate note, as well as the names of those who have been discharged due to an order from Fidel because of a disturbing matter that I'm sure he will tell you about. I haven't received the bullets, but I did receive the thousand pesos.

Greetings,

[Unsigned]

To the Civic Institutions of Buey Arriba
Sierra Maestra, October 12, 1957

To the Civic Institutions of Buey Arriba:

We have received a statement from these institutions for which we have always maintained the respect that correct behavior deserves. The shopkeepers who have signed it are calling for the release of the soldier Leonardo Baró Merodio, whom we have as our prisoner, arguing that we should consider this request in the spirit of democracy. Before responding to the request, I have to ask a question that each member of the Civic Institutions should be asking themselves: in the name of this same democratic spirit for which we struggle, can I ask that you resuscitate the 14 peasants killed in Peladero or the five that were burnt alive in El Hombrito?

I put this specific question to you — without mentioning the indefensible, savage bombardment of villages in the Sierra Maestra, the genocide in the city of Cienfuegos, or the mysterious deaths across the island that are an everyday occurrence under this government of terror — because the events I mentioned occurred in areas around Buey Arriba and which you therefore cannot ignore.

I remind you that the captured soldier belonged to the company led by Captain Merob Sosa, who was directly responsible for these murders and was promoted to commander due to the supposed "victories" he obtained at the cost of the innocent blood of defenseless peasants. I also remind you that no one should ever fear for the physical safety of any of our prisoners, and that the author of this note released two prisoners in Bueycito after a request by these same institutions on August 1, 1957. I also remind you that our action was unable to guarantee the physical safety of the local people who were jailed and mistreated in that town.

Despite all this, we would have freed the soldier Baró if it weren't for the fact that he knows too much about our movements and tactics, which makes him a threat to the [guerrilla] column. Experience tells us that freed prisoners end up becoming spies for the army, telling the officers everything they want to know. This is exactly what happened with the 16 from Uvero.

Nevertheless, I have clear instructions from our commander-in-chief, Fidel Castro. These instructions were read by the Civic Institutions' envoy, Mr. Pablo Chacón Hernández, who can testify to what I'm about to say. The instructions ordered me to free the prisoners as long as there is absolute certainty that they will not pass on information to the army that could harm us. It states that an acceptable solution for us would be that an accredited member of any embassy from this continent (as long as they represent a democratic country) takes responsibility for the prisoner.

It does not have to be a functionary, but it does have to be an accredited person and they cannot represent the following countries: Dominican Republic, Nicaragua or Venezuela.

The conditions that this person must accept are:

a) The prisoner cannot be interrogated by or make contact with members of the army, and reunions with family members must be held in front of embassy personnel.

b) Outside the country, they cannot respond to any questionnaire sent to them by the government.

c) The prisoner cannot return to Cuba until the end of the current civil war, and only with our consent.

We would like to point out, moreover, that Mr. Chacón was able to reach us due to the respect we have for the Civic Institutions and their word of honor not to reveal any information about us that could aid the enemy. Complying with these conditions is vital to ensuring future negotiations for other prisoners.

On a personal note, I hope that these negotiations will have a happy ending so that soon no Cuban mother will have to suffer the distress of having a son taken prisoner or the terrible anguish of knowing that her son is dead or was brutally tortured because of his ideals.

A respectful greeting to the Civic Institutions of this country and a personal greeting to the president of this organization in Buey Arriba; thanks to his personal requests, other prisoners have been freed.

Commander of the Fourth Revolutionary Column[4]

---

4   By this time, Che had become a commander, leading the recently formed second guerrilla column (designated "Column Four" to deceive the government about the strength of the revolutionary movement), which operated in the zone of El Hombrito, to the east of Pico Turquino in the Sierra Maestra mountains.

To *Mario*[5]

Sierra Maestra, November 23, 1957

Dear *Mario*,

I'm writing, as always, to make a number of requests. I have already written to Santiago recommending they appoint you to the post of provisioner, as we agreed.

The main things we need are: mimeograph paper, ink, stencils. I have attached a few copies of the newspaper and statements we have distributed to peasants. The marks that you will notice are due to the poor quality of the paper, which is not suitable for this task, and the poor state of the mimeograph. It would be good if you could reproduce them there, in particular the newspaper. We need books to consult on the history of Cuba and the lives of [José] Martí, [Antonio] Maceo and [Máximo] Gómez for the newspaper.

In terms of health care, we have a project to build a hospital, for which we already have the materials and are only waiting for the government's offensive to die down a bit before we begin. We are engaging in almost daily fire fights with [Batista's] National Guards. I have attached a list of the materials we need. To obtain these you can consult the doctor you told me about. Let me know what you can't get so that I can request those items from Havana.

To complete the machine we talked about, we need some six sections or more of rubber (like the piece I have sent you) that is

---

5   Mario was the *nom de guerre* of an unidentified underground activist in the July 26 Movement in the towns near the Sierra Maestra where Che's column was active.

3 feet long, and more rubber like the stuff you already sent and also some that is similar but longer, which I believe you can get.[6] Moreover, we need: two pieces of 1-1/3 x 4 feet of angular aluminum; 10 feet of 1 inch aluminum tubing; a box of 1/4 x 2 inch bolts with butterfly nuts and standard nuts with washers; a 3/4 x 10 or 12 inch spiral spring; four square feet sheets of aluminum that are 1/8 inch thick.

The following are also important: a 14" lathe; a packet of 35" scroll saws; a set of drill bits from 1/16 to 1/2; a complete set of medium type hooks; two ball hammers, small and medium size; a big screwdriver.

I'm also sending you a video camera to repair. I need an instruction booklet for the camera, a good photometer and film; also a flash that can be used on a 35-mm Leica camera.

When you come you will discover a lot of great things here, if our distinguished friends don't destroy them.

I don't think I have anything else to add.

Greetings

Che

---

6   This is possibly a reference to materials required for a small electricity generator or a sewing machine that were part of a group of small workshops Che established in his operational zone in the Sierra Maestra to ensure the self-sufficiency of his troop and the local population.

To *Daniel*

[No date, but probably written in the first days of December 1957]

Dear *Daniel*,

Here we are again in our area, enjoying the air of La Mina. We find ourselves facing the same problems we left behind: that is, Bayamo is not providing us with what we need when it comes to some fundamental requests such as rubber for "homemade" mortars, which promise to be good, and bureaucratic-style delays, such as not providing certain supplies because the order didn't come with my signature, etc.

Now I'm making a big order and I need it to be filled entirely and quickly. The importance of this sometimes escapes people who tend to underestimate us and our capacity to inflict damage on the enemy. Right now, for example, the soldiers are in two areas that are perfectly vulnerable to attacks with mortars but we can't attack them because we haven't received the mortars yet. It is quite feasible to make them; our armory has made some ingenious landmines, which is incredible given the scarcity and poor quality of our materials. Moreover, we obtained the dynamite ourselves, because it often doesn't reach us from outside. We are waiting to see the results of the first mines we laid for trucks, which if successful will inaugurate a new era in the struggle here in the Sierra. You can now see the fundamental change in the method of struggle; here things are worse, we have a war of position, the guerrillas operate by harassing the enemy in their own territory while the majority take cover, bunkered down against aerial attacks on fixed terrain.

All of this is due to the previous attack in El Hombrito and the small blow dealt by the Pazos guys, which I'll tell you about in case this information is useful: the marines bunkered down in Ocujal — about 100 of them — have the habit of going out in small groups to look for cattle in the neighborhood, and our guys saw them and surprised a group of three men led by a lieutenant near the mouth of Las Brujas creek. The lieutenant received two bullets in the thorax and fell to the ground badly wounded; one of the soldiers was injured but he got away. An M1 and a pistol dealt with the wounded lieutenant. Lieutenant Roberto Sotomayor headed up the action.

Now I'll tell you about the visitors we have had, which might interest you and which everyone should know about.

First, I'll say that Piferrer returned to see me, after he failed to receive me when I told him I was coming. Once again, he demonstrated his complete willingness to collaborate with anyone on whatever conditions, including a complete break with [Carlos] Prío if that was asked of him, something I abstained from giving an opinion on.[7] Many of his criticisms seem to ring somewhat true and I believe the time has come to make a decision on Bayamo. My suggestion is to create a post that can be easily controlled by people in whom the Movement has confidence. The post could be responsible for providing supplies to the Sierra and Piferrer could occupy it, after he comes to some agreement with the leadership. Up to now the man has done everything asked of him.

I also received a visit from two lawyers from Camagüey named Carlos Varona Duque Estrada and Agustín Tomé Agüero, who came to see Fidel but they were not willing to make the trip to find

---

7   Carlos Prío Socarrás was the president of Cuba (1948–1952). His admin-
     istration was mediocre and corrupt, which resulted in lost popularity
     among the people. General Fulgencio Batista successfully led a military
     coup against President Prío on March 10, 1952.

him. They represent a dissident group in Camagüey and came to offer their services to the revolution, independently of what the other group does, based on the fact that there has been no action in that province yet. Concretely, they are offering to organize a general strike, burn the cane fields in the province and make an immediate contribution of $5,000 and monthly contributions of $1,000. They are backed by two groups, one of them a workers' group led by Alfredo Álvarez, a bank workers' leader, who they said the Movement had condemned to death but then reversed its decision. The other one is called "Mazorana," an ex-marine, who heads up an action group. I simply took note of what they said and told them that the Movement does not accept the cooperation of dissident elements.

Nevertheless, they are waiting for some kind of response. The way to do this is to go to the office of one of the two and say, "We are emissaries from the Sierra." Piferrer brought these people to us.

Another person who came by was a José Luis Carballo, who has collaborated with the Movement for some time and carried a vague message from Melba Hernández and an offer to organize the burning of cane in Havana province.[8] I directed him to see Fidel.

There are two very curious guys here right now. One is a journalist, or supposed Yankee journalist, who says he is from the *New York Herald Tribune.* I forget his name, but the man is staying at the home of a peasant friend of ours, and he said he won't walk any further. I don't know if he thinks that this will frighten me and that I'll rush off to see him or what. The other is a man who Piferrer also introduced (the journalist also contacted us through him). This one is Mexican, an active army lieutenant, who is currently on leave for a year. He said he has come to fight and has brought with him some very murky projects for obtaining arms from his country.

---

8   Melba Hernández (1921-2014) was one of the two women who participated in the July 26, 1953, attack on the Moncada barracks in Santiago de Cuba.

I'll add his name to this letter later because I cannot remember it right now. It would be good if you can find out some information about these two and let me know as soon as possible what I should do with them. I am also writing to Fidel to let him know.

It would also be good if you can use the Movement's channels to find out some information about Antonio Matanzas, who lives in the area of Alto Songo and has popped up around here selling lottery tickets. I have held him as a prisoner for a month and the reports I have indicate that he is an individual with few morals, but nothing seems to suggest he is or might have been a soldier.

Now I'll tell you about our projects, those we've already begun work on and for which we need the backing of the *Llano*.[9] The mimeograph machine (1903 model) is small and not very good. Despite everything, we have issued the attached statement, which has been posted around for the soldiers to see. I would have liked the message to come from Fidel himself, but he didn't do it and so I came up with what I could. The main thing is that we are continuing to place mines on the roads and the bombs will confirm the message. The newspaper has been written and made into stencils, but the lack of ink means we can't print it yet, and the lack of paper means we can only do a run of 700 copies. It also suffers from the fundamental weakness of not carrying an article written by Fidel. Luis Orlando has said he will devote himself to the newspaper. Please send everything we ask for in this regard as I think the newspaper can be very useful. What we need to improve it is a stencil artist who can stay in a safe place and not have to move about much.

We have a project to install an electricity plant and a hydroelectric plant, the latter is more efficient than the other as it provides light all day, which is why I have asked for electricity.

---

9   The *Llano* [literally, the plain] refers to the urban underground wing of the July 26 Movement.

Tomorrow we will work on the first of two or three ovens that will be used to make fresh bread for the troops; for this we need yeast.

We have already asked those dummies who left us to establish farms to send chickens and pigs. To hasten the process we could do with an electric incubator or the materials to make one, which are basically a coil and a thermostat. These are not on the general list I've attached.

It is urgent that you dispatch materials to make boots and backpacks, as we already have the machines and the operators ready to work them. You don't need to send the whole order at once but please begin by sending parts of it so we can start work.

We are considering making our own uniforms here, making use of the various sewing machines that the peasants left behind when they fled. If you can, please send us fabric.

We need school materials, mainly for learning how to read and write but also for higher grades. This is not included in the attached list.

We continue to use large amounts of dynamite making the mines; this is an item of vital importance, don't scrimp on this.

The troops' aim is very bad, as shown in the practice we did when you were here with the few bullets that Fidel didn't steal from us. This is something we must pay attention to now that we are in a more comfortable situation.

We are still waiting for film for the camera so that we can send footage to you. I can't guarantee the quality of the movies (I am the cameraman) but time improves everything; I should say that now I rarely break teeth and only the occasionally jaw.[10]

Something important that we'll need soon is heavy clothes to keep the troops warm.

---

10   Dentistry was part of the medical care Che gave to the guerrilla troops.

To finish, some delayed news: Fidel gave orders to burn the cane immediately and Pazos has come up with a crazy project: do you think any pilot would dare to bring their *clipper* here? If so, what do they need to land? I have written more than enough, so I'll end here. […]

[Unsigned]

To *Darío*[11] and *Daniel*

Sierra Maestra, December 4, 1957

Dear *Darío* and *Daniel*,

I received both letters and will respond to both (no exaggeration), but before that, I want to say two things: first, we are shooting it out with the National Guard soldiers on an almost daily basis, they are determined to climb up to El Hombrito and we are determined to make sure that they don't. On the 29th we had an encounter [with the military] that lasted 12 hours; we completely surrounded Sánchez Mosquera,[12] but at 4:00 in the afternoon their reinforcements arrived and we had to lift the siege at 6:00. Ciro [Redondo][13] died in the battle, a true hero in the fighting; we couldn't recover his body. In that respect, the official news is correct, although they forgot to mention that they stole $750, which no doubt some official took for himself. But there is a mistake where they said "nothing to report" on their side, because

---

11   Darío was one of Armando Hart's (1930–2017) *noms de guerre*. Hart joined the Orthodox Party Youth in 1947 as a young lawyer. He later became a leader of the July 26 Movement in Oriente province until he was captured in 1958. Released on January 1, 1959, he became Minister for Education (1959–1965), Organization Secretary of the Cuban Communist Party (1965–1970), Minister of Culture, and a member of the Central Committee and Political Bureau of the PCC.

12   Lt. Colonel Sánchez Mosquera was an officer in Batista's army who was infamous for his brutality.

13   Ciro Redondo García (1931–1957) participated in the July 26, 1953, attack on Batista's barracks and was captured and imprisoned. He joined the *Granma* expedition and was a member of Che's column, but he was killed in action on November 29, 1957.

I can tell you that we took three prisoners; killed one [soldier] for sure, and another two almost certainly; and they suffered a proportional number of injuries. The second news is that, as a result of these actions, the previous ones and earlier clashes, we have little ammunition left and we urgently need to replenish our stocks somehow. To the list I sent I would only add 30-06, but we need a lot of them (say 5,000) and we need more 44 bullets.

Now to respond to the letters. You are mistaken if you think my lack of discipline would lead me to make a pact or make contact with people without authorization. I followed your advice when responding to the people in Camagüey and told them that I could not negotiate with them, promising only that I would pass on their details to you, as I did. I listened to what they had to say and I passed that on. I have lost all contact with them and only accepted the personal offer of one of them to send the elastic bands that have already arrived. [...]

The case of Piferrer is different because Daniel knew him and he agreed to make contact with you, which I now see never happened. The moment you give the order, I'll break off all contact with him. I only want you to consider our indigent state, as we haven't received the promised funds, or even the materials we need. I have to look after 200 men who eat like horses, have no shoes, and we haven't even been sent shoes or the materials we asked for. They are naked, without [waterproof] plastic sheets or backpacks (because we lost a lot of backpacks in the battle I mentioned), and nothing has arrived. [...]

The atrocities carried out by the soldiers in this area are appalling. In a place called Agua de Revés they burnt 15 houses, 23 in Mar Verde, two in Pinalito, another one in Dos Brazos de Peladero, after they had already destroyed the rest during previous incursions. The people are completely terrorized and I don't know if we'll be able to obtain what we need if everyone leaves. We had begun to establish farms but the soldiers ate everything and I don't know how long we will be able to sustain this.

We are now waiting to see the results of the arson and the strike, but even there things have happened which I can't quite explain. Fidel sent strict orders to begin burning the cane at a particular time and I sent some emissaries to pass on that message to the main sugar farms in my area. Some have already returned reporting that they haven't been able to comply with the order because the municipal leadership said they had not received any such order. I don't know why this has occurred, but it raises a serious concern because if the Movement cannot agree upon a set date for such an important action, then imagine just how difficult it will be to do so on less important matters.

I hope that the support committee is now functioning, although I'll give them time to rest a bit and organize themselves while I wait for the bullets. Remember: bullets and money are our two weak points, then comes [waterproof] plastic sheets, warm clothes and shoes.

A warm greeting for everyone from

Che

To *Darío*

Sierra Maestra, December 30, 1957

Dear *Darío*,

I'm sending four explanatory letters. I received your letter from the Sierra as well as one from the DN [National Directorate of the July 26 Movement] that I don't think was written by you, as it would not have been physically possible given the dates.[14]

In your letter you apologize for having involuntarily offended me and retract your words if they caused offense. That is absolutely unnecessary. For me there is no such thing as personal offense. I'll confess that I thought that my ideology was the reason behind the delays in the supply of goods. Now it's my turn to apologize, as those thoughts are truly offensive. However, this didn't occur for

---

14   This letter is part of an exchange that took place in early December 1957 between Che and Darío (Armando Hart) and Daniel (René Ramos Latour) regarding the roles of the different wings of the July 26 Movement — the *Llano* (the urban underground) and the Rebel Army, the latter usually referred to as the *Sierra* — and how each reacted to the announcement of the Miami Pact in October 1957, signed by representatives of the Movement in exile without consultation with the leadership in Cuba. This pact undermined both the military and political struggle against the Batista dictatorship and was repudiated by Fidel in December 1957. The polemic between Che and the others arose due to the fact that, as Armando Hart explained, Che's "socialist ideas had already crystalized, whereas among many of those in the *Llano* [those ideas] were still gestating, and not without doubts and contradictions." This debate became public in January 1958 after Hart and several others were captured and a draft of a letter to Che was found. See the appendices of this book, and also Guevara, *Reminiscences of the Cuban Revolutionary War*, op. cit. and Guevara, *Diary of a Combatant*, op. cit.

no reason. Until then, we had received nothing we had asked for, except for a letter from you in which you discusssed many things but didn't mention our requests (I now understand that this was not your fault) and one from Daniel, in which he said the things were coming, but much later. [...] I am neither a communist nor a Soviet spy nor an agent provocateur, but much, much less am I an anticommunist. I believe anticommunism is a sewer where everything that is rotten congregates (take a look at the champions of anticommunism if you don't believe me). I consider myself to be a man of honor and won't sink into that sewer. Moreover, I knew, because you confessed to me, that you had refused to work with them on tasks of revolutionary unity (you told me this when [Herbert] Matthews)[15] was here. And I knew about your conversation with representatives of an embassy or, better said, a consulate, through the letter from you-know-who. I also learned, from the same source, that the ambassador had made a special point about Raúl's [Castro] ideology.

Things are different now because I am leading a [guerrilla] column and my ideological position is known to the embassy. All this leads me to think about what I said, although I changed my view after receiving Daniel's letter in which he refuted my suggestion that everything you were telling me was false. I also told Fidel this, but, nevertheless, I have put my post at his disposal, as I cannot renounce my ideals and in no way do I want to be an obstacle to victory, as I believe it always best for a government to be run by a group of young men who are apt to change when confronted with reality rather than the murderer who governs the non-liberated parts of Cuba.

That's how things stand today. If I wrote the letter, the contents of which you already know, it was because Fidel reaffirmed his

---

15   *New York Times* journalist Herbert Matthews interviewed Fidel Castro in the Sierra Maestra in February 1957.

confidence in me and I had to clarify things because, if there is one thing I don't want to be it's a martyr. The only matter left to clarify is that I have no aspiration to hold any future political post and that I will only continue to collaborate if my services are clearly required in the new government. I will never, in any way, shape or form, act as an obstacle. I have too much pride in the historic nature of my revolutionary vocation for that.

I believe I have clarified things. I'm sorry that I haven't been able to give this explanation to you in person. I think that would have been better for everyone. I send you greetings with the utmost affection, willing to clarify anything regarding this issue.

Che

To *Daniel*

Sierra Maestra, December 30, 1957

Dear *Daniel*,

I am responding to your letter in order to conclude this exchange of ideas that I believe has been useful. To be clear, I just want to state clearly that I did not accuse you of treason, although I maintain that the entire DN is at fault for having publicized a document that had been signed behind its back, thereby making it appear official to the members of the Movement. If I had been in your place, even thinking the way I do, I would also not have dared to contradict clearly and firmly an individual with the prestige that Pazos has.[16] But there is a big difference between this and publicizing it without waiting for a decision from Fidel. The other thing I want to clarify is that I don't believe in exporting revolutions. That is why I would never look kindly on a change of master, even if this came about as the result of socialist interference in our (if you allow me to call it this) island. You can choose to believe me or not, as I don't have documentary evidence or proof of this. It's up to you. As for me, this polemic or whatever you want to call it is over, but given your letter represents the sentiment of the entire DN and Darío sent me some separate notes, without having read my letter, I have clarified a few points with him.

Regarding the supplies sent: first, I have to say I was not at all satisfied; whether I'm being disrespectful, that is your somewhat

---

16   Felipe Pazos was a bourgeois oppositionist to General Batista and one of the signatories of the Miami Pact.

personal opinion. You have to understand that I cannot arm the troops with the bullets you sent me, as there were only enough 30.06 for 10 people. Even if we calculate that they use half the amount of bullets (it is more but let's say half), there is only enough to arm 20 of them. We don't need bullets for the M1 here, as Fidel gave me a lot and I only have three of those rifles; naturally, I gave them back to him as he has a lot of them and they used up a lot of the ammunition. The cartridges and bullets for revolvers are good and we need them, but they are for irregular troops, of which we have about 100; they cannot be used in open combat as the difference between these weapons and a Garand is enormous.

Regarding your lament for the guys from the *Llano* [urban underground] who laid down their weapons, including the 15 in Mayarí you refer to: I had no news about this but Fidel should know. I don't know if the latest recruits have been incorporated, but anyway, a similar number should come to the Sierra or serve as the nucleus of another front. You may not know this but I'm one of the most enthusiastic supporters of establishing another front although on various occasions Fidel has opposed this, giving the example of Faustino and [the failed attempt to do this in] Miranda.[17] (I remember well how I "pushed" for the latter when *Nicaragua* proposed it, and I continue to defend this, in spite of previous failures.)[18] With respect to our ammunition stocks, I must remind you of something I forgot to mention: I received one hundred 44 bullets that are extremely useful here. I recall you saying that one can find anything you need, although at a cost. If

---

17   Faustino Pérez (1920–1992) was a doctor who participated in the *Granma* expedition. He became the head of the July 26 Movement's action and sabotage section in the urban underground during the revolutionary war.

18   Nicaragua was the *nom de guerre* of Carlos Julio Iglesia Fonseca, a member of the national leadership of the July 26 Movement.

that's still the case, I would prefer that you use some of the money that was to be sent to me to buy more of those bullets

About Márquez, the doubt remains. The man who recommended him is the head of the Movement in Palma Soriano (or was in Los Cocos, when I saw him). It would be good to clarify this point because, after taking him prisoner, we can't let him go and It is very hard to confirm from here. He showed me a piece of paper from a sergeant or someone like that, recommending him. That paper, according to him, was what allowed him to move around without problems.

I should tell you, for your and everyone's satisfaction, that we have finally received an important consignment that includes a new mimeograph and paper. They tell me that there's still a lot more to come and then even more. The things we need most here are fabric to make uniforms (it would be even better if there were some patterns) and cables to make electronic explosives, which would be fantastic to use here (it would be even better if we were sent the detonators themselves). The rest of the stuff, except for the weapons, can wait as we can continue to make boots and uniforms even with Sánchez Mosquera around (he is already in La Mina and threatening to come up here within a few days).

I think the change in Bayamo has been very beneficial for the Movement. The relative ease with which things happen now, I'm sure, will convince you of the negligence of the previous leadership. I must criticize the fact that a young student called Pepe is trying to pass himself off as the chief and even went as far as to threaten to kill a man I sent to Contramaestre for the cane burning. I think I've already warned you that all the men who went to burn the cane fields did so complying with Fidel's order. I'm saying this because in some quarters this was interpreted as interference in the affairs of the *Llano* and many of the guys were prevented from carrying out the burning.

To finish, I want to clarify that I truly appreciate the heroism of those who are fighting in the *Llano*. Everyone who has been there and returned, without exception, has spoken to me about the harsh conditions faced there.

Please do me the favor of passing on the other letter for *Darío*. Receive a cordial greeting from someone who considers you a compañero in the struggle and as such holds you in high esteem.

Che

To Calixto[19]

Sierra Maestra, July 13, 1958

Dear Calixto,

I haven't written before in order to avoid the kind of interference that usually happens here but I'm very interested in clarifying with you various problems that have arisen in recent times.

I had such bad luck with the letter I wrote you in that the imbecile of a messenger gave it to you-know-who to pass on to you. In that letter, I spoke rather harshly about certain people, who, later on, quoted my letter in a meeting. It was a private letter; if you read it out loud like they said you did, then that was wrong. Obviously, I'm pretty sure that others read the letter before it got to you, which is why I never asked for an explanation.

Subsequently they brought along as evidence a semi-public manifesto that was unequivocably signed by you. I believe that this little pamphlet containing your denunciation was your worst mistake. You should have remembered that, despite all ideological differences, they are compañeros in the struggle who share a common objective, even if we have tactical differences and very different final goals. I read the pamphlet, which could have been a genuine representation of revolutionary thought had it not been for you identifying those you accuse, something that is really incredible for a man of your standing.

---

19 Calixto Morales (1929) was a *Granma* expeditionary who fought in Fidel Castro's Column One and then in the urban underground. He later joined Che's column in Las Villas.

In the end, all these problems and any others can be clarified and discussed directly with us. I thank you and ask you not to forget to send me some good poetry.

Revolutionary greetings,

[Unsigned]

LETTERS WRITTEN FROM THE CAMAGÜEY PLAINS AND LAS VILLAS PROVINCE

To Fidel Castro

Camagüey plains, September 8, 1958, 1:50 a.m.[20]

Fidel,

After some exhausting long nights, I'm finally writing to you from Camagüey, with no immediate perspective of accelerating our pace, an average of three to four leagues a day, and with only half the troops on horseback and without saddles. Camilo is nearby, and I was waiting for him here at the Bartles rice farm, but he didn't show up. The plains are formidable: there are not so many mosquitos, we haven't seen a single *casquito* [soldier] and [Batista's] planes seem like inoffensive doves. Radio Rebelde can be heard with great difficulty via Venezuela.

Everything indicates that the soldiers don't want war and nor do we. I confess that I am scared of carrying out a withdrawal with 150 inexperienced recruits in this unknown zone, but an armed guerrilla unit of 30 men could do wonders in the area and revolutionarize it. By the way, I spoke to the rice workers' union in Peonero and spoke about the tax but they rejected it. It's not that I backed down but it does seem that the quota is excessive. I said we could discuss it and left it until our next visit. Someone with a

---

20 On August 31, Che had left the Sierra Maestra in Oriente province, leading his guerrilla column westward toward the center of the island.

social consciousness could work miracles here and there are plenty of woods to hide in. Regarding my future plans, I can't tell you anything in terms of the route we'll take, because I don't know myself; it depends more on particular circumstances and luck. We are currently waiting for some trucks to see if we can dispense with the horses, which were well suited to Maceo's pre-aircraft times but which [make us] highly visible from the air. If it weren't for the horses, we could happily travel during the day. There is mud and water everywhere and the *fidelazos* [lengthy speeches] I've had to make to ensure the convoy arrived in good shape could have come straight from a movie. We had to cross various creeks, tough going, but the troops are behaving well, even though the punishment squadron is growing fast and promises to be the largest one in our column. The next report will reach you over the airwaves, if that's possible, from the city of Camagüey. That's it, except to repeat the fraternal embrace to those in the "Sierra," which we can no longer see.

[Unsigned]

To Fidel Castro

Camaguey plains, September 13, 1958, 9:50 p.m.

Fidel,

After some accident prone days, I'm still writing from Camagüey, where we are about to cross through the most dangerous part, or one of the two most dangerous parts, of our trek. Camilo already crossed last night with a lot of technical difficulties but without any military problems. Since the last report I sent you, some unfortunate things have happened. Due to a lack of guides, we fell into an ambush on the estate of Remigio Fernández in La Federal, in which Marcos Borrero, a captain, died. We reduced the number of soldiers by eight, killing three and taking four prisoners, whom we had planned to keep with us until we had an opportunity to release them. One escaped and blew the whistle. Some 60 soldiers appeared and, on advice from Camilo who was close by, we withdrew, without engaging in any real combat, although we did lose a man, Dalcio Gutiérrez, from the Sierra. Herman was slightly wounded in the leg and Enriquito Acevedo was more seriously injured in both his arms. Acevedo, Captain Ángel Frías and Lieutenant Roberto Rodríguez (*El Vaquerito* [Little Cowboy]) were outstanding.

Later, they tried again to advance and we surprised a passing truck with only four men in our ambush. We took down at least two of them. We retreated to La Federal and then left immediately, taking Enrique with us for treatment. The following day the B-26s fired on us. Camilo was able to move faster and we are now waiting for them to send some trucks to pick us up.

Strange things are happening around here, suggesting that it would be a good idea to send us immediately a leader with experience and "toughness" in these parts. On no account should he come with more than 30 armed men and they could get whatever they need here. It would be worthwhile operating in the region of Naboas where the climate is very favorable due to the spoils of the Francisco sugar mill. There is constant vegetation all the way from Santa Beatriz to Santa Cruz, which is good for a group of this size. You should watch what the leadership in Camagüey is doing, promising to enlist everyone and we are being assaulted by unarmed groups asking to join us. I've asked around about the issue of the crazy guy and essentially it seems he has a terrible psychosis of war.

There are many more problems I would like to raise with you, but I don't have time as I have to go. They say there are lots of soldiers along the road but by the time this report arrives, you will know [what has happened] by other means.

Greetings to everyone,

[Unsigned]

To *Gómez*[21]

Camp of the Revolutionary Directorate, Las Villas[22]

Sierra del Escambray, October 23, 1958[23]

Dear *Gómez*,

I'm taking advantage of the messenger to send you a few lines of greetings. I'm now where I am supposed to be but my hopes of emulating your feats have been shattered as I have come up against a situation which is not for little Napoleons but for a Talleyrand. Nevertheless, we will attempt to continue making progress while maintaining the honor of that quartet [of fallen compañeros] that included poor Ñico and the now deceased Universo.[24]

When you get a chance, tell me about [what's happening in] your zone because I need to learn from all other experiences to overcome the thousand obstacles I'm confronting here, despite my great willingness to achieve something positive.

---

21   Raúl Castro used the *nom de guerre* Gómez. He had been a student leader at the University of Havana and participated in the attack on the 1953 Moncada barracks. He returned to Cuba with the *Granma* expedition. He became a central leader of the revolutionary government, Minister of the Armed Forces and succeeded his brother Fidel as president of Cuba from 2006 to 2018.

22   The Revolutionary Directorate was established by student leader José Antonio Echeverría, who was killed in an armed attack on Batista's presidential palace and Radio Reloj in Havana on March 13, 1957.

23   After a six-week trek from the Sierra Maestra in the east, Che's column reached the Escambray mountains in central Cuba on October 16, 1958.

24   Antonio López ("Ñico") was one the Cuban revolutionaries Che met in Guatemala in 1954 and was killed during the revolutionary war in Cuba.

I need to learn from common experiences while trying to deal with thousands of obstacles preventing me from doing something good, I assure you I have a lot of willpower.

I heard that our friend Lucas has gone his own way; you failed in not applying Triple Zero, but there is always time.[25]

Give a hug to all the combatants I know and those I don't know on your front, especially to Efigenio, Jiménez, Pena, Fajardo and another tight one for compañera Débora [Vilma Espín].

Receive a fraternal embrace from

Che

---

25 A reference to someone who had apparently betrayed the guerrillas and whom Che urges should be captured and brought to justice.

To Fidel Castro

Camp of the Revolutionary Directorate, Las Villas
Sierra del Escambray, October 23, 1958

Fidel,

I didn't send you this report earlier because the complicated political situation means that a more detailed study is required, and I didn't want to waste time simply reporting that I had arrived.

The complexity of the situation means that I must provide you with a historical summary of the situation. To begin, I'll report on our trek and then turn to an analysis of the current situation.

Trek through Las Villas

September 13. That night I sent you the last report explaining the dangers we faced. The July 26 Movement contacts had assured us that the guides would arrive, something that didn't happen. Reviewing our situation, I decided nevertheless to continue with the guide we had, improvising. The final result was that sunrise forced us to go to a post in Cuatro Compañeros. We had not taken all the recommended precautions and, although we had no casualties, a state of confusion arose. With no knowledge of the area, we headed for a hill we could see in the half-light of dawn, but to get there we had to cross a railway line that the soldiers were advancing along from two directions. We had to engage in combat to ensure all the compañeros behind us could make it. Captain Silva was injured, but he has continued, with exemplary stoicism, to lead his men despite suffering a fracture in the articular cartilage of his right shoulder. This situation lasted two and an half hours, until 9:30 in the morning, when I gave the order to withdraw, having lost compañero Juan Hernández, whose right leg was destroyed by a 100-pound bomb. We suffered some other minor injuries at the bottom of the hill as a result of the bombardment and machine-gun fire from two B26s, two C47s and two small planes; this lasted for 45 minutes.

We regrouped over the following days and discovered that 10 of the men who had become separated were now in Camilo's column and only one had disappeared, nicknamed Morenito, whose first name and surname I'll include at the end. Without taking even a day's rest, we passed through Remedios, a Cadenas rice farm, a few unimportant cays, Lagunas de Guano. All of this without any guide, occasionally picking up a Camagüeyan peasant to help us, and having to face the consequences of various tip-offs.

September 20. That day we heard radio reports from Tabernilla about the barefoot column led by Che Guevara. It turns out that in one of the backpacks they found a book with the names, addresses, guns, bullets and equipment of each member of the entire column. Moreover, a member of this column, who is also a member of the PSP [Popular Socialist Party], left his backpack behind containing documents from that organization. Over the next days, we crossed the San Pedro River and the Durán or Altamira, reaching a place known as El Chicharrón. There, an individual who had joined us in Camagüey deserted and, shortly after, while crossing a dangerous railway line, we lost José Pérez, who had joined the column before we left Oriente, and who, I suspect, deserted with his rifle.

We then crossed a rather dangerous embankment and we camped in the rice growing region where the big estates of the Aguilera brothers are. We had no guide and were trying to follow the sporadic tracks of compañero Camilo. We walked through quagmires, almost without stopping, from the 20th. On more than one occasion, we had to abandon some of the horses we had with us. The *mazamorra* [maize porridge] began to cause discontent among the troops.

September 29. We left the last Aguilera rice farm behind and reached the lands of the Baraguá sugar mill where we discovered that the army had completely blocked off the railway line we had to cross. They saw us, and our rearguard was forced to repel the soldiers with a few shots. Believing that the shots had come from soldiers hidden along the railway line, and following our usual practice, I ordered that we wait until nightfall, thinking we could cross then. By the time I found out about the skirmish, and that the enemy was fully aware of our position, it was too late to try because the night was dark and rainy, and we didn't know where the enemy was. We had to retreat, camping in a muddy area further down the mountain to fool the planes that, effectively, directed their attacks against wooded hills located not far from our position. The exploratory team headed by Lieutenant Acevedo discovered a way around the enemy line, as they had neglected a lagoon that they thought no one could cross. We walked nearly 2 kilometers through this muddy lagoon, trying to minimize as much as possible the sound of 140 men splashing, until we crossed a railway line close to 100 meters from the last post from where we could hear the soldiers' conversations. The splashing noise, which was impossible to avoid completely, along with the bright moonlight, more or less convinced me that the enemy was aware of our presence, but the low combat morale that we constantly observed among the dictatorship's soldiers made them deaf to any suspicious sounds.

We walked the entire night and part of the next day through marshes of weedy water. A quarter of the troops had no boots and or ones that were in a bad condition.

October 3. In a cay near the Baraguá sugar mill, we captured the butcher at that mill and notified his family that nothing would happen to him but that he would have to act as our guide for a few days. It seems that the woman wanted to change husbands, as she tipped-off the National Guard, which led to a visit from some B26s carrying their usually cargo. Nothing came of this, but we had to walk all night in a lagoon full of rushes with sharp leaves that horribly injured the feet of some of those who had no boots. The troop's morale was being affected by the impact of hunger and the maize porridge. We never had the chance to stop and rest because the soldiers were following our tracks, with a lot of help from the planes. We viewed each peasant we came across as a potential snitch. We were in a psychological state akin to the early days in the Sierra Maestra. We were unable to establish contact with the July 26 organization, as a couple of supposed members refused our request for help and we only received money, some [waterproof] plastic sheets, a few shoes, medicines, food and a guide from members of the PSP [Popular Socialist Party], who told me they had also asked the Movement for help and were apparently told, although this seems unlikey to me: if Che sends a written note, we'll help; if not, tough luck to Che.

October 7. We made contact with three guides from the Escambray who had a string of complaints about [Eloy] Gutiérrez Menoyo[26]

---

26   Eloy Gutiérrez Menoyo was a member of the Revolutionary Directorate and a commander of the Second Front of the Escambray. He refused to collaborate with the Rebel Army in Las Villas until the last days of the war against Batista. After the revolution he became active in the counterrevolutionary movement.

and told me that Bordón[27] had been taken prisoner and that there was now an internal situation of virtual open conflict between the different groups. I suspected that behind this there was a lot of dirty laundry that needed airing, and I sent one of them to bring Bordón to meet with me. That day, in an effort to clean out the scum from the column, I ordered the discharge of anyone who chose to leave: seven took this opportunity and I'll list their names so that they go down on the dark side of the history of this revolution: Víctor Sarduy, Juan Noguera, Ernesto Magaña, Rigoberto Solís, Oscar Macías, Teodoro Reyes and Rigoberto Alarcón. The previous day, Pardillo from Joel's platoon disappeared; I suspect that he deserted.

From then on, the air force followed us with total precision, bombing the woods we had left the previous day as they tried to cut us off at the Jatibonico River. During one of those bombing raids a retro propulsion jet exploded in mid air. I imagine you heard about this on the radio. On October 10, planes carrying a machine gun attacked the hill where we were. They were just small planes and there were no casualties. The next day, the vanguard group seized a sugar refinery that was in contact with a nearby rice farm. We discovered that the army knew about our situation from the conversations we intercepted. The exact location of "the rats" had been identified, according to the army's reports we intercepted (although, foreseeing this, we abandoned the hill and hid in a house surrounded by fields where we stayed for the day without moving). They didn't think we were capable of walking the two leagues to the Jatibonico. Of course, that's what we did that night. We swam across the river, although almost all of our weapons got wet, and then we carried on for another league until we found

---

27   Victor Bordón Machado (1930–2014) was a member of the Orthdox Party Youth and the July 26 Movement. He joined Che's column in Las Villas in October 1958.

a safe refuge on a hill. Crossing the Jatibonico symbolized the passage from darkness into the light. Ramiro [Valdés] said it was as if an electric switch had turned on a light, and that is exactly how it was. From the day before, the bluish mountains [of the Escambray] could be seen in the distance, and even the most dejected highlander became extremely anxious to get there.

We then spent an exhausting day walking through deep mud; we traversed rice fields and cane fields, and crossed the Zaza River, which must be the widest in Cuba; we passed the last cordon of soldiers on the road from Trinidad to Sancti Spíritus by night on the 15th, and then began our tedious political task.

I have heard about Vega's disaster; undoubtedly it was the result of inexperience. The same would not have happened to Ramiro. But let's wait a bit; we will demonstrate that his presence here is a positive for the revolution. Now to the second part.

Report on the political-military situation in Las Villas

The first groups of rebels were essentially a group of refugees who had been aligned with the July 26 Movement but forced to flee because of political difficulties in the urban underground. They did nothing, militarily speaking, in the hills. The first organized group to arrive here was the Revolutionary Directorate, a nucleus of some 20 men under the military command of Eloy Gutiérrez Menoyo. It seems that the troubles with Faure Chaumont [sic] began almost as soon as Menoyo took up arms.[28] In the midst of their tussle, Bordón arrived with arms given to him by the July 26 Movement. The hostility of the other group was obvious. Bordón separated his people out, moved to a different area and remained

---

28   Faure Chomón Mediavilla was a leader of the Revolutionary Directorate who took part in the March 13, 1957, assault on the presidential palace in Havana. He later joined Che's column during the revolutionary war.

there, apparently carrying out some good political work among the peasant population. The situation between Gutiérrez Menoyo and the [Revolutionary] Directorate reached crisis point, the forces were separated, and the Directorate took control over the Trinidad-Sancti Spíritus area.

Gutiérrez Menoyo and his group decided to set up the so-called Second Front of the Escambray. They proposed the addition of a general staff to the provincial leadership of the July 26 Movement, with Eloy Gutiérrez as chief and with each of the 14 chiefs of the guerrillas having the rank of commander, in a situation of parity among them. The provincial leadership, concretely Sierra [Enrique Oltuski], after consulting with Faustino and some other members of the National Leadership (I believe it was our Eloy, but I'm not sure), made a counterproposal to create a general staff composed of Gutiérrez Menoyo, Bordón and Plinio Prieto, representing the OA |Organización Auténtica].[29] This general staff would decide by majority vote what military actions to undertake. By this time, the Caracas Pact had been signed and there was an agreement to send $100,000 to the different fronts of struggle, of which $35,000 was for the front in the Escambray.[30] The only recognized combat organization there, however, was the Directorate. Sierra therefore wrote a document requesting that the money be divided between the two groups, the Directorate and the Second Front (which included the three commanders mentioned above). He dispatched the document to be signed and it was sent back deleting the part about parity and naming Eloy Gutiérrez Menoyo as chief of the Second Front of the Escambray. Given the

---

29   Sierra was the *nom de guerre* of Enrique Oltuski (1930–2012) who was the coordinator of the July 26 Movement in Las Villas and after the revolution worked with Che in the Ministry of Industry.

30   The Caracas Pact was signed in Venezuela on July 20, 1958, by 11 Cuban political parties and organizations.

rush, Sierra said he signed the document that then went to the Caracas Pact commission, thereby placing the July 26 Movement under Gutiérrez Menoyo's authority. It's not clear what role was played by Diego, the commander of the militias, in all this.[31] The seriousness of the situation does not end there, as a new document was drafted, which I've attached, in which point C of the final resolutions gives the chief of the General Staff the right to set the national and international strategy of the Second Front. This document was signed by Bordón, as commander of the Second Front. It seems that some of the leaders of the July 26 Movement advised Bordón to send this with Anastasio Cárdenas to the Sierra Maestra to legitimize the pact. But Bordón didn't go to the Sierra, but returned saying that he had gone and that he was the only commander that Fidel recognized. This was when Menoyo stripped him of his weapon and took him prisoner, forcing him to sign a document in which he promised to leave the region. The provincial leaders of the July 26 Movement convinced him to not do this, and to stay as leader of those who remained loyal to him. This provoked Menoyo into issuing an ultimatum, saying that he would expel Bordón from [the Escambray] in five days if he didn't leave. The provincial leadership issued an order to resist the attack and Bordón didn't come to me, as he had been ordered to on four different occasions. I had most recently ordered him to come down to see me bringing all his men, but I have had no news that he has moved from where he was.

On reaching the Escambray, I received a note that I have attached, signed by commander Jesús Carreras, the tone of which you will notice immediately.[32] On the way, as we looked

---

31   Diego was the *nom de guerre* of Víctor Dáz Paneque, director of action in the urban underground in Las Villas province.

32   Jesús Carreras Zayas was a commander of the Second Front of the Escambray, who after 1959 joined the counterrevolution.

for somewhere to set up our base camp, I passed by three camps belonging to the Second Front and noticed the following: a cordial reception on the part of the troops and a cold welcome from the chiefs, who seemed to be carrying out espionage and who had disappeared before we arrived. I went to Jesús Carreras' camp, who absented himself just moments before I got there. I left him a letter explaining my surprise, but just at that moment, I read a circular stuck up at the camp, point 10 of which said essentially that any troops not belonging to the organization were prohibited from entering the territory they controlled, that the first time they would receive a warning and that if they didn't comply, they would be expelled or killed. I brought the guys together and explained the seriousness of this clause and the need for them to be on alert because we understood that the territory of Cuba was open to everyone who wanted to fight the dictatorship. We'll never fire the first shot, but our tradition of struggle … blah, blah, blah. That was when Carreras turned up, apologizing for the word "order," which I accepted. He said he was not very good at writing and that he didn't mean what he had said, that there was no threat intended and that the edict I had read was solely aimed at those belonging to the Directorate because "they steal our stuff." I said that the only way to work together was by recognizing the military leadership of the July 26 Movement, which at first he didn't accept. I then met with commander Alfredo Peña, ex-army chief and former member of the July 26 Movement, who confessed that he had been left with no men to lead. This gentleman had a letter from you, dated March, where you said you would help him if he accept the structure of the July 26 Movement. He is a perfect imbecile but ambitious like all of them. I haven't spoken with Gutiérrez Menoyo yet but he didn't carry out his ultimatum against Bordón.

My conversations with the [Revolutionary] Directorate were different: they are not willing to unite with Gutiérrez Menoyo's group. We reached an agreement in which they would set up their base camp in the area they currently control and we would set up ours somewhere else, leaving for future negotiations the delineation of territory, the imposition of taxes, etc. We've proposed a joint action but I don't see a lot of enthusiasm for this on their side. They are waiting for some big equipment and don't want to move until then, according to what they told us. There are only a few of them and they are not well armed.

The OA [Organización Auténtica] does not exist up here, but as always they have messed things up and designated the worst elements of the Second Front (Peña) to be their official representative. As usual, I have offered guns.

The PSP [Popular Socialist Party] sent a representative. I told them that the way to unity was for their guerrillas to follow the orders of the July 26 Movement and that I could not accept commander Torres, who was imposed by another organization, if he had not complied with the unity agreement signed by all the sectors in Escambray.[33] They agreed to this.

The fat gentleman who visited us in the Sierra, the second time with Lino, has business dealings in Las Villas and came to see me to offer a transmitter and a mimeograph. I accepted them. You sent a letter to Camilo with him, and I opened it to see what it said. Your orders coincided with what I had asked for; I took out 1,000 pesos. His willingness to collaborate is magnificent. He has had differences with the provincial leadership who refused to recognize him. Our eternal problem.

The provincial leadership has committed the gross error of signing these documents; it suffers from a slackness. I wanted to bring together all the coordinators from the local towns and only the general coordinator came; the rest said "they couldn't make

---

33   Félix Torres González was a leader of the PSP, who later achieved the rank of commander in the Rebel Army.

it." Cienfuegos seems to be the only city up to the task when it comes to provisioning the Rebel Army. I spoke with the workers' delegate, telling him about the need to attack those towns that have no internal organization that backs us, and gave him instructions. I don't plan to take measures or have serious conversations (serious in terms of length) until after November 3.

Our arrival in Las Villas has had the benefit in these last few days of awakening all the organizations that have been ready to fight.

The name of the person who disappeared that I promised to give you: Santos Ferrales Milanés from the Mabay sugar mill.

I need you to respond to me quickly regarding whether the sugar tax will be charged in a consistent manner or if I should collect it in this province. I'm thinking of establishing a treasury here to administer the money collected from these taxes and I have ambitious projects that I'll tell you about later. (I have just heard the harmonious sound of a bazooka. Given the amount of energy it takes, it is the heroine of the troops.)

I should also tell you that the reception we got from the civilian population was simply tremendous and if it were not for Camilo, I would surely have given the Bronze Titan [independence hero Antonio Maceo] a dirty look.

A hug from the tourists of the Escambray to the sedentary ones in the Sierra Maestra.

[Unsigned]

To Fidel Castro
Sierra del Escambray, November 3, 1958

Fidel

I'm sending you a preliminary report, written on the run, of events to date and of the difficulties we've encountered along the way, attaching copies of the letters.

After the last report I sent, I was held up for a few days due to the prevarication of the [Revolutionary] Directorate, who finally resolved to support the attack on the Güinía de Miranda barracks (now Lino Pérez) without the help, in any case fictitious, of that [other] group, who didn't even provide a guide for them. The barracks were said to be an easy target, with 20 or so soldiers willing to surrender. This would have been the case if the bazooka had not misfired four times. The fifth hit the target and the barracks surrendered, with an unknown number of soldiers escaping. The battle cost us two dead, whose names I have included separately, six injured, two of them with fractures, and the loss of a significant amount of ammunition. All of this for eight rifles, one of which I gave to a guide from the Directorate, and very little ammunition. The action was in no way profitable, but politically it was a strong blow that demonstrated our desire to do things properly.

Two days later, we headed for another small barracks defended by 50 soldiers, but I told the troops to hold their fire until 3:00 am, as we didn't have enough ammunition to capture it through a direct assault because it is open terrain for two leagues all around. The bazooka was not in position in time so we had to

Self-portrait, Buenos Aires, 1950.

Heading off on his solo trip around Argentina, 1950,
on a motorized bicycle.

Preparing La Poderosa, II (Mighty One, II) for the trip around Latin
America with Alberto Granado, as described in Che's book and movie of
the same name, *The Motorcycle Diaries*.

Che's parents, Celia and Ernesto (Sr.), arriving in Havana, soon after the overthrow of General Batista in January 1959.

Aleida March and Che Guevara, January 28, 1960.

Fidel, Che's daughter Aleidita and Che, Revolution Plaza, Havana, 1964.

Che and Aleida, 1965, with their children (left to right): Ernestito, Camilo, Aleidita and Celia.

Che in Bolivia, several months before he was captured and killed in
October 1967.

Che in his office at the Ministry of Industry, Havana, 1963.

lift the siege. We did a forced march to the Banao barracks, which has 30 soldiers, along the Trinidad-Sancti Spíritus highway, but lost a day due to the stupidity of the guides who said it was five hours away whereas we walked for 12 without getting there. Despite everything, we carried out the operation the following day, but the bazooka failed, forcing us to retreat without having fired a shot.

I called together the action chiefs in the surrounding localities to give them general instructions on what they had to do and asked them for details of friendly and enemy banks. I decided to attack a few of them, one of them a Canadian bank, with the intention of leaving IOUs that informed customers that the revolution would take responsibility for repaying their money. But the leadership of the *Llano* [urban underground] opposed this (because no action chief said anything and neither did Diego, but Sierra did). Moreover, they boycotted the actions or were scared [to participate]. We'll have to work this out later. We were unable to do anything in Sancti Spíritus, as you will see in the letter. In Fomento, they performed very poorly and gave up when Bordón got there.

Cabaiguán, whose chief is one of Faustino's brothers, responded very well, but unfortunately, one of the many stupid guides, remnants of what the Second Front left us after it disintegrated, got us lost yesterday, which meant we couldn't attack. We will do so today, but now with the whole world expecting it. I want your express authorization to do whatever we need to do with the banks, or otherwise a clear "no," so that we can put an end to this matter. I also want your support to get rid of all the useless chiefs. I think it would be positive in the current situation to get our hands on a bank. If you are afraid that "good people" will be turned off by such an action, we should at least attack an English bank or something similar. That is my opinion but I will wait for your confirmation or correction or for you to call me in front of the revolutionary tribunal, which I discuss in an attached letter. Given the opportunity, I'll clean things up with more enthusiasm than Al Capone.

My intention is to give the troops two days' rest, reorganize those who are still here, give instructions for the creation of everything we need in the general headquarters established a cannon shot away from Sancti Spíritus, and go with part of my troop and my beloved bazooka to destroy those barracks. I'm waiting for news from Camilo, as I haven't heard anything from him since I gave him instructions to act, which were different from your instructions, which had become superfluous.

The political situation is more or less the following: the Directorate, nothing to report; the Second Front lost almost all its guerrilla fighters in the zone because they joined our ranks bringing with them their habits of drunkeness, firing bullets into the air, doing whatever they want, but no guns. I have already established a school for new recruits which all these men will have to attend; there are more than 200 of them at the moment and their number is rising at an alarming rate. Apart from the school, we need the government to launch a purifying offensive. I set up the "telephone emulation" in the zone, which consists of all the patrols and action groups in the towns bringing me electrical wiring and telephones in a sporting competition. We'll try not to leave any trace. It is incredible what we could do if we had action chiefs who were less concerned about their own hides and organized their militias better.

Bordón was removed as commander and made a captain, not the best move that could have been made but more appropriate; this was done on Ramiro's advice. I'm thinking of demanding control of the administration of the zone where I am at the moment and to come down with an iron fist on the abuses currently being committed, abuses sometimes committed against peasants, and at other times within our own ranks; for example, within the space of a few days, boots were stolen by two guerrillas from the Second Front.

The names of our dead: Alberto Cabrales and Carlos Amengual. I'd like to hear a brief mention of them on the radio as they came from Oriente and were the first to die here. Angelito and Silva have turned out to be great captains. The two were slightly injured in Güinía. I intend to prepare Angelito to become the head of the Yaguajay front, with some intelligent person from there to advise him. But before making a decision, I am waiting for news from Camilo who already knows that area. The soldiers we captured and released in the small barracks (which was a fort) are: Maximiliano Juviel Hugando, from Trinidad, 58 years old, acting corporal; Israel Rodríguez Torres, 25 years old, enlisted in December 1957; Juan Díaz López, 21 years old, enlisted in March 1957; Mario Aday Espinosa, 21 years old, enlisted in December 1957; Manuel Armando García Morales, enlisted in January 1958; two injured, one of whom later died, and one dead, all belonged to Regiment # 3, Squadron 39. Between five and 15 soldiers escaped via a trench that appears to have been dug for that purpose.

We have been promised a couple of transmitters but I'm not sure if they will come or not. If we get them, we will call at 5:00 in the afternoon for 20 or 40 minutes until we establish contact. We will quickly try to announce our presence on Radio Miami. Sierra told me he was personally going to Miami to seek guns. I want to know if he can do that on his own or not. For now, we cannot rely on another airstrip apart from the ones that belong to the Directorate or the other people. But we will be able to come to some kind of agreement with them in a few days after we show them what we can do. Tell me your view of the situation and if you believe the government is on the verge of collapse or not. In my next report, I'll include my first balance sheet.

A warm embrace to the heroes of the Oriente from your younger brothers.

[Unsigned]

Additional note, November 5

We haven't been able to add to the old glories of the July 26 in these days. The honorable leadership of the honorable gentlemen pharmacists of the people have not had the dignity to lend me their support. Fomento was a failure thanks to the cowardice of those people who refused even to give us a guide for the action. Cabaiguán was our fault: Angelito was in charge of opening fire on the barracks, Joel was to advance through the center of town and Ramiro on the other, so as to destroy the refinery. But as there were lots of soldiers, he didn't do this and the others, waiting to hear gunfire from their side, withdrew at 4:00 in the morning without firing a shot. The only thing we demonstrated was our ability to take over all of these small towns, thereby forcing them to keep 300 to 500 soldiers in each one. I don't believe it prudent to tell you my military plans but we must make sure that not a single [military] barracks is left across the entire [Escambray] region. I'm waiting to hear the results of the attack on Jíquima that I ordered last night and which appears to have been successful because today there were five planes bombing that area. Ramiro was going to lead that action.

With regard to unity, this appears to be something impossible to achieve. [William] Morgan sent an ultimatum to one of the captains I have in that area.[34] They sent a group to disarm them and instead the entire group came over to join our ranks. Then they sent another one, and they too suffered the same fate. Finally,

---

34   William Morgan was a member of the Second Front of the Escambray, who later became an agent of the US intelligence services.

Morgan, who is a commander [in the Second Front] and a North American, came to say that if by Sunday [November 2] we didn't hand over all our weapons they would attack. I don't know what the result was, but I sent the attached letter to Gutiérrez Menoyo, with a Fidel-style ending.

To the Provincial Leadership of the July 26 Movement in Las Villas
Liberated Territory, December 3, 1958

To the Provincial Leadership of the July 26 Movement

Compañeros,

I am writing to clarify a number of points relating to the Movement.

Before anything, I have to inform you that I have already signed a pact of relative unity with the Revolutionary Directorate, of which I'm attaching a mimeographed copy.[35] Moreover, in converstions with Camilo Cienfuegos, Félix Torres and leaders of the PSP, we have reached an agreement for Félix Torres to send a public letter renouncing his independence as guerrilla commander, putting his group of men, known as "Máximo Gómez," at the disposal of the July 26 Movement. Under these conditions, we have accepted the integration of those guerrilla fighters, with Torres being granted the status of captain. The group will be led by captain Ángel Frías from my column, if Camilo is forced to abandon the region. Thus, the only group with whom we haven't been able to reach any kind of agreement is the Second Front, although our relations with them have greatly improved in these last few days and they warmly received captain Julio Chaviano, who is there with them.[36]

---

35   This was the Pact of Pedrero, signed by the July 26 Movement and the Revolutionary Directorate on December 1, 1958, which established the basis for united military action and political administration in the liberated zones. A few days later the PSP also signed this unity pact.

36   Shortly after this letter was written, on December 12, 1958, Che Guevara

Regarding the Yaguajay front, Camilo Cienfuegos has passed on to me the complaints made by the coordinator of that town, who has asked to be replaced or be given precise instructions on how to better carry out his duties. The coordinators of Remedios, Zulueta and Caibarién should go and see Commander Camilo Cienfuegos and deal with him directly on certain issues.

I also want to let you know that we have almost completely restructured the Action Organization, which will now be composed of three chiefs: René Rodríguez from here, Macho Parra from Yaguajay and Eliecer Grave de Peralta from Chaviano (which for now includes the city of Santa Clara). Each action chief will head up a group and have at their disposal all the urban and semi-urban militias, through the existing structures.

The Revolutionary Army has been divided into four groups: the first is under my direct command; the second covers the area of Yaguajay, up to the highway that connects Caibarién, Remedios and Camajuaní; the third corresponds to Bordón's old jurisdiction in Escambray; and the fourth, the Oeste zone. The third and fourth groups are headed up by captains Erasmo Peraza and Julio Chaviano.

We will soon send the sketch of the badges that the Revolutionary Army of the July 26 Movement should use, with the aim of demonstrating our unity.

The first group of militia fighters trained by the special section of the school is now operating in Fomento.

The propaganda section is now running at full throttle, although it has faced some theoretical hurdles, as I had to confiscate an issue of *El Miliciano* that didn't fulfill the objective with which this publication was created [illegible in the original] printed a special edition, a newspaper specifically aimed at soldiers, called *A ti*

---

and Eloy Gutiérrez Menoyo signed a memorandum of understanding on behalf of the July 26 Movement and the Second Front of the Escambray.

soldado de la tiranía [To you, soldier of the dictatorship], of which I have attached a copy. I have also attached a copy of Military Order Number Five and a small internal memo, "To members of the July 26 Army."

In terms of combat actions, we repelled an attempt by the army to take our positions in El Pedrero; four were injured in combat. The enemy retreated to Fomento to our right flank, leaving behind as they fled a tank they didn't use and a great deal of bullets plus various other pieces military equipment. Those who tried to get through the center were pushed back to Santa Lucía; they also tried to attack us from the right flank, using an encircling maneuver, but they were also pushed back to Santa Lucía. In reprisal, the enemy burnt 21 houses belonging to local peasants.

Sabotage of [the military's] communication lines continues, with our forces having completely destroyed the rail bridge over the Calabazas River and the main road bridge over the Tuinicú River. We also destroyed a bridge and parts of the road along the Trinidad-Sancti Spíritus highway. We have promoted two soldiers to captains: compañeros Erasmo Rodríguez and Alfonso Zayas; we also promoted various combatants to the rank of lieutenant, whose names I won't give as I only know their nicknames or first names. The column's requests will be sent through the usual channels.

I have attached the program of the July 26 Movement that compañero Eloy [Gutiérrez-Menoyo] asked for and a letter for Fidel.

With revolutionary greetings, I bid you farewell.

[Unsigned]

LETTERS AS A LEADER
OF THE REVOLUTIONARY GOVERNMENT
(1959-1965)

Introduction

Che's correspondence from this period of his life as a leader of the new Cuban revolutionary government includes his letters to a broad range of individuals, among them artists, international political and literary figures, old friends and current colleagues. These letters reveal the intellectual rigor, creative thinking and tenacious dedication he applied to the extraordinary range of responsibilities he assumed in the early years of the Cuban Revolution.

In regarding the revolution as a work in progress, Che's most severe criticism and biting sarcasm is directed at what he perceives as examples of bureaucratism, "ideological parrotry" or any tendency — intentional or otherwise — to embellish or cover up inconvenient truths, including any attempt by others to rewrite his own story.

He consistently argues that a revolutionary communist leader must reject any special privileges and that they are obliged to work harder and more consistently than all others. He firmly but politely rejects any appeals from anyone for special consideration or favors, such as jobs or trips to Cuba. He is absolutely scrupulous when it comes to financial accountability and any avoidable waste of precious resources.

In a letter written in April 1960 to the writer Ernesto Sábato, Che makes an early effort to explain the nature and ideology of the revolution underway in Cuba, which his fellow Argentine has apparently asked him to clarify. Che points out that all attempts to theorize the Cuban Revolution will inevitably lag behind the rapid pace at which it is unfolding. Unfortunately, the Che Guevara Studies Center archive in Havana only retains few copies of the original correspondence to which Che is replying.

In the process of confronting the immediate challenges presented by his roles as head of the department of industrialization in the National Institute of Agrarian Reform, and subsequently as Minister of Industry, president of the National Bank and many other key responsibilities, Che never loses sight of the longer-term goals of the revolution: the transformation not just of the economy but also how individual Cubans might become the active and conscious human beings who would create a new, more just society, outlined in his essay, "Socialism and Man in Cuba."[1]

In early 1965, Che leaves Cuba to lead a small group of Cuban internationalists to support the ongoing independence struggle in the Congo, the former Belgian colony in Central Africa. Prior to leaving, Che writes a long letter to Fidel outlining some of his views on some of the key problems Cuba faced in transitioning from a capitalist economy to a new, socialist society and political culture. This letter, like many others in this section, is published here in full for the first time.

Included here are also several letters from Che to his partner Aleida and their rapidly expanding family, written during some of his frequent, extended trips abroad representing the Cuban revolutionary government. Che's tone is sometimes passionate and sometimes witty or teasing, often at his own expense.

---

1   "Socialism and Man in Cuba," in *Che Guevara Reader* (Seven Stories Press, 2021).

To Trapito [Víctor Trapote][2]

January 12, 1959

Trapito,

The victorious rebels here are living well off the few crumbs left by the former regime.

Your only good sculpture is getting married here. I have been told that your work is too sensitive and that you are not coming. No worries, we don't need you. There are plenty of *gallegos* [Spaniards] here and they can be easily replaced.

Nevertheless, if you care even a little about your daughter, then come, as I forgive you.

Much to do around here.

Greetings and a hug from this uncompromising dogmatist,

Che

---

2   Víctor Trapote ("Trapito") was a Spanish sculptor exiled in Mexico, whom Che had met during his time in Mexico. His daughter, Irina Trapote, was marrying Commander Ramiro Valdés.

To Juan Hehong Quintana
Havana, February 5, 1959

Mr. Juan Hehong Quintana
A-6, Primera No. 371
Oeste, Cárdenas

Esteemed friend,

I thank you for your gesture. It is always good to see that youth are willing to sacrifice themselves for such noble causes as the freedom of the Dominican Republic. But I believe that today, our role in the struggle is here, in Cuba, where we still have enormous difficulties to overcome.

For now, dedicate yourself to working enthusiastically for our revolution. This will be the best help that we can offer the Dominican people, that is, the example of our complete triumph.

Receive greetings from

Dr. Ernesto (Che) Guevara
Commander-in-chief, Military Department, La Cabaña
Havana

To Remberto Martínez Jiménez

Havana, February 5, 1959

Mr. Remberto Martínez Jiménez
Martí No. 263 Norte
Sancti Spíritus, Las Villas

Esteemed friend,

It was a pleasure to read your letter. You are full of courage and good will, which are the basic traits of any good person, the kind of person that Cuba needs now more than ever to bring our revolution to a happy conclusion.

If you dedicate yourself in these moments to cooperating with us, carving out your own future through study and work, then, when the time comes, the Dominican Republic will also be free, as it will be able to count on the help of upright and mature people, such as you will no doubt be.

My best personal greetings,

Dr. Ernesto (Che) Guevara
Commander-in-chief, Military Department
La Cabaña

To José E. Martí Leyva

Havana, February 5, 1959

Sr. José E. Martí Leyva
Mártires No. 180
Holguín, Oriente

Esteemed friend,

I read with real pleasure your generous offer to fight for the freedom of our neighbors, the people of Santo Domingo.

Having fully considered this disinterested and noble offer, I urge you to keep alive your enthusiasm for the future, when an opportunity will arise. Meanwhile, take advantage of your years in school and make of yourself a useful man, something we have great need of in Cuba and I'm sure that you will be one of them. Devote yourself to drawing. Promise me.

My cordial greetings,

Dr. Ernesto (Che) Guevara
Commander-in-chief, Military Department
La Cabaña

To William Morris

Havana, February 5, 1959

Mr. William Morris
45 N. E. 9th St.
Miami, Florida

Esteemed Sir,

I received your letter to pass on to our commander-in-chief, which I have done. But I would like to say that if any vestiges of racial discrimination remain in this country, our revolution will put a complete end to them.

You can be absolutely sure that within a few years any difference between white and black will be solely a question of skin color, as it should be.

Receive a revolutionary embrace from

Dr. Ernesto (Che) Guevara
Commander-in-chief, Military Department
La Cabaña

To Pedro Revuelta
Havana, February 5, 1959

Mr. Pedro Revuelta
Obrapía 516
Havana

Distinguished Mr. Revuelta,

Thank you very much for your kind letter dated January 28, which was filled with your extremely beautiful verses and songs, which I sincerely appreciated.

I have taken note of your complaint about journalists and am using the opportunity to encourage you to remain on guard, in your symbolic trench, as the struggle is not over.

Receive a fraternal greeting from this revolutionary who never became a poet.

Dr. Ernesto (Che) Guevara
Commander-in-chief, Military Department
La Cabaña

To Luis Paredes López
Havana, February 5, 1959

Mr. Luis Paredes López
José María Paz
Pabellón No. 8, piso No. 9
Depto. 93, Villa Celina
Buenos Aires

Esteemed friend,

I am always happy to receive letters from people who take an interest in what is happening now in the Americas.

Of your entire exposition, I would say my attention was especially drawn to the issue you raise regarding executions. I believe this is a big error. Executions are not only a necessity for the people of Cuba but an imposition by the people. I would like you to inform yourself through unbiased media outlets in order to be able to appreciate this problem in all its dimensions.

Receive an affectionate embrace from your eternal friend,

Dr. Ernesto (Che) Guevara
Commander-in-chief, Military Department
La Cabaña

To Carlos Franqui
Tarará, March 10, 1959

Compañero Carlos Franqui
Director of the newspaper *Revolución*
Havana

Compañero Franqui,

I saw in the magazine *Carteles*, in the section "Behind the News" a note written by Antonio Llano Montes that has interested me as it insinuates something about my stature as a revolutionary with the apparently inoffensive phrase: "Commander Guevara chose to live in Tarará."

I won't analyze here who the journalist is or say anything about [his history]. It is not my intention to make accusations or counter-accusations. I feel only obliged to make a public explanation, especially to those who have confidence in me as a revolutionary.

I should explain to readers of *Revolución* that I am ill, an illness not contracted in gambling houses or by staying out late at cabarets, but rather by working for the Revolution beyond what my body could take.

The doctors recommended that I stay in a place away from daily visitors and [the Department of] Assets Recovery has lent me this house near the aforementioned beach until the colleagues caring for me say I am well enough to leave. I occupy a house that belonged to members of the former regime because my wage of $125 as an official of the Rebel Army is not enough to rent something big enough to house me and my staff.

The fact that this house belonged to a former Batista crony naturally means it is luxurious. I chose the simplest one available, which nevertheless is an insult to popular sensibilities. I give Mr. Llano Montes and, above all, the people of Cuba, my promise that I'll leave here as soon as I am well.

I would appreciate it if you could publish these words so that our people will be better informed about the actions of those who have assumed responsibility on their behalf.

Che

To Dr. Miguel Angel Quevedo
Havana, May 23, 1959

Dr. Miguel Angel Quevedo
Director of the magazine *Bohemia*
Havana

In my opinion,

Appealing to your democratic spirit and respect for the norms of freedom of the press, I am sending these lines in response to the miserable international gangster [Jules Dubois] who bears the pompous title of editor of the Latin American page of *Bohemia* magazine.

It is not my intention to defend myself against the fallacious imputations and the insidious reference to my Argentine citizenship. I am Argentine and I shall never renounce my country of origin (if you will excuse my audacity in the comparison, neither did [independence hero] Máximo Gómez renounce his Dominican homeland). But I feel Cuban, independently of whether the laws certify it or not: as a Cuban, I shared the sacrifices of the people throughout the armed struggle and today I share their hopes of bringing them to fruition.[3] I am not a communist either (if I was, I would proclaim it to the four winds, just as I assert my status as fighter for the people's cause and reaffirm my hopes that the arms of the people of each oppressed country will rid the Latin American scene of every trumped-up dictator). The fact is that

---

3   Ernesto Che Guevara was granted Cuban citizenship on February 9, 1959.

the masters of Jules Dubois, United Fruit and other fruit, mining, livestock, telephone and electricity companies, in other words, the exploiters of the people, have given the order to roll out their classic lies.

Let neither slaves nor masters be deceived. Fidel Castro's words were irrevocable: "If they attack us, we'll even arm the cats." Moreover, it's obvious, Mr. Dubois, that if the cats are to be armed, they must be taught to use those arms, and don't think that you or any other lackeys who might come to this country will find a flock of frightened sheep. You will find a vibrant and united people ready to fight an armed struggle right down to the last cartridge, as our prime minister [Fidel Castro] stated in his last press conference.

The people of the Revolution, beyond the different tactics that might exist at certain moments, are firmly united and no threat, no maliciousness, will be able to divide them in their struggle to achieve together the great goals of the Cuban people: Agrarian Reform, Tariff Reform, Fiscal Reform, which means the industrialization of the country and the resulting improvements in the people's standard of living, national liberation and international dignity.

Please receive my respects, Mr. Quevedo, although I cannot congratulate you on the jackal disguised as a sheep, whom you have permitted to appear in the pages of your magazine.

Ernesto Che Guevara
Commander-in-chief, Military Department

To Valentina González Bravo
Havana, May 25, 1959

Ms. Valentina González Bravo
Narciso López No. 35
Morón, Camagüey

Esteemed Miss,

I read your letter in which you ask me to provide you with an official "July 26" [Movement] regulated indoctrination system. I admire your interest in improving yourself. I congratulate you for the effort you have made and the reasons that motivate you.

Nevertheless, I don't that it's possible to write according to a regulated indoctrination system and, besides, there is no such thing as an official July 26 one. I believe that writing is a way of dealing with concrete problems and something that, according to one's sensibilities, develops over the course of one's lifetime.

Continue working as victory will crown your efforts. Overcoming adversity is, in the profession you have chosen, one of the best ways to better oneself.

Cordial greetings,

Dr. Ernesto (Che) Guevara
Commander-in-chief, Military Department
La Cabaña

To Loreto Cabrera Cruz

Havana, May 27, 1959

Mr. Loreto Cabrera Cruz
San Roque
C. de Ávila, Camagüey

Esteemed friend,

I received your letter in which you informed me that the Ernesto Guevara School Committee has approved the decision to change its name to Zenén Marín, a compañero who was assassinated on September 24, 1958. I believe this to be a very good decision.

Receive a cordial greeting from

Dr. Ernesto (Che) Guevara
Commander-in-chief, Military Department
La Cabaña

To Pedro Revuelta
Havana, May 27, 1959

Mr. Pedro Revuelta
Obrapía 516
Havana

Esteemed friend,

I am very happy to acknowledge receipt of your letter dated the 11th of the current month, which has left me well informed.

All your letters are well received, as are all those from citizens who care about Cuba. I invite you to continue these enjoyable little chats.

With nothing more to say, receive a cordial greeting "from one poet to another" from

Dr. Ernesto Che Guevara
Commander-in-chief, Military Department
La Cabaña

To María Teresa Díaz Dicon
Havana, June 1, 1959

Ms. María Teresa Díaz Dicon
Hotel Bouchard 487
Buenos Aires, Argentina

Madam,

It was a pleasure to receive your letter, to which I am responding today.

In reality, given the challenges we face in meeting Cuba's needs, we cannot reject anyone who offers services that could be of great use to advancing the Revolution.

As such, I see no problem in your coming here, and you will be well received; but I want to clarify that all appointments are made according to a strict selection criterion and you will have to submit yourself to this norm.

Receive a cordial greeting from

Dr. Ernesto Che Guevara
Commander-in-chief, Military Department,
La Cabaña

To José Ricardo Gómez

Havana, June 7, 1959

Mr. José Ricardo Gómez
Las Heras 126
Ezeiza, Argentina

Esteemed friend,

Although somewhat late, I am responding to your kind letter. You will understand that I have a heavy workload and it is hard for me [to find time] to write. I'll go straight to the heart of your letter and answer your questions.

The first 80 rebels [arriving in Cuba on the *Granma*] got our guns in Mexico City; these were mainly rifles, machine guns and grenades made in the United States. After disembarking, there were only a few survivors and we had to focus on fleeing and surviving rather than on organizing ourselves. We took refuge in *bohíos* (that is what we call peasants' houses here) and hiked mostly at night. In reality, we didn't carry out mass attacks [on Batista's armed forces] but instead launched assaults as small groups of strategically positioned guerrillas.

I hope you are much better. Receive a cordial greeting from

Dr. Ernesto Che Guevara
Commander-in-chief, Military Department
La Cabaña

To Aleida March[4]

June 22, 1959

Dearest Aleida,

I began writing to you in Madrid, continued in Rome, and then I had to start again. We are working hard and understand that we are not in a position to dictate our itinerary. That is why we have been taken to visit museums and other places like the pyramids, etc., which were not as pretty as we expected, but which we nevertheless found very interesting. We have a program that continues right through June 26 here in the UAR [United Arab Republic] and then we continue along the set route, but with a few extra countries thrown in.

We have had some success right from the start in terms of our trade mission, and received a very warm welcome from the Egyptian government.

Although you won't believe me, I think about you all the time. I hope you are dedicating yourself entirely to the [typewriter], stenography and your English studies, so that you can accompany me on every trip I do, that is, if I get another chance.

They decorated me with the Order of the Republic. A very big

---

4   From June 12 to September 8, 1959, Che represented the Cuban revolutionary government on a trip to the countries that had signed the Bandung Accord, which was the antecedent of the Nonaligned Nations Movement. Only days before he left, on June 2, Che married Aleida March de la Torre, whom he had met during the revolutionary war in Las Villas where she was a member of the July 26 Movement. During this trip, Che wrote many letters to his new bride, some of which are included in the following pages.

medal that looks great on me, and not just because I say so. I went to the silver market to buy you a bracelet but I didn't see anything resembling what I wanted for you, although I am bringing you a few other little things. So far the trip has gone very fast; we haven't had much of a chance to see anything, and it's the same in the UAR. I'm sleeping very little and my eyelids are starting to stick together. Tomorrow we leave for Gaza and I want to tell you about recent events.

Gaza was very interesting, insofar as we saw the misery and the hopelessness in which the refugees from Palestine live.

I went to visit the Brazilian officials who are looking after those areas. I established new diplomatic norms of confraternity between peoples by falling asleep on the shoulder of the Egyptian official who was accompanying me.

The following day I went to Damascus, from where I had hoped to bring you one of those famous fabrics, but I didn't like any of them, and here you'll have to rely on my taste. After a full, hectic day, we went to Alexandria, the city of Cleopatra, where the great hospitality continued. Today I returned to Cairo but I can't continue writing now as I have to go out. Until later.

At night we went to a reception where, once again, I demonstrated my diplomatic skills.

Another day: today we visited some armaments and explosives factories, where they gave me a rifle and a machine gun made in Egypt. Every day is full of work and every day, I miss you more — I'm joking!

We are staying in a great palace that belonged to one of the former big wigs, with a set of servants who bow their heads and run to do whatever one tells them, just like in the movies. This would have been a good way for you to pick up some tips.

To finish: Simón left two articles for *Verde Olivo*;[5] give them to Raúl so that he can do whatever he wants with them. I didn't have a chance to read them.

I bid you farewell so that I can send this letter, because if not, I'll never send it. I'm sending you a kiss the size of an elephant to comfort you in my absence [...].

Che
Written at night

---

5   *Verde Olivo* was the magazine of the Rebel Army (later the Revolutionary Armed Forces).

To Aleida March
June 27, 1959

Dearest Aleida,

I have attached a list of presents. They told me in Rome that the Christian martyrs always carried gifts with them to appease the lions (I don't know why I'm telling you this, as it has nothing to do with anything.) Send me a list of the people who you gave something to so that I know. No doubt you will think that your mother is not on the list, but you are wrong: both of them are, it's just that I could not find a muzzle that was the right size. I'll probably be able to find one in India.

I should mention that, when it comes to epistolary relations, Havana is the same distance from Cairo as Cairo is from Havana. I leave on the 30th for India, where I hope to receive news from you. Write to me at the Ministry of [Foreign] Relations in my name.

Alfredo can tell you about what we are doing and how well I've behaved myself. Now, there's nothing left for me to write as a model husband.

A small hug so that you don't become too unaccustomed, greetings to all.

Che

[...]

To Aleida March

June 30, 1959
[Somewhere in India]

Darling,

Everyone has received letters from home except me. It's time for you to show some sign of life. We ended our stay in Egypt with a formal farewell, reviewing companies of soldiers who moved like machines.

The witch butterfly is now moving along nicely.[6]

I have decided to write short letters so that I can send them more often and so that you can have some idea of what we are doing, even if this means that I explode, because as you know rhetoric is not my strong point.

In the last few days we visited various factories of all types and met with political and economic characters who would not particularly interest you. We said goodbye to [President] Nasser and had a farewell dinner with the entire diplomatic corps, where I suffered a barbarity but survived valiantly.

They say that in India the protocol is far more rigid than in Egypt, and that frightens me. But nevertheless, we will have to push on.

Don't forget to tell me what you want me to buy for you especially and to send me a list of the people to whom you want to give a small gift.

---

6   The *tatagua*, or witch butterfly, is associated with the imminent death of a relative or other unpleasant event.

Your other half truly misses you, especially now that I have hives all over my body thanks to the food.

A big kiss,

Che

To Aleida March
July 12, 1959

Aleiducha,

I'm using this, the best opportunity I'll have, to send you a few lines, but I suggest you read this letter alone so that no one will see you cry. Your two letters were nothing more than a litany of complaints; I read them from start to finish three times.

The only thing I liked is that, after getting your own private library, you said to me: I "suggest," etc... a perfect word, you are heading in the right direction.

I love you a little, but not that much. At least I didn't begin to cry after receiving two such unfriendly letters. This will take some time. Today marks one month and we have only visited two countries; there are still two important ones to go, Japan and Indonesia, but nevertheless the trip will take another month. We will be in Japan for a few days, send me something there, even if it is just a postcard. [...]

I won't tell you everything I've been doing because you'll say it's all very boring etc. and if something appeals to you, you'll say why didn't I bring you one and so on.

Continue to send me news but write more clearly because I can't understand any of your writing. I can't send you more stuff, as I don't have anyone to send it with.

Give me all the news about how things are at home. If the people are studying, etc.

We heard the news about Pedro Luis[7] but we didn't believe it, based on the falseness of various other news reports we have received.

Here only the bad news from US newspapers is circulated; absolutely no one defends us.

I'm dead tired. If I leave this letter for another moment, it will be a long time before it's sent, which is why I'm finishing here.

A kiss the size of the distance that separates us,

Che

---

7   Pedro Luis Díaz Lanz was chief of the Cuban air force until he defected in July 1959.

To Aleida March

[No date]

Dearest Aleida,

I'm taking advantage of the journalist Rabilero's departure to send you these lines. Today we are under the strange impression that Fidel has resigned, although we don't know exactly what has happened as there's lots of contradictory news in the media.[8]

Anyway, we are speeding up our trip, which will mean we will get to Cuba with the proposals.

I can't write much because time is short.

I only want to tell you that I bought you a beautiful kimono that has a special enchantment for me because of the enchanting geisha who modelled it.

I bought another one for your mother, but as they are my size I can only imagine how they will fit.

Instead of news, which Rabilero will pass on to you, I'm sending a kiss and a hug with all the enthusiasm of a month's delay.

Give the doll to Hildita[9] and send the $100 for this month if you have been paid.

Another embrace,

Che

A kiss… Aleiducha

---

8   On July 16, 1959, Fidel Castro resigned as prime minister after a clash with President Manuel Urrutia, whom he said was impeding the progress of the revolution. Urrutia then resigned and was replaced by Osvaldo Dorticós. Fidel resumed the post of prime minister on July 26.

9   After the revolution, Che's daughter Hildita, who had been born in Mexico, came to live in Cuba along with her mother Hilda Gadea.

To Aleida March
[No date]

Darling,

I am writing to you aboard an Indonesian Garuda plane that is taking us to Singapore and, as always, I'm sending this letter with someone to make sure it arrives.

In Indonesia, they gave us a reception worthy of who we are: great heroes of the liberation of the Americas. We visited the island of Bali, a precious jewel that looked like a Gauguin [painting], complete with its dead painter and the islander guarding his memory. It's a real paradise and a total contrast to Jakarta, the capital, which is a shithole and extremely hot.

I received your letters here through the Egyptian embassy as well as the diplomatic pouches. I don't know if you really love me or if you're not inclined to fill your letters with loving words. Anyway, I have to confess that I do love you and am not bothered by not hearing from that inhospitable nest in Santiago [de las Vegas]. I am a materialist; I associate spiritual things with material things, and that is why I love every part of you [...]. I love everything about you and my feelings cannot be carved up or divided.

This trip is becoming tiring, monotonous and disconcerting. As soon as one begins to acclimatize [to a place], we're off again. The lack of sleep is the same as in Cuba, but the air of transience in everything dampens our work spirit.

[…] a hug the size of an elephant, with the vigor of an enraged lion that has been starved for nearly two months.

Che

To Aleida March
August 6, 1959

My darling,

I am using these two minutes and the lack of postcards to send you these words from Kandy, the second largest city in Ceylon [Sri Lanka].

We were received here like kings and are staying in the home of the prime minister.

Perhaps there is not a lot for us to learn here, but there is a firm resolve to work together, along with a positive sense of friendship towards the Revolution.

Yesterday I was thinking about things and took a while to get to sleep. There is still more than a month to go on this trip and the separation is starting to weigh on me. I have not received any letters from you and I am getting desperate for one. The best thing would be to write and send it to Cairo; from there, old García will send it on to me.

Make sure all the guys are studying and tell Hernando to manage with the teacher's salary, which I imagine is up in the air. You haven't told me if Villegas is attending college and if he and Alberto are competing.

A little kiss,

Che

To Company of International Airports, S.A.[10]

Havana, November 30, 1959
"Year of Liberation"

Company of International Airports, S.A.
Prado No. 262
Havana

Attn: Mr. Raúl García González, Treasurer

Esteemed Sirs,

I was greatly surprised by your note of the 26th of this month as I am not aware of any debt I have accrued. I ask that you send me the details and, if possible, specify the government department in the name of which the purchases were made and from whom you are demanding payment.

Sincerely,

Commander Ernesto Guevara

---

10   Unfortunately, the Che Guevara Studies Center archive does not retain the original letter to which Che is replying. This letter does, however, show his strictly ethical approach to all business dealings and anything related to money.

To Miguel Grau Triana

Havana, March 18, 1960
"Year of the Agrarian Reform"

Dr. Miguel Grau Triana
Aguiar No. 108, downstairs
Havana

Sir,

I have the pleasure of acknowledging receipt of your letter from the 16th of this month, informing me of your microscopic research of x-rays.

I'm sorry I cannot comment on your work, as this would require a thorough study that would take a fair bit of time, which I don't have due to my current occupation which has removed me from the field of medicine.

I suggest you pass this on to our Ministry of Health, as it is an issue that pertains to that ministry.

I am returning your report to you so that, if you wish, you can keep it private.

Yours sincerely,

Commander Ernesto Che Guevara

To Ernesto Sábato

Havana, April 12, 1960
"Year of the Agrarian Reform"

Mr. Ernesto Sábato
Santos Lugares
Argentina

Esteemed compatriot,

Some 15 years have passed since I first met your wife and your son (who would be about 20 now) in a place called "Cabalando," in Carlos Paz. Later, when I read your book, *Uno y el universo*, which fascinated me, I could never have imagined that you — who (for me) bears the most sacred title in the world, that of a writer — would one day be asking for my views, renewing an acquaintance as you put it, due to the position I now find myself in because of certain events and personal experiences.

I mention this simply to remind you that, despite everything, I belong to the land where I was born and that I'm still capable of feeling deep down all its joys, all its hopes, and also all its disappointments.

It is difficult to explain to you why "this" is not a "Liberating Revolution."[11] I should say perhaps that I noticed the quote marks on the words you used to denounce it almost as soon as it began, words I undertood as referring to what happened in Guatemala, a

---

11   Che is contrasting the Cuban Revolution to the 1955 military coup that overthrew Argentine President Juan Perón.

country I left feeling defeated and rather disillusioned.[12] Everyone who was personally involved in that strange adventure felt the same as I did, their revolutionary commitment deepening through our contact with the peasant masses in a deep interrelationship that developed over two years of cruel struggle and great effort.

We are not "liberators" because we are not part of a plutocratic army; we are instead a new popular army, one that has taken up arms to destroy the old [regime].[13] Furthermore, we are not "liberators" because our banner of struggle was not neutral; in any case, it featured a large landowner's fence being destroyed by a tractor, similar to the logo of our INRA [Institute of Agrarian Reform] today.[14] We cannot be "liberators" because our "little servants" cried tears of joy on the day that Batista fled and we entered Havana, and today they continue to oppose all the protests and all the dishonest conspiracies of the "Country Club" folk — the same "Country Club" people you know there, and who, on occasion, were your compañeros in the campaign of hatred against Peronism.

The role intellectuals played here was far less concealed than in Argentina. Here, the intellectuals were nothing but toadies, who did not disguise their real position as apathy like they did [in Argentina]. Moreover, they didn't even pretend to be intelligent. It was a matter of pure and simple slavishness in the service of a disgraceful cause, nothing more. They just ranted and raved. [...]

To recommend, as you asked me, a book on Cuban ideology

---

12 Che had witnessed the 1954 CIA-backed overthrow of the popularly elected government of President Árbenz in Guatemala.

13 Che is arguing that the Rebel Army did not see itself as acting on behalf of the Cuban people but rather as an armed force of the Cuban people.

14 INRA was established in 1959 to carry out the economic and social policies associated with the agrarian reform. This also resulted in the creation of the Ministry of Industry on February 23, 1961. INRA was replaced in 1976 by the Ministry of Agriculture.

is something I'll only be able do in a year or so. Today, the best I can offer you as an attempt to theorize this [Cuban] revolution is [my] book on guerrilla warfare.[15] It could be [regarded as] the first serious attempt, but it is largely practical, like everything produced by inveterate empiricists. It is almost a juvenile exposition, in simple language; it does not try to explain the bigger picture that interests you. Maybe I'll be able to expound on [my ideas] in another book I plan to write, if national and international circumstances don't oblige me to take up a gun again (a task I scorn as a politician but which enthuses me as someone who loves adventure). Anticipating what may or may not come (the book), I can say, in an attempt to summarize, that this revolution is the genuine creation of improvisation.[16]

When we were in the Sierra Maestra, a leader of the communist [Popular Socialist] party visited us and told us that he admired how much we improvised and how we had been able to bring together all the groups that operated independently into a centralized organization. He commented that this was the most perfectly organized chaos in the universe. Certainly this revolution is like that because it has rapidly outgrown its early ideology. Fidel started out running as a candidate for deputy of a bourgeois party,[17] a party as bourgeois and respectable as the Radical Party in Argentina. [The Cuban Orthodox Party] followed the line of its former leader, Eduardo Chibás, who was similar to [Radical Party leader Hipólito] Irigoyen. Those of us who followed Fidel were a group lacking political experience but with a lot of goodwill and basic honesty.

---

15 A reference to Che Guevara's book, *Guerrilla Warfare*, first published in Cuba in 1960. Ernesto Che Guevara, *Guerrilla Warfare* (Seven Stories Press, 2022).

16 Some of Che's ideas outlined in this letter were elaborated in his "Notes for the study of the ideology of the Cuban Revolution" (October 1960) and "Cuba: Historical exception or vanguard in the anticolonial struggle?" (April 1961), both published in *Che Guevara Reader*, op. cit.

17 A reference to the Orthodox Party that was founded by Eduardo Chibás.

We proclaimed: "In [19]56 we will be heroes or martyrs." Not long before that, we would have been proclaiming, as Fidel did: "Shame against money."[18] Our simple slogans encapsulated our simple ideas.

The war [against Batista] revolutionized us. There is no more profound experience for a revolutionary than the act of war, not the isolated act of killing or carrying a rifle or initiating some kind of battle, but the total experience of war, knowing that an armed [guerrilla fighter] who no longer fears another armed man is equal to an [army's] combat unit or any other armed soldier. As leaders, we explained to the defenseless peasants that they too could take up arms and show the soldiers that an armed peasant was worth as much as the best of them. We learned along the way how an individual's effort is worthless unless it is accompanied by the efforts of everyone around them. We also learned how revolutionary slogans have to respond to the actual desires of the people, and we learned how to absorb the people's deepest desires and convert them into banners for political agitation. Each one of us experienced this and came to understand that the peasant's yearning for land was the strongest stimulus for the struggle in Cuba. Fidel understood this and much else besides; he became the extraordinary leader of the people that he is today, the gigantic uniting force of our people. Above all else, Fidel is a unifier par excellence, the undisputed mediator who overcomes all differences. and shatters with his disapproval. Some of those with money or ambition might try to use or challenge him, but Fidel is always feared by his adversaries.

That is how this Revolution was born, that is how its program emerged and that is how, little by little, our theory developed as we went along; our ideology always lagged behind events. By the time

---

18   The slogan of Chibás's campaign against government corruption.

we launched our [first] Agrarian Reform Law in the Sierra Maestra, we had already redistributed land there. Even after learning a lot through practical experience, our first timid [agrarian reform] law didn't dare touch the most fundamental issue: the expropriation of the *latifundistas* [large landowners].

The [Latin American] media has not dismissed us out of hand for two reasons: first, because Fidel Castro is an extraordinary politician who never reveals his hand beyond what is necessary, and he knew how to win the admiration of sympathetic reporters from large media companies who would normally take the easy option of sensationalism. On the other hand, North Americans always apply certain tests or yardsticks to assess everything and they used this same approach in analyzing [our Revolution]. Thus, when we said, "we will nationalize all public services," they thought we meant "we will avoid this if we receive reasonable support." And when we said "we will eliminate the *latifundistas*," they believed we were saying, "we will use large farms as a good base from which to fund our political campaign and to line our own pockets," and so on. It never entered their heads that what Fidel Castro and our Movement said — so dramatically and sincerely — was the honest truth when it came to our intentions. Thus, in their eyes, we were the biggest fraudsters of this half century because [they believed] we said one thing but did something else. Eisenhower said we betrayed our principles, and this is partly true: we betrayed their image of us, like in the story of the lying pastor, but in reverse, because they never believed [what we said].

Today we are using a new language because we continue to advance at a much faster pace than our thinking and our ability to structure our thoughts. We are in continuous motion and theory trails far behind, so slowly that, after writing the manual

I'm sending you,[19] within a very short period of time, I realized it was almost of no use for Cuba. It may, however, be useful for our country [Argentina], if applied with intelligence, without haste or embellishment. That is why I am afraid to try to define the ideology of the Movement; by the time I get around to publishing, the entire world will think the book was written years ago.

As the external situation becomes more acute and international tensions rise, due to its need to survive, our Revolution must intensify, and each time that the Revolution intensifies the tensions increase, and this leads to a further intensification until we reach a breaking point. We'll see how we can extract ourselves from this quagmire. What I can assure you is that our people are strong because they have fought and won and they know what victory tastes like; they have tasted bullets and bombs and they have tasted oppression. They know how to fight with exemplary integrity. At the same time, I can assure you that when the time comes, despite the modest remarks I've shared with you on this topic, we will have theorized very little, having had to resolve many challenges with the agility that guerrilla life taught us. I know that on that day, as an honored intellectual you will be focused on the enemy, our common enemy, and that we will be able to count on you to be there, struggling alongside us. This letter is rather long and not without a small amount of posturing that simple people like to indulge in. Nevertheless, I have attempted to demonstrate to you, a thinker, that we are also that which we are not: thinkers. Anyway, I'm at your disposal.

Cordially,

Ernesto Che Guevara

---

19   Probably a reference to the *Manual de Capacitación Cívica* that Che prepared for the political education of members of the new Cuban armed forces, published by the newly created Ministry of the Armed Forces in 1960.

To José Tiquet

Havana, May 17, 1960
"Year of the Agrarian Reform"

Mr. José Tiquet
Publicaciones Continente, S.A.
Pasco de la Reforma No. 95
México, D.F.

Esteemed friend,

I implore you to forgive me for the delay in answering your letter. This was due not so much to negligence on my part but to a lack of time. It would give me great pleasure to bear the cost of your trip to Cuba, but I don't possess the means to do so. My income is limited to my salary as a major of the Rebel Army, which, in accordance with the austerity policy of our revolutionary government, consists only of the amount necessary to maintain a modest standard of living.

Your letter was no bother at all. On the contrary, I was glad to receive it.

Affectionately yours,

Commander Ernesto Che Guevara

To José R. Silva

Havana, July 5, 1960
"Year of the Agrarian Reform"

Commander of the Rebel Army José R. Silva
708 Manord
Alexandría, Va.

Dear compañero,

I refer to your letter of June 23, for which I'm very grateful.

I agree with what Dr. Anderson told you as today's orthopedic equipment is marvelous.

For now, don't think about anything except getting better so that, as you say, we will soon be able to have you back here again and hard at work.

Aleida sends her regards. A hug from your compañero,

Commander Ernesto Che Guevara

To Mr. Lorenzo Alujas

Havana, August 9, 1960
"Year of the Agrarian Reform"

Mr. Lorenzo Alujas Piñeiro
Avenida 62 No. 3914
Cienfuegos, Las Villas

Sir,

I received your letter of the 24th of last month informing me of the criticism that has arisen due to my signing bank notes with my *nom de guerre*, something that I was already aware of.

Although I am in no way concerned about how the counter-revolution is using this, I understand the reason why you have written to me. It therefore gives me the pleasure of explaining to you that, although this is not the usual manner in which bank presidents sign [bank notes] — they are usually men with a very different ideology from mine and who, moreover, have obtained their posts in very different circumstances from that which placed me at the head of our National Bank — [my simple signature as "Che"] in no way diminishes the importance of the document; rather it shows that the revolutionary process is not yet complete and, furthermore, that our value system still needs to change.

Yours sincerely,

Commander Ernesto Che Guevara

To the General Administration of the Bank of China

Havana, October 13, 1960

"Year of the Agrarian Reform"

To the Directors of General Administration
Bank of China
Peking [Beijing]
People's Republic of China

Esteemed Sirs,

A branch of the Bank of China has been operating in Havana for some years with the authorization of the National Bank of Cuba, dated June 9, 1952, and which the Kuomintang gang administered.

The directors of the Bank of China chose to abandon the bank and left our country after the General National Assembly of the People of Cuba, held on September 2, 1960, approved the historic Declaration of Havana, which took the opportunity to normalize diplomatic relations between the legitimate governments of Cuba and [the People's Republic of] China.[20]

As a consequence of this, a Legal Intervention of [the Bank of China] was decreed, which, it should be noted, was found to be in a rather irregular state of affairs.

---

20   On September 2, 1960, a mass rally in Havana's Revolution Plaza adopted the "Declaration of Havana" in response to the "Declaration of San José" issued by the Organization of American States (OAS) that condemned the Cuban Revolution. The "National General Assembly of the People of Cuba" called for the end of exploitation of human beings and the plundering of the underdeveloped world by imperialism.

The Revolutionary Government of Cuba seeks to complete the unification of the banking system in our country and move toward the creation of a state bank. This is why, acknowledging that the property of the Bank of China belongs to the Chinese people and its sole legitimate government, we wish to express our desire to buy the office of the Bank of China, in light of our aim to nationalize all foreign banks.

We are sending you a copy of the balance sheet of the Bank of China in Havana as of last October 21 [1958] and reiterate our desire to take control of all property, shares, liabilities and obligations of this branch from that date.

Fraternal greetings to you,

Commander Ernesto Che Guevara, President

To Gustavo Jiménez

Havana, December 30, 1960
"Year of the Agrarian Reform"

Mr. Gustavo Jiménez
Nayarit 73
Mexico 7, D.F.

My dear Gustavo,

On returning from my trip abroad on an official government mission, I discovered your affectionate letter reminding me of old times, which gave me great pleasure.

My life is now very different from those days. Everything can be summed up in one word: work, work and more work. The Revolution requires all of our time. If you get the chance to visit us you will get an idea of what we are doing here.

I got married more than a year ago to a Cuban and we had a little girl last month.

Pass on my greetings to your parents.

Affectionately yours,

Commander Ernesto Che Guevara

To Fernando Barral

Havana, February 15, 1961
"Year of Education"

Dr. Fernando Barral
Papp J.18
Budapest IV
Újpest, Hungary

Dear Fernando,

It is truly a pity that we haven't been able to see each other for even a few minutes. I write with the haste and brevity imposed by my many diverse jobs. I hope you will understand. To come to the point, although you didn't mention it in your last letter as you had in the previous one, I assume that you want to come to work in these parts. I can tell you now that there is work here for you and your wife; that the salary will be adequate but will not cover luxuries; I expect that the experience of the Cuban Revolution would be something of great interest to people like you, who must one day return to work again in their native land. Of course, you could bring your mother; all necessary personal facilities for your work would be made available. The university is being restructured and there is room for you there if you are interested.

Naturally, you will find everything here more irrational than over there, since a revolution overturns and disrupts everything; little by little everybody must be placed in the job they are best suited to. The only important thing is not to hamper anyone's work.

To sum up, *aquí está tu casa*. If you want to come, let me know how that might happen and tell me the steps we need to take, if any, in order for your wife to come.

Since we have followed such different paths for many years, as far as personal circumstances go, I can tell you that I am married and have two daughters. I have had some news of old friends from mama who visited me a few months ago.

A fraternal embrace from your friend,

Commander Ernesto Che Guevara

To Robert Starkie

Havana, June 12, 1961
"Year of Education"

Mr. Robert Starkie
Rocamora Bros. Ltd.
35 Wingold
Toronto 19, Ontario

Sir,

I am responding to your letter of May 19 this year, which I received a few days ago. We consider that there are two aspects of your offer that interest us.

You offer to set up factories to produce insecticides for general use, for veterinarian use, for use in agriculture, especially for fruits, fungicides, fumigators for the soil and warehoused goods. You could say that we are interested in setting up all of these factories in Cuba, but in our country we have condemned the exploitation of man by man and [therefore] eliminated the possibility of anyone setting up new privately owned factories. This means we cannot accept a foreign company establishing factories here.

If you are interested in selling the machinery, together with a long-term contract to supply the raw materials that we cannot obtain here, and using a form of payment that is acceptable to our country, which lacks convertible currency at the moment, we would be very interested to discuss this with you.

Yours sincerely,

Commander Ernesto Che Guevara

To Rolando Díaz Aztaraín

Havana, June 27, 1962
"Year of Planning"

Commander Rolando Díaz Aztaraín
Captain of Corbeta
General Staff, Navy of the Revolutionary War

Subject: Transfer of compañera Carmen Durán Suárez to the Treasury

Compañero,

Notwithstanding the fact that you currently find yourself performing other functions, I want to point out to you the poor manner in which the transfer was handled of the above-mentioned compañera, who was earning a monthly wage of $99.54 in this ministry, as we communicated to you in our letter dated June 1, 1962.

Despite this, on June 4, the compañera's wage was raised to $143.00 a month, violating the JUCEPLAN [Central Planning Board] resolution and causing the disruption and problems that generally arise as a result of an anarchic system of wage rises.

With nothing more to add, I send you revolutionary greetings, Homeland or Death. We will win.

Commander Ernesto Che Guevara

To Laura Bergquist

Havana, October 15, 1962
"Year of Planning"

Laura Bergquist
Senior Editor
Cowles Magazines and Broadcasting Inc.
488 Madison Avenue
New York 22, N.Y.

Esteemed Laura,

Thank you for your note. I see that, even if only for professional reasons, there are still people in the United States who are concerned with finding out the truth.

I can guarantee you an interview if you give me enough notice. The possibilities of conducting the research that you propose can be coordinated from here, although I cannot promise anything.

Thank you for the greetings from I.F. Stone and receive mine.

Homeland or Death. We will win.

Commander Ernesto Che Guevara

To Anna Louise Strong[21]
Havana, November 19, 1962
"Year of Planning"

Anna Louise Strong
Tai Chi Chang
Peking, China

Esteemed compañera,

I received your letter of September 10.

I understand the problems you are facing. We invited you to Cuba fundamentally because we would have been delighted to have you with us and for you to get to know our Revolution. You are in no way obliged to write [while you are here], although I think you are being modest in terms of your qualifications. On the matter of your trip, my invitation remains permanently open for as long as you like and to do as you please (from writing a thousand-page book to nothing, which also has its enchantments).

I have attached some copies of your book about the communes [in China] that was very popular in Cuba. Unfortunately, I have to tell you that the dangerous gears of our bureaucratic machinery crushed your book on Laos.

The situation here in Cuba is one of a state of alert; the people

---

21   Anna Louise Strong was a US journalist and political activist, who reported on the Russian and Chinese revolutions. She sent her book, *The Chinese Conquer China* (1949 edition) to Che with the dedication, "For Che Guevara: With admiration and best wishes."

are standing firm, expecting some kind of aggression.[22] No one is considering taking a step back. Everyone is ready to do their duty. If we end up succumbing (which would be at a very high cost of lives), in every corner of our island you will be able to read a message similar to that of Thermopylae.[23]

Anyway, we are not rehearsing final [dramatic] gestures in preparation for a last stand: we choose life and we will defend it.

Receive a revolutionary greeting from your friend,

Homeland or Death. We will win.

Commander Ernesto Che Guevara

---

22 Che's letter was written in the immediate aftermath of the Cuban Missile Crisis of October 1962.

23 A reference to the legendary heroism of Spartan troops who defended the pass of Thermopylae to the last soldier.

To Antonio Venturelli

Havana, November 19, 1962
"Year of Planning"

Antonio Venturelli E.
13, Ave. Sainte Cecile
Meyrin, Geneva, Switzerland

Esteemed compañero,

I received what you sent and I believe it is important for us.

We are focused on a discussion on the need to bring prices in the socialist sector in line with prices in the world market, especially for a country like Cuba, where industrial and even agricultural production are dependent on imports.

Nevertheless, I also considered it a fraternal gesture for which I thank you.

Receive an affectionate greeting of
Homeland or Death. We will win.

Commander Ernesto Che Guevara

To Carlos Franqui[24]

Compañero Carlos Franqui
Editor, *Revolución*
Havana

Compañero Franqui,

I didn't like the photo supplement published the other day. Allow me to tell you this very frankly and to explain why, hoping that these lines will be published as my "outburst."

Leaving aside minor matters that don't reflect well on the newspaper's seriousness, such as those photos of a group of soldiers aiming at a supposed enemy with their eyes turned to the camera, there are some fundamental errors:

1. The extract from my diary is not entirely authentic. The facts are as follows: I was asked (during the war) if I had kept a diary of the invasion.[25] I had, but in the form of very rough notes made for my personal use; and at the time I had had no opportunity to work on them. I don't remember now under what circumstances a gentleman from Santa Clara came to take charge of editing my notes; he turned out to be

---

24   This letter was written in response to the publication in *Revolución* of a special photo supplement entitled "Che in the Escambray: Diary of an Invasion" in its December 24, 1962, issue. This letter was published in *Revolución*, December 29, 1962.

25   "The invasion" refers to the movement of Che Guevara's guerrilla column from the Sierra Maestra in the east toward Las Villas province in central Cuba during the revolutionary war.

quite "flamboyant" and was inclined to embellish events by means of adjectives.

What little value those four notebooks might have had is destroyed when they lose authenticity.

2. It is false [to suggest] that the war took second place for me to meeting the needs of the peasantry. At that time, winning the war was the important thing, and I believe I devoted myself to that task with all the dogged determination of which I was capable. After reaching the Escambray mountains, I gave two days' rest to the troops who had been on the march for 45 days under extremely difficult conditions, and then we resumed operations, seizing Güinía de Miranda. If a mistake was made it was in the opposite sense: little attention was paid to the difficult task of dealing with the "cattle rustlers" who had taken up arms in those cursed hills. Gutiérrez Menoyo and his crew vexed me no end and I had to put up with it in order to devote myself to the main task: the war.

3. It is false to say that Ramiro Valdés was my "close collaborator in organizational matters." I don't know how that could have got past you as editor, knowing him as well as you do.

    Ramirito [Ramiro Valdés] was a Moncada [veteran]; he was imprisoned on the Isle of Pines; he came on the *Granma* as a lieutenant; he rose to [the rank of] captain when I was made a commander; he led a column as a commander; he was second in command of the invasion, and then he led the operation in the eastern sector [of the island] while I marched toward Santa Clara.

I believe that the historical truth must be respected: to fabricate it at whim leads to nothing good. For that reason, and because I was an actor in that part of the drama, I decided to send you these criticisms, which are intended to be constructive. It seems to me that if you had checked the text these errors would have been avoided. I wish you happy holidays and a coming year without too many big headlines (because of what they bring).

Che

To Nicolás Guillén[26]

Havana, February 28, 1963
"Year of Organization"

Nicolás Guillén, President
National Union of Cuban Writers and Artists [UNEAC]
Calle 17, No. 351
Vedado, Havana

Compañero,

In answer to your letter of the 14th regarding the book containing my war diary,[27] I'll say the following:

1. I think that the title can stay the same.

2. You can do whatever you think is best.

Receive a revolutionary greeting from

Commander Ernesto Che Guevara

Homeland or Death. We will win.

---

26   Afro-Cuban Nicolás Guillén was one of Cuba's most prominent poets.

27   Che's "war diary" referred to here was a collection of essays he wrote, based on the actual diary he kept during the revolutionary war. These essays were published by UNEAC as *Pasajes de la Guerra Revolucionaria* [Reminiscences of the Cuban Revolutionary War] after most of them had been serialized in *Verde Olivo* and other Cuban publications. Che's original diary was published for the first time as *Diary of a Combatant, op.cit.*

To Editorial Grijalbo, S.A.

Havana, April 1, 1963
"Year of Organization"

Editorial Grijalbo, S.A.
Apartado No. 28568
Mexico 17, D.F.

To whom it may concern,

Thank you for sending me a copy of *History of Philosophy* translated from Russian (even though I didn't receive it; I don't know which of the two state bureaucracies to blame).

I accept detailed criticism. Believe me when I say that we are more than willing to correct the current state of affairs, although I cannot make any firm promises, as the imperialist encirclement is impacting on our access to freely convertible currency.

Receive a revolutionary greeting from

Commander Ernesto Che Guevara

Homeland or Death. We will win.

To Guillermo Lorentzen
Havana, May 4, 1963
"Year of Organization"

Compañero Guillermo Lorentzen
Havana

Compañero,

I have received your letters for which I thank you.

I was born in Argentina, I fought in Cuba, and I started to become a revolutionary in Guatemala.

This autobiographical synthesis will perhaps serve as some justification for my involvement in your [country's] affairs.

The guerrillas are fighting in Guatemala. The people have taken up arms in a certain way. There is only one possibility of slowing the development of a struggle that shows every sign of developing into a Cuban- or Algerian-type of revolution.

Although I'm not sure they will bother to use it, imperialism has the possibility of "free elections" with Arévalo.[28]

That's how we see the matter. Do you doubt this?

A revolutionary greeting,

Homeland or Death. We will win.

Commander Ernesto Che Guevara

---

28   Juan José Arévalo was the first democratically elected president of Guatemala (1945-1950).

To Peter Marucci
Havana, May 4, 1963
"Year of Organization"

Mr. Peter Marucci
Editor of *The Telegraph* and *The Daily Mercury*
Canada

Compañero,

First, allow me to confess that in our country bureaucracy is strong and well entrenched; it absorbs paperwork into its immense bosom, incubates it and, all in good time, sees to it that it reaches its destination.

That is why I am only now answering your kind letter.

Cuba is a socialist country: tropical, fierce, ingenuous and cheerful. It is socialist, without relinquishing any of its unique characteristics, while adding to its people's maturity. It is worth getting to know. We hope you will come, whenever you like.

Sincerely,

Homeland or Death. We will win.

Commander Ernesto Che Guevara

To Aleida Coto Martínez

May 23, 1963
"Year of Organization"

Dr. Aleida Coto Martínez
Assistant Director of Primary Education
Puerto Regla, Guanabacoa region
Ministry of Education
Havana

Esteemed compañera,

Thank you for your letter.

Sometimes we revolutionaries are lonely. Even our children regard us as strangers. They see less of us than of the soldier on sentry duty, whom they call "uncle."

The compositions you sent me took me back for a moment to the composition that we wrote for the president's visit to our town, when I was in the second or third grade. The difference between what those children expressed and what the children of today's Revolution express gives us confidence in the future.

Revolutionary greetings,

Homeland or Death. We will win.

Commander Ernesto Che Guevara

To the Compañeros of the Motorcycle Assembly Plant
Havana, May 31, 1963
"Year of Organization"

Compañeros of the Motorcycle Assembly Plant
Unidad 0-1 ECA [Consolidated Automotive Company]
Lorraine No. 102
Santiago de Cuba

Compañeros,

There is an error in your proposals. Workers responsible for the production of any item have no right over it. Bakers have no right to more bread, cement workers have no right to more bags of cement, nor do you have any right to motorcycles.

The day of my visit, I saw that one of the three-wheelers was being used as a kind of little bus. Just as I was criticizing that, a member of the Communist Youth was leaving on a motorcycle to do some work for that organization, something I was doubly critical of, given the improper use of the vehicle and the incorrect attitude of using time paid for by society for tasks that are supposed to represent an extra, totally voluntary contribution of time to society.

In the course of the conversation, I said I would look into the question of the conditions of payment and whether or not it would be possible to give vehicles to some workers and technicians.

Since responsibility for all the tasks of distribution and sale of vehicles has been turned over to the Ministry of Transportation, I don't see the possibility of that happening.

With revolutionary greetings,

Homeland or Death. We will win.

Commander Ernesto Che Guevara

To Lisandro Otero

June 23, 1963
"Year of Organization"

Compañero Lisandro Otero
Secretary of Cultural Activities
UNEAC [National Union of Cuban Writers and Artists]
Havana

Compañero,

No one can know to what point praise of himself is merited. Whatever the case, I don't like it and think it unnecessary.

I shall refer to some errors of content and form:

Content: My forbears who [are said to have] "shown signs of hatred for the oppressors of the people" were, in fact, members of the great Argentine cattle monopoly, and the struggle against Rosas was never mass-based. Moreover, those who opposed Juan Manuel Rosas cannot be described as progressive from a Marxist point of view.

Incidentally, I had no social awareness as an adolescent and I did not participate in any political or student struggles in Argentina.

Form: This is not [really] a book but a collection of notes.

With revolutionary greetings,

Homeland or Death. We will win.

Commander Ernesto Che Guevara

To Daniel Gispert

Havana, September 2, 1963
"Year of Organization"

Dr. Daniel Gispert, General
of the Liberation Army
Carretera del Cuervo, Luyanó
Havana

Sir,

I acknowledge receipt of your letter of the 26th, addressed to the prime minister, compañero Fidel Castro Ruz.

Regarding your interest in not proceeding for now with the sale of the entity Industrias Gispert S.A., of which you are the owner, it is my duty to inform you that in accordance with the policy of the Revolutionary Government, the time has come to integrate all sectors of production into the national economy, no matter how small the factory, in an orderly and steady process.

Given this, we must push ahead with the purchase of Industrias Gispert S.A. by the Cuban state, with the certainty that the Revolutionary Government will provide all the guarantees and facilities that your case requires.

Sincerely,

Commander Ernesto Che Guevara
cc Prime Minister

To José Matar

Havana, September 19, 1963
"Year of Organization"

Mr. José Matar
National Coordinator
National Leadership of the CDR [Committees for the Defense of the Revolution]
Misiones 25, Havana

Esteemed compañero,

Although too late to go in your special edition, I am responding to your request for me to give you my opinion on this organization.

From what I know up to now, its fundamental feature is the disorganization of its Executive Bureau, proven by the fact that I received a letter dated July 22 asking me to send my opinions before the 31st of the same month. The letter was stamped as having left the organization on July 12 and I received it in this office on September 17.

Perhaps the disorganization is the fault of this Ministry [of Industry]. In that case, you should let the CDR on the ground floor know.

With revolutionary greetings,
Homeland or Death. We will win.

Commander Ernesto Che Guevara

To Manuel Navarro Luna

Havana, October 18, 1963
"Year of Organization"

Compañero Manuel Navarro Luna
Hotel Colina
Calle L y 27
Vedado, Havana

Compañero,

With great shame I must now respond to you and your request.

It turns out that on receiving your book, I simply flicked through it, hoping to find an opportunity to read it more closely later.

I have attached the report on the case of this compañero. It is simply a question of a difference in our evaluation of the situation. I have full confidence in our technicians and in their spirit of justice. I don't think you can get much better than them in that field.

I am sorry that your sole request cannot be fully satisfied.

I congratulate you on the book, although in reality I knew some of the individual poems, which were written some time ago and well before this latest period, due to their publication in [various] newspapers and magazines.

Receive an affectionate greeting from someone who holds you in high regard.

Commander Ernesto Che Guevara

To Arturo Don Varona

Havana, October 28, 1963
"Year of Organization"

Dr. Arturo Don Varona
3rd y 6 Rpto. Vista Hermosa
Camagüey

Doctor,

I acknowledge receipt of your report, but I believe that the number of *caballerías*[29] is too great to comply with any article of the [agrarian reform] law.

Nevertheless, I will not disguise my concern because the state has often been a less efficient administrator than the private producer.

From your address, I take it that you are not one of those producers who lives in permanent contact with agriculture, but your administrative experience probably allows you to manage the farm, as I can see in the figures. I ask that you don't take this as a bad joke but, perhaps, your incorporation into INRA [Institute of Agrarian Reform] would reinforce that organization. Everything depends on your ability to appreciate the depth and justice of the moment that we are passing through and therefore to evaluate with a critical eye the multiple errors that a genuinely popular revolution might commit.

Yours sincerely,

Homeland or Death. We win will.

Commander Ernesto Che Guevara

---

29   In Cuba, one *caballeria* was equivalent to about 33 acres.

To Pablo Díaz González

Havana, October 28, 1963
"Year of Organization"

Compañero Pablo Díaz González
Administrator
Campo de Perf. Extr. de la Cuenca Central
Aptdo. 9 Majagua
Camagüey

Pablo,

I read your article. I must thank you for how well you portray me — too well in my opinion. Furthermore, it seems to me that you also portray yourself rather well.

The first thing a revolutionary has to do in writing history is to stick to the truth as tightly as a finger in a glove. You did that, but it was a boxing glove, and that's not right.

My advice is to reread the article, eliminate everything you know is not true and take care with everything you don't know for certain is the truth.

Revolutionary greetings,
Homeland or Death. We will win.

Commander Ernesto Che Guevara

To Carlos Rafael Rodríguez[30]

Havana, October 28, 1963
"Year of Organization"

Compañero Carlos Rafael Rodríguez, President
National Institute of Agrarian Reform
Havana

Compañero,

I have attached the papers belonging to Argelio Rosabal, the [Seventh Day] Adventist of whom I spoke to you and whose earthly prize had become a [prison] sentence.

Given the brilliant Young Communist that you are, you will no doubt know how to flout the law or lull me to sleep.

(The dogs and cats thing will come separately.)[31]

Revolutionary greetings,

Homeland or Death. We win will.

Commander Ernesto Che Guevara

---

30 Carlos Rafael Rodríguez (1913–1997) was a Cuban revolutionary political leader and economist. He was president of INRA in the 1960s and, in later years, he was vice-president of Cuba's Council of State in charge of international relations and a member of the Political Bureau of the Cuban Communist Party.

31 This reference is not clear, but it may refer to the fraternal debate at the time about political economy to which both Che and Carlos Rafael contributed.

To Lydia Ares Rodríguez

Havana, October 30, 1963
"Year of Organization"

Ms. Lydia Ares Rodríguez
Calle Cárdenas 69
Calabazar, Havana

Compañera,

Your letter has been forwarded to the Ministry of the Interior, since that is the agency responsible for solving such problems.

In any case, I appreciate your attitude toward work and toward the Revolution; but I must tell you that, in my personal opinion, your son must serve his sentence because the commission of a crime against socialist property is the gravest offense, independently of any extenuating circumstances.

I am sorry to tell you this, and I regret the suffering it will cause you, but I would not be fulfilling my revolutionary duty were I not to explain this frankly.

A revolutionary greeting,

Homeland or Death. We will win.

Commander Ernesto Che Guevara

To Lisandro Otero

Havana, November 10, 1963
"Year of Organization"

Compañero Lisandro Otero
Secretary of Cultural Activities
National Union of Cuban Writers and Artists
Calle 17 No. 351
Vedado, Havana

Compañero,

Regarding your correspondence of October 29, I can inform you of the following:

I have no problem with *Pasajes de la guerra revolucionaria* [Episodes of the revolutionary war] being translated into any language.

In cases where the request comes from one of the socialist countries, I ask that you pass on my approval with the express recommendation of not charging for any rights.

Revolutionary greetings,

Homeland or Death. We will win.

Commander Ernesto Che Guevara

To Juan Ángel Cardi

Havana, November 11, 1963
"Year of Organization"

Compañero Juan Ángel Cardi
Calle 17 N° 54 Apto 22
Vedado, Havana

Compañero,

I acknowledge receipt of your communication dated last October 3, in which you enclosed chapters from nine of your unpublished novels.

I have no objection to your using whatever you feel is appropriate from [my] Las Villas diary. Remember, however, that when it was published, it was embellished by the florid language of an ass-licker.

I read the chapter of *Pléyade* like someone examining a photograph of a familiar place but not recognizing it. It creates the impression that you have never been in the Sierra [Maestra] and have not even spoken with those who were there at the time. If you would permit me, I should like to tell you in a fraternal spirit that you have not captured the grandeur of those times in all its depth.

This is my impression, not literary criticism, but simply the observation of someone who is looking for a likeness in an old photograph — a souvenir of a group of friends, for example — but who finds that some technical defect, or time itself, has rendered the subjects of the photo unrecognizable.

If this observation is of any use to you, I am gratified; if not, please don't be offended by my frankness. I don't know how old you are, nor [anything about] your vocation as a writer. The only passion that guides me in this field of yours is to convey the truth (and don't take me here for a hard-line defender of socialist realism). I look at everything from this point of view.

My greetings and wishes for your success in your literary odyssey,

Commander Ernesto Che Guevara

To Oscar L. Torras de la Luz

Havana, January 3, 1964
"Year of the Economy"

Mr. Oscar L. Torras de la Luz
Director, Department of Accountancy, School of Economics
University of Havana
Havana

Compañero,

I thank you for your package. I am studying accounting, which makes me a student. I'll give you my opinion once I have read it.

Due to everything else, I believe that if it is good, it will fill an important vacuum in our country.

Sincerely,

Homeland or Death. We will win.

Commander Ernesto Che Guevara

To Regino G. Boti

Havana, February 2, 1964
"Year of the Economy"

Dr. Regino G. Boti[32]
Minister of Economy and
Technical Secretary of the Central Board of Planning [JUCEPLAN]
Havana

Ref. Wire-Relays

Compañero,

I acknowledge receipt of your detailed letter. I have extracted from it the following conclusions in ascending order:

1. The Consolidated Mechanical Company is functioning badly (various directors and subdivisions. This has occurred from the first date noted until now.)

2. The Consolidated Plastics Company is functioning badly (various directors ... etc.).

3. The Ministry of Industry is incapable of doing its job because its employees are inefficient and no one has come up with adequate measures to resolve this.

---

32 Regino G. Boti (1923–1999) was a Cuban economist, recognized for his role in the Economic Commission for Latin America and the Caribbean (CEPAL). As Che's close friend and collaborator, their correspondence, as shown in this letter, was often peppered with ironic remarks, sarcasm, innuendo and witticisms.

4. The highest authority for directing the economy should know about the most minimal pieces being built to justify a mold, along with the inefficiencies you have pointed out that make this job dangerous.

I greet you compañero Minister, with the battle cry of the Central Board of Planning: Long live the epistolary war! Death to productive work!

Revolutionary greetings,

Homeland or Death. We will win.

Commander Ernesto Che Guevara

To Charles Bettelheim[33]

Havana, February 6, 1964
"Year of the Economy"

Charles Bettelheim
Ecole Practique des Hautes Etudes 54
Rue de Varenne, Paris 7
France

Esteemed friend,

I'm sending you the latest issue of our magazine [*Nuestra Industria*]. The articles you sent had to be divided up due to our format, and your article will appear in the next issue. I think it is of great importance for elucidating some aspects of relations with both worlds. (The contract with the Soviets is very interesting in this regard.)

I would be grateful if you could pass on a copy to compañero [Arghiri] Emmanuel, and if both of you could closely read my article and make some pertinent criticisms.

Receive a revolutionary greeting,

Commander Ernesto Che Guevara

---

33 Charles Bettelheim (1913–2006) was a French Marxist economist, and professor of Political Economy. He was the director of the École Pratique des Hautes Études in Paris. At the time he wrote this letter, Che had initiated a polemic in Cuba about political economy in which various revolutionary leaders participated. This debate soon assumed an international character involving Marxist economists such as Ernest Mandel and Charles Bettelheim.

To Josefina Cabrera[34]

Havana, February 11, 1964
"Year of the Economy"

Dr. Josefina Cabrera
Havana

Esteemed friend,

Like you, I felt a sense of contempt towards the so-called "sensible left" after reading Benítez's article, and found your letter very useful.

I would like to take the opportunity to pass on my respect and my solidarity, which I was unable to do personally when the remains of your husband arrived, due to a lack of notice.

I would have liked to have to expressed this in person, but my fear that the days will go by without my being able to do so obliges me to write these lines.

I am an enemy of the formal aspects of condolences, but I understand that you need our solidarity and are a worthy recipient of it. May the remains of your husband that rest in Cuba dignify us all. It is our obligation to keep his memory alive because of what he represented as a man, a scientist and revolutionary.

Receive a fraternal hug from your eternal friend,

Commander Ernesto Che Guevara

---

34   Josefina Cabrera was the widow of Mexican cardiologist Professor Enrique Cabrera Cossio who moved to Cuba in 1962. He died at the age of 45, probably of cancer, on January 6, 1964, when Che was in Moscow. The national hospital in Havana now bears his name.

To María Rosario Guevara

Havana, February 20, 1964
"Year of the Economy"

Ms. María Rosario Guevara
36, rue d'Annam
(Maarif) Casablanca, Morocco

Compañera,

In truth, I don't know what part of Spain my family came from. Of course, my ancestors left there a long time ago, with one hand in front and another behind;[35] and if I don't keep mine in the same place, it is only because of the discomfort of the position.

I don't think you and I are very closely related, but if you are capable of trembling with indignation any time an injustice is committed in the world, we are compañeros, and that is far more important.

A revolutionary greeting,

Homeland or Death. We will win.

Commander Ernesto Che Guevara

---

35   A saying in Spanish suggesting extreme poverty.

To Luis Amado Blanco

Havana, February 25, 1964
"Year of the Economy"

Mr. Luis Amado Blanco
Ambassador of Cuba to the Holy See
The Vatican, Ruggero Fauro No. 25
Rome

Compañero,

I acknowledge receipt of *Revista de Occidente* [a Spanish literary magazine].

I see from your tone that you are reproaching me for my silence regarding your previous letters. You are right to do so. I am guilty, simple as that. Your book has not appeared anywhere and every time I have to face your silent criticism, I desperately try to find a way to put off this moment.

I thank you for your interest in a whole series of problems regarding industry. The case of Bacardí is being studied by a government commission that, due to the character of the commission and also the government, will take a long time and end up doing nothing.[36]

Revolutionary greetings,
Homeland or Death. We will win.

Commander Ernesto Che Guevara

---

36   The international dispute over the trademark of Havana Club rum continues to this day.

To José Medero Mestre

Havana, February 26, 1964
"Year of the Economy"

Mr. José Medero Mestre
Juan Bruno Zayas No. 560
Esq. Ave de Acosta & O'Farrill
Víbora, Havana

Compañero,

Thank you for your interest and your comments. In order to convince me, you have touched a sore spot: you quote my adversaries. Unfortunately, because of the time required I cannot continue this polemic by mail. Future issues of *Nuestra Industria Económica* will carry articles by a select number of Soviet technicians showing their concern with similar questions.

Just one statement for you to think about: counterposing socialist efficiency to capitalist inefficiency in factory management is to confuse wishes with reality. It is in distribution that socialism achieves unquestionable advantages, and it is in centralized planning where it has been able to overcome its technological and organizational disadvantages with respect to capitalism. With the break-up of the old society, an attempt has been made to establish the new one with a hybrid. Man as wolf, the society of wolves, is being replaced by another genus that no longer has the desperate urge to rob their fellows, since the exploitation of man by man has disappeared. But he still does have some urges of that type (although quantitatively fewer), due to the fact that the lever of material interest is still the arbiter of the well-being of the individual and of the small collectivity (factories, for example). And that is where I see the root of the evil. Conquering capitalism with its own fetishes, having removed their most magical quality, profit, seems like a tricky business.

If this is very obscure (my watch says it's past midnight), perhaps another shuffle will make it clearer: the lever of material interest under socialism is like Pastorita's lottery; it can neither light up the eyes of the most ambitious nor budge the others out of their indifference. I don't pretend to have exhausted this topic, much less to have given the papal "amen" to these and other contradictions. Unfortunately, in the eyes of most of our people, and in mine as well, apologetics for a system can have more impact than scientific analysis of it. This does not help us in the task of clarification, and our whole effort is aimed at inviting people to think, to treat Marxism with the seriousness this towering doctrine deserves.

Because of this, and because you think, I am grateful for your letter; the fact that we don't agree is of little importance.

If you ever have anything else to tell me, remember, I am not a teacher; I am just one of many people struggling today to build a new Cuba, but one who had the good fortune to be at Fidel's side during the most difficult moments of the Cuban Revolution and some of the most tragic and glorious moments in the history of the worldwide struggle for freedom. That is why you know who I am, while I don't remember your name. It might have been the other way around, except that in that case I would have had to write you from some remote part of the world, wherever my wandering bones might have carried me, since I was not born here.

That's all for now.

Revolutionary greetings,

Homeland or Death. We will win.

Commander Ernesto Che Guevara

To Luis Corvea
Havana, March 14, 1964
"Year of the Economy"

Compañero Luis Corvea
Calle 146 No. 25701
Bauta, Havana

Compañero,

I acknowledge receipt of your letter in which you inform me that you have done 354 hours of voluntary work in the period between December 1962 and December 1963.

In the same letter, you make mention of my speech from last January 11 in which I referred to voluntary labor. I would like to repeat here one of the ideas that I expressed on that occasion, and which I believe encapsulates the essence of this very honorable activity.

I said that "the importance that voluntary labor has is reflected in the *consciousness* that is acquired and in the stimulus and example that this attitude represents for all the compañeros." Communist education must be based on this consciousness, and vanguard volunteer workers are those who best fulfill the ideals of a true communist. Our revolution has confronted big problems; it has had to defend itself from dozens of aggressive acts by our enemies and directly from Yankee imperialism. There are still many evils that we have to struggle against to merit a better future, and we must be conscious of the fact that this future, this new society, without classes, based on living in abundance, can only be achieved with sweat, with work and sacrifice.

Compañero Corvea, I warmly congratulate you and hope that these words act as encouragement for you to continue working more and better each day and, through your example, to lead your workmates down the road of constructing the communist society.

Homeland or Death. We will win.

Commander Ernesto Che Guevara
Minister of Industry

To Eduardo B. Ordaz

May 26, 1964
"Year of the Economy"

Dr. Eduardo B. Ordaz
Director
Psychiatric Hospital
Havana

Esteemed Ordaz,

I acknowledge receipt of the magazine. Although I have very little time, the issues it covers seem very interesting and I'll try to read it.

But I do have a query: How are you able to print 6,300 copies of a specialist magazine, when we don't even have that many doctors in Cuba?

This has raised a doubt for me that has brought me to the verge of neuro-economic psychosis. Are the rats using the magazine to deepen their knowledge of psychiatry or to fill their stomachs? Or perhaps every patient gets a copy of the publication?

In any case, there are 3,000 copies too many; I beg you to consider this.

Seriously, the magazine is good; the number of copies is intolerable. Believe me, because crazy people always tell the truth.

Revolutionary greetings,

Homeland or Death. We will win.

Commander Ernesto Che Guevara

To Leo Huberman and Paul M. Sweezy[37]

June 12, 1964

"Year of the Economy"

Mr. Leo Huberman and Mr. Paul M. Sweezy

Monthly Review

333 Sixth Avenue

New York 14, N.Y.

Esteemed friends,

Today, June 12, I have read your kind request of May 24. I believe it is unnecessary for me to point out the admiration I felt for compañero [Paul] Baran and how constructive his book on underdevelopment was for our nascent (and still weak) economic culture.

I would have added nothing to what you and other compañeros could say about our deceased friend, but I regret not having been able to fulfill what I believe is a fraternal duty.

Revolutionary greetings,

Homeland or Death. We will win.

Commander Ernesto Che Guevara

---

37 Paul Sweezy (1910–2004) was a US political economist and professor at Harvard University who published many books together with Paul Baran (1909–1964), including *Monopoly Capital: An Essay on the American Economic and Social Order*. He closely followed developments in Cuba after 1959 and visited the island many times, establishing relations with intellectuals and revolutionary leaders, including Che. He co-authored *Socialism in Cuba* with Leo Huberman (1903–1968), a US socialist writer and activist and author of *Man's Worldly Goods*.

To Ezequiel Vieta
June 16, 1964
"Year of the Economy"

Mr. Ezequiel Vieta
Calle 18 No. 316
Miramar, Havana

Esteemed compañero,

It is true, I had not read your note. I feel somewhat ashamed because you treat me so well. The book is a compilation of notes written with the intention that others would then also write about their experiences and published them in *Verde Olivo*.[38] One day I'll finish it. I didn't want to publish it in parts, but they didn't listen to me and I don't see how anyone could understand it without having an intimate knowledge of the history of the Revolution.[39]

I hope that some day I can talk about the complete history of these two years of genuinely heroic deeds that I had the luck to live through. In the meantime, I thank you for your kind words about me, although I don't agree with them. There you are.

Revolutionary greetings,

Homeland or Death. We will win.

Commander Ernesto Che Guevara

---

38   The publication of Cuba's Revolutionary Armed Forces.
39   A reference to the first publication of his essays on the guerrilla war in Cuba, *Pasajes de la Guerra Revolucionaria* [*Reminiscences of the Cuban Revolutionary War*, op. cit.].

To Fabio Vargas Vivanco

June 16, 1964
"Year of the Economy"

Mr. Fabio Vargas Vivanco
Moscow V 330
Avenida Lomonosov No. 31
Corredor 2 Hab. 329
U.S.S.R.

Esteemed compañero,

I recall the events you mention, but I don't remember you. But that is the least of my concerns.

I cannot do personal favors, but the Revolution usually provides impersonal opportunities. I'll pass your letter on to the Minister of Education who deals with scholarships.

If you "sneak in" I will see you around these parts. If not, fraternal hugs, you didn't make it... So until we meet again.

Homeland or Death. We will win.

Commander Ernesto Che Guevara

To Regino G. Boti

June 17, 1964
"Year of the Economy"

Dr. Regino G. Boti
Minister of Economy
Havana

Compañero,

I refer to your memo dated May 25, to which you attached a request from Mr. Carlos A. Fidalgo, requesting the purchase of a mechanical lathe of some 120 cms.

Your letter was such a surprise that it has taken me 20 days to recover and respond.

As you would know, according to the ineluctable regulations of the Budgetary Finance System, a pure and direct enunciation of Marxism and its sole representative in these lands, the basic means of production are not commodities.[40] This is based on the concept of exchange within the state sector, which, if the state is not the sole owner of means of production, it should increasingly become so, and must never allow for the possibility of the exploitation of man by man by handing over a [single] tool, particularly one like this.

To clarify, putting myself at your level of comprehension: I'll

---

40   See "On the Budgetary Finance System" in *Che Guevara Reader*, op. cit. See also Ernesto Che Guevara, *El Gran Debate* (Ocean Sur, 2018) and Ernesto Che Guevara, *Retos de la Transición socialista en Cuba* (Ocean Sur, 2008).

never consent to transforming what is state investment into a commodity. I'll be faithful to the end to the Budgetary [Finance] System. If you have friends, go and ask them for the means of production [...].

Long live the Budgetary [Finance] System!

Death to neocapitalist heresy!

Homeland or Death. We will win.

Commander Ernesto Che Guevara

To the Cuban Trading Company of Works of Art and Culture
June 25, 1964
"Year of the Economy"

Cuban Trading Company of Works of Art and Culture
Ministry of Foreign Trade
Havana

Compañeros,

I acknowledge receipt of the [phonograph] records.

Although they are far from perfect — I am referring to their presentation — the improvement is noticeable.

Perhaps I am putting my foot in it, given that among the signatories to the letter are a number of writers, but allow me to suggest that you look over your text; in my opinion this is a good way to avoid looking silly. If any of you participated in this, don't worry; I am not qualified to be a judge when it comes to this issue.

I won't speak about the content. I am not allowed to give even the most timid opinion about music because my ignorance approximates at least 273 degrees.

Thank you for bothering to show me these achievements.

Revolutionary greetings,

Homeland or Death. We will win.

Commander Ernesto Che Guevara

To Hubert Jacob
June 30, 1964
"Year of the Economy"

Mr. Hubert Jacob
Hotel Sierra Maestra
Bloque B, Apto. 251
Havana

Sir,

I read the letter that you handed to me personally.

You threatened to cause a scandal in order to grab attention. That's fine by me. These are not the kinds of threats that will get you a meeting with me. A meeting with a government minister is not an inalienable right of a functionary; rather the minister grants it as a courtesy. At least that is the practice here.

Any complaints you have regarding the injustice you say you have suffered can be passed on to the Director of Technical Collaboration or the chief of personnel of this organization.

Sincerely,

Commander Ernesto Che Guevara

To Santiago Morciego and Manuel Hernández

July 3, 1964
"Year of the Economy"

Santiago Morciego and Manuel Hernández
Granja No. 5-34 «Dalcio Gutiérrez»
Carretera de Vertientes, km. 14
Camagüey

Compañeros,

I can confirm that compañero Gutiérrez was part of my column, his name was DALCIO.

From a peasant family in the Sierra Maestra, he and his brother enlisted in my column and were part of the invasion [of central Cuba from the Sierra Maestra]. He was injured in the stomach during the battle of La Federal and we had to operate on him, virtually without anesthesia, to try to save his life, something we were unable to do.

His life as a combatant was short, but he always sought to be on the front line, which is where he was when he was injured on the last day of his life.

Revolutionary greetings,
Homeland or Death. We will win.

Commander Ernesto Che Guevara

To León Felipe
August 21, 1964
"Year of the Economy"

Mr. León Felipe
Editorial Grijalbo, S.A.
Avenida Granjas, 82
Mexico 16, D.F

Maestro,

A number of years ago, when the Revolution took power, I received a copy of your last book, signed by you.

I have always been aware that I never thanked you for this. Perhaps you will be interested to know that your *El Ciervo y otros poemas* is one of the two or three books that I have beside my bed. I have had little time to read it because in Cuba sleep, free time (or rest) is, essentially, a sin of *lesa dirigencia*.[41]

The other day I attended an event of great significance for me. The room was crammed with enthusiastic workers and there was a sense of the new human being in the air. That little drop of failed poet I carry within me came out and I recurred to you in order to polemicize at a distance. That is my homage; I beg you to interpret it that way.

If you feel tempted by the challenge, the invitation is still open. With sincere admiration and appreciation.

Commander Ernesto Che Guevara

---

41   A play on the term *lèse-majesté*, (*dirigencia* meaning leadership).

To Elías Entralgo

August 31, 1964
"Year of the Economy"

Elías Entralgo
President, University Extension Commission
University of Havana
Havana

Esteemed compañero,

I have received your kind invitation, which demonstrates to me — without your intending it, I'm sure — a radical difference of opinion on the question of what a leader should be.

I cannot commit myself to give the lecture which you've invited me to give; if I were to do so, it would mean not giving all my available time to working for the Revolution. Besides, for me it is inconceivable that a leader of the government and the party should be offered monetary remuneration for work of any kind.

Among the many compensations I have received, the most important is that of being regarded as a Cuban [citizen]; and this cannot be calculated in *pesos* and *centavos*.

I'm sorry to have to write to you in this way; I urge you to give it no other importance than that of an expression of hurt feelings caused by what I consider to be a gratuitous affront, nonetheless painful for being unintentional.

Revolutionary greetings,
Homeland or Death. We will win.

Commander Ernesto Che Guevara

To Juana Rosa Jiménez
September 11, 1964
"Year of the Economy"

Compañera Juana Rosa Jiménez
4ta. del Oeste e/ 5 y 6 Norte
Placetas, Las Villas

Dear *China*,

I received your letter. I remember you well and I was very happy to hear from you.

If you asked me for a job, I might be able to come up with a way to get you one, although at the moment this would not be easy without violating norms, something I don't normally do.

In terms of moving to Havana with your family, this would not make much sense, unless you were doing so simply because you wanted to live in the capital. I am not able to help you with this request.

Try to resolve your problems in Las Villas. I can help you with any basic requests.

Receive a greeting from your old boss,

Commander Ernesto Che Guevara

To Julio González Noriega
September 15, 1964
"Year of the Economy"

Compañero Julio González Noriega
Director, Directorate of Information
Ministry of Foreign Trade
Havana

Esteemed compañero,

I received your sincere business letters in which you correctly acknowledge the moral stimulus as secondary [to material incentives] — the logical order in Auto-Financing Management system.[42]

I thank you for the free delivery and, to repay you the attention in the same manner, I'll grant you a meeting of five minutes, completely free of charge, on Thursday the 17th at 2:00 p.m.

I should warn you, however, that if the meeting goes over time by more than five seconds, I'll have to charge you the modest price of $2.25 per additional minute, or a copy of what you offered me regarding plastics, on agreement between the two parties.

Before your visit, you should communicate with my secretary, on letterhead along with a $0.25 stamp, your acceptance of the

---

42   The Auto-Financing [or Economic Calculus] system was operating in the Soviet Union at this time, of which Che Guevara was severely critical, and to which he counterposed the Budgetary Finance System. See his letter to Fidel Castro of March 26, 1965, in this volume.

conditions I have outlined here. I bid you farewell with the ministry's new motto: "The Budgetary [Finance] System also does business."

Dr. Ernesto Che Guevara

To Pedro Pérez Vega[43]

September 23, 1964
"Year of the Economy"

Pedro Pérez Vega
Finca No. 102
«Mártires de Artemisa»
Artemisa, Pinar del Río

Esteemed Pedro,

I think your idea is correct.

If your news about the salary is correct, I have no objection to your request.

I'm sure you will not fail me. Pay attention in studying the subjects you still need to complete here in Cuba and don't forget that during the year you have here you must continue to lead by example in your work.

Revolutionary greetings,

Homeland or Death. We will win.

Commander Ernesto Che Guevara
cc Ángel Gutiérrez

---

43   Pedro Pérez might have been a foreign student studying in Cuba. Unfortunately, Che's archive does not contain Pérez's original letter.

To Manuel Moreno Fraginals

October 8, 1964

"Year of the Economy"

Compañero Manuel Moreno Fraginals
Avenida 9na. No. 6403 (altos)
Esq. 64 y 66, Marianao

Esteemed compañero,

I am now acknowledging receipt of your book, which you were kind enough to sign and send me.

Not long ago I finished reading the last page. I want to let you know that I cannot recall ever having read a Latin American book like yours that brings together a rigorous Marxist method of analysis, historical meticulousness and passion, which all combine to make it such a thrilling read.

If the other volumes maintain the same quality, I have no fear in stating that *El Ingenio* will become a Cuban classic.

Revolutionary greetings,

Homeland or Death. We will win.

Commander Ernesto Che Guevara

To Charles Bettelheim
October 24, 1964
"Year of the Economy"

Compañero Charles Bettelheim
Sorbonne et 54
Rué de Varenne, Paris 7.

Esteemed compañero,

I received your letter and I am sending you separately the magazines you asked for.

I would be very grateful if I could further discuss with you "our differences."

Although a bit beyond the stage of chaos, perhaps in its first or second day of creation, I have a world of ideas that contradict one another, intertwine and, occasionally, organize themselves. I would very much like to add them to our common polemical material.

Awaiting your visit, I bid you a revolutionary farewell,

Homeland or Death. We will win.

Commander Ernesto Che Guevara

Letter to Fidel Castro[44]

Havana, March 26, 1965

"Year of Agriculture"

Fidel,

[I want to] bring to your attention my thoughts on some of the core problems of the State. I'll try to be as concrete as possible and constructive in my criticism, so that it may serve to address some problems that remain serious.

I would also like to give you a brief explanation of my conception of that entelechy known as "The Budgetary Finance System." I also want to say something about the Party and, finally, make some general recommendations.

So this exposition will have four points:

1. Errors in economic policy

2. The Budgetary Finance System

3. The functioning of the Party[45]

4. General recommendations

---

44 Written by Che Guevara a few days before he left for the Congo, this letter — together with his February 25, 1965, speech in Algeria and his letter to the Uruguayan newspaper *Marcha* (which became known as "Socialism and Man in Cuba") — is one of three texts Che wrote in which he addressed the Cuban Revolution's foreign policy, its ideological development and the problems of the socialist transition, as well as the practical challenges Cuba faced. Che hoped his contributions would aid the subsequent development of the Cuban revolutionary process and other revolutionary processes that might arise in the future.

45 Che is referring here to the United Party of the Socialist Revolution (PURS), the precursor to the Cuban Communist Party which was launched in October 1965.

When we began our apprenticeship in this march toward communism we set up, with the help of the Czechs, the Central Planning Board (JUCEPLAN). I think it's clear to all of us that [central] planning is a condition implicit in socialism and in this period of transition [to socialism] we have now entered. The problem is that so far we have been unable to organize planning in such a way that it acts as a conductive channel, rather than an uncontrollable valve that sometimes allows gases to escape and closes hermetically at other times, with the risk of bursting the boiler.

Despite all the errors in the plan, and despite the erroneous orientation and conception of the Board, I think we all agree that there is a certain chain of command in the economic sphere that must be respected. We agree that the government comes up with the ideas for economic-political development, ideas that emerge from the initiatives of the leaders and also, if circumstances permit, those of the population. They are meant to be submitted to the Board for analysis, to make them mutually compatible and to make a recommendation. The government is meant to approve or amend these figures as the basis for the plan, and the Board is then tasked with drafting the plan in consultation with all the administrative entities, in the case of an annual plan, but on the basis of a strategic plan in which key entities may have an advisory role.

We have been operating as if this fiction were a reality. But what has been happening in practice? The government's supposed transfer of ideas for development was just a compilation of some disconnected ideas that the Board put together, adding its own ideas, and which were then passed back to the government. After an extremely superficial analysis these guidelines for development were approved. Sometimes certain changes were made, always to the annual plan, because the strategic plans had failed prior to being implemented. The Board starts drawing up its plans with the intention of minimizing imbalances, but simultaneously it comes under pressure from all the productive and non-productive units. As a result, the plan becomes unbalanced, it falls behind schedule and we have had to dash off overseas to ask for help, for understanding, etc., etc. The Board then takes it upon itself to complicate things with its own errors.

I think we have made a lot of mistakes of an economic nature. The first of these — the most important — is the improvised way in which we have put our ideas into practice. This has resulted in a zig-zag policy, which I would describe as improvisation and subjectivism. We set targets that could only be achieved on the basis of impossible growth rates. At the beginning, these impossible growth targets were planned organically on the basis of economic modelling that forecast growth rates of up to 15 or 20 percent annually. This changed later, but the dispersion and lack of centralization of economic decision-making allowed every entity to pursue its own plan, the targets of which were achievable in isolation, but which were unrealistic on a broader level. This is why 90 percent fulfillment of a plan is considered a real accomplishment in our country. It is also why a series of unjustified investments has been made, investments that were modified or canceled prior to completion, again without adequate justification. Cases in point are the promotion of rice and its subsequent curtailment; the promotion of corn and its subsequent curtailment; the cases of millet, cotton, hogs and some other livestock investments that seem unjustified to me; investments in fishing and a good part of the poultry policy. All this is in the agricultural sector alone.

We have made similar investment errors in the industrial sector. The Antillana de Acero steel mill, for example, is a monster that we start to sketch beginning, as we always do, with the nose, and then the monster's paws won't fit on the sheet of paper. The cement industry policy, based on a conception of the development of the domestic economy that is very ambitious, has proven unrealistic. We have built factories for the canning industry that are not operational at present. Other factories require raw materials imported from the West and therefore do not actually resolve our problems. The most typical example is the National White Goods Production Industry (INPUD) plant, although in terms of construction and the rationalization of production it's one of the best we have built. But there are countless other examples that we are all aware of and which have the same [problems].

In many cases, there is also [the problem of] obsolete technology, the Polish radios, for example. To top it all off, we were going to make the same mistake with televisions until we put a stop to it. These are all costly investments. Another example is building fishing boats that cannot be justified at present, due to the high price and scarcity of timber. Using iron may be justified, even if our boats cost more than those on the world market, as long as it is accepted as a loss-making venture at present and part of a learning process.

Also under the heading of unjustified investments is the acquisition of container ships when the enterprise lacks the organizational ability to make use of them. The ships, which should have been reducing our hard currency expenditure, have become yet another drain on the coffers while doing almost nothing to resolve problems. While the need for buses was more pressing, the same could be said about the large numbers that were acquired when proper maintenance could have resolved some problems; perhaps we could have bought fewer buses. In the absence of the minimal conditions to acclimatize cattle, the livestock policy has these same pitfalls, as does buying fishing boats in numbers that exceed our organizational ability. There are other, minor cases, such as tourism. We once thought that tourism would be the big source of hard currency and many millions of pesos have been sunk into it.

Erroneous general guidelines have also been adopted. In the industrial sphere, we could cite the policy of import substitution, which was the first policy we implemented, the search for a self-sufficiency that remains illusory for now. We're aware of the mistakes in sugar cane harvesting, and in importing animal feed for cattle and hogs. I also think buying fertilizers at exorbitant prices is the result of an ill-conceived policy. The same is true of prohibiting the export of some traditional products, exports that we could have easily maintained: seafood comes to mind right now, as well as certain kinds of cigars and agave rope.

I insist that even if we divide all these errors into two categories — the more serious and the less serious errors — the core problem is the zig-zag policy, which is the result of a superficial and subjective analysis of all the economy's problems. But the economy has shown that it operates according to certain laws and that breaking these laws is very costly.

We can identify other categories of less serious errors. For example, something that has clearly had a big influence on our economic management at times is the failure to demand the accountability of leadership cadres. They are not monitored and, because of this, they are not criticized in a timely fashion until they suddenly step down at some point. This is one of the big problems faced by the State that I want to take up as well.

We have also seen a free-spending policy that must be corrected immediately and drastically; this has been doing great harm to the economy because we can no longer avoid indiscriminate cost-cutting.

In general, there has been a lack of a conscious approach to the role of organization as the cornerstone of our development strategy. When administrative chaos reaches extreme levels, only then do we start making certain structural changes. Expense accounts are frozen or other actions are taken in the search for solutions, while at other times leadership cadres are dismissed. The latter is a step forward: a good cadre obviously does an infinitely better job than a mediocre or a bad one. But we must also take into account the fact that, no matter how good the cadre is, if the general organizational framework is a hindrance then they can only do so much.

The [various] levels of decision-making are very ill-defined. This has been one of my constant preoccupations during my stint as minister of industry, but we have really only succeeded here up to the level of director and, in some cases, head of department. Further down the hierarchy, at the factory level, there has been a great lack of clarity, which we have resolved through administrative centralization that is often excessive.

In other productive entities the lack of demarcation has, I think, been even greater. But because administrative discipline has also been lacking, anarchy reigns supreme. Individual solutions to novel problems are the order of the day, at times giving rise to a passive, wait-and-see attitude on the part of the productive unit.

All this organizational chaos has been particularly acute in the services sector and in agriculture, where the structural changes have been more far-reaching — at least more far-reaching than those in industry, where the old structure has been retained. In any case, factories have been consolidated, larger productive units have been created while others have been eliminated, but the organizational structure has been retained. In these [new and reorganized productive units] almost everything has had to be changed, with frankly disastrous results to date. For all these reasons, the information hasn't flowed as it should have and, as a result, there has been a total loss of any control. We have sometimes tried to resolve organizational problems with schemas — the famous organizational charts you so despise — without addressing the capability of the cadres, and with a system personnel training that is deficient in many ways. [...]

To all this must be added the errors of the Central Planning Board. As I said, its first mistake was to copy the Czech organizational structure, which the Czechs themselves have now abandoned; but this need not concern us because they have replaced it with one that is far worse and clearly capitalist. What *should* concern us is the fact that we were contemplating exerting an extreme degree of control over a whole series of indices, something the Cuban planning apparatus was incapable of.

As I see it, the Board's role is to elaborate the government's economic policy in a concrete way and to oversee all aspects of the implementation of that policy. How detailed that elaboration can be and how much control can be exerted over its implementation cannot be specified, or at least I cannot specify this concretely, and I think our ignorance in this regard is what has led us to the present state of affairs. But in order for the Board to do these things, it has to have decision-making powers that it has never had, and which it still does not have.

The Board has been unable to direct the economy. We have all seen this inability. I think it has reached a point where that inability has become fatal. But none of us who have served on the Board has been able to organize what I once tried to set up, namely an oversight and analysis body sufficiently serious so that the running of the economy would, at some point, naturally fall into its hands, having proven itself correct through its ongoing work, and through its recommendations and analyses.

The [Economic] Calculus method is now obsolete.[46] The tech-

---

46   A reference to the methodology employed in a rival, Soviet-inspired system of economic management, known as Economic Calculus or Auto-Financing system, in which state enterprises were self-financing and guided by the criterion of profitability. By contrast, in the Budgetary

nological revolution has reached the economy as well: the new mathematical methods [i.e. computers] enable far more profound analyses. Moreover, calculation methods can be borrowed from a good part of the bourgeois economy, methods that the socialist economy has so far ignored and from which it has taken only the most negative and capitalistic methods, such as that of market regulation.

Thus, the Board's economy-wide projections, which were presumptuous and divorced from reality, served only to undermine its own credibility in the eyes of entities that were elaborating their own plans and had their feet on the ground. From the first episode of the 24 million pairs of shoes and the export of a vast amount of timber, projected in the first plan, up to today, the Board has been losing credibility, and the mid-level cadres have now lost all confidence in it. You have no idea of the great lengths to which we have had to go in order to stick to the plans and complete them on schedule, something I have insisted on for all levels of the Ministry [of Industry]. Yet everyone, including me, knew that the plan would be adjusted, even before it was fully implemented, and that's exactly what happened.

Given all this, everyone involved in the management of the national economy, in every sector, feels very disillusioned and their confidence in the central authority is waning. Now, with [the incorporation of President Osvaldo] Dorticós, there have been some qualitative changes with respect to that authority and, what's more, specific changes in terms of its management methods. But this is yet to have an effect, and if there are no structural and conceptual changes (that is, structural changes in accordance with a new concept) grounded in the reality of the country, and if the

---

Finance System advocated by Che state enterprises were funded out of the state budget. These two systems were both operating in different ministries in Cuba at the time.

Board is not given the real executive authority it needs when its job is to draft the plans then nothing much will change.

The Board now receives a very substantial amount of economic data. I know, from my own experience in [the Ministry of] Industry, that this data suffices for in-depth analysis. But the Board's analytical capacity, which has always been very limited, is now almost nonexistent. Then there's the fact that the same body, or rather the same cadres in the upper echelons of the apparatus, are incapable of helping Dorticós to implement the plans, however insignificant they may be. Hyper-individualism and clique politics have completely distorted the structure of the Board, so much so that the key problem is obscured, namely that the Board is ineffectual, disorganized and conflict-ridden. It is so paralyzed that, although paralysis may appear to be the core problem, in reality, the core problem — and that which has a bearing on these secondary questions — is that the Board does not run the economy. That being the case, even though the restructuring of the Board is a good thing, even if it results in improved organization, etc., etc., in no way can it be said that things will improve simply by restructuring the Board as a body.

While it seems correct to me in principle, I can't comment on the new reorganization plans because I don't know enough about them. But I must point out that, important as this is, it's not the key issue. The key issue is the real authority that the body tasked with drafting the plans and overseeing their implementation will have, and its ability to impose its will on those responsible for their implementation.

Some of our most serious mistakes have been made in the Ministry of Foreign Trade [MINCEX]. There's no need to talk about the practical errors, the hard currency shambles that is simply due to the complete disorganization and lack of vision of the Board, the [Central] Bank and, in this case, of MINCEX.

We ourselves have seen MINCEX as an entity whose job it is to export sugar to wherever and to buy things. It's true that sugar is our chief export, but it is precisely this policy that has been blind to our economy's most basic needs. Our economy is an open one; we are maintaining that structure and we'll have to do so for a long time to come. The imported component of industrial inputs is very significant: 19 percent of the [Ministry of] Industry's gross industrial production. So much so that a decline in foreign trade has an immediate impact on industry, on agriculture, on investments, on domestic trade, on transport, etc.

Our weak and distorted industrial base does not allow us to supply the agricultural sector, or the population in general, and [therefore] we must purchase goods on the overseas market. But balance sheets have been nonexistent in revolutionary Cuba; and while the balance-sheet method [of planning] may be described as artisanal, it has its benefits and, as a concept, we must make use of it. We compartmentalized imports and exports: exports were the amounts of sugar we could produce plus the sum total of certain other products that producers, such as INRA and our Ministry [of Industry], wanted to export. Imports were the sum total of the needs of each and every one of the entities that had a certain amount of clout (and almost all of them have had such clout, because almost all of them have had some kind of special plan that must be carried out). Now we are saddled with an enormous debt and, what's worse, a debt for food, for consumer goods and ill-conceived investments. So no matter how much help we get from the [industrial] installations that were built with the loans that incurred the debt, that debt can never be paid back.

Our import capacity declined significantly due to the shortfall in sugar [production], yet we didn't do our utmost to squeeze one more centavo out of everything. MINCEX has pursued a policy of bulk sales to big customers. It totally disregarded the small supplier or consumer which, furthermore, could eventually become a market that would complement our own. In Africa, for example, this can be done, and I think in Europe and in other places as well. But I know that in Africa we could have had small operations that would have been insignificant in comparison to our huge foreign trade figures, but which would have been a step in the right direction.

MINCEX was incapable of long-term planning. It's true that the limitations of the annual trade plans, the most macabre form of economic paralysis that could be imagined, have made its work far more difficult. But it has lacked the agility to create what it belatedly recognizes we needed years ago: a continual flow of essential raw materials, as we have achieved with petroleum, for example, where the problem is now reduced to one of adjusting quantities annually while the basic amounts are already assigned. This can be done with every country in the world; the capitalists also engage in this type of planning.

To sum up: our entire economy has lacked the conception of foreign trade as its bedrock, and all the rest flowed from this.

We need new directives and our first priority must be to make the most of every dollar obtained or saved; [we must] then save as much as we can on freight charges, paying those charges but without squandering resources.

Until now we have not pursued a strict policy of, firstly, seeking ways to replace the [US] dollar with another convertible currency and then analyzing the potential to substitute it domestically.

There is much that MINCEX can do, but not on its own. It must be organized hierarchically and integrated with the administrative apparatus of the domestic economy, with the [Central Planning] Board running the latter in reality rather than just on paper. The method adopted by the Ministry [of Industry], whereby MINCEX can inspect all the tobacco destined for export, should be extended to all relations between the foreign trade apparatus and the domestic economy, and vice versa: the Ministry should be able to inspect MINCEX's external operations and assist it. This system of relations should also be established within the domestic economy itself, so that, for example, the Ministry controls INRA's production of the tobacco required by the Ministry, while INRA does the same for the agricultural machinery, etc., produced by the Ministry for INRA.

I have already discussed unjustified investments, but I also want to draw attention to a specific case that is symptomatic of problems in the economy as a whole and the way in which investments are made. We begin paying for equipment [purchased] from the socialist countries as soon as we sign the contracts. These contracts are honored, the goods are shipped, and then they are stored here, sometimes for years on end, in various warehouses or left out in the open; meanwhile the workforce, for which the equipment or materials were designated, is urgently reassigned to another project at the last minute. Thus, projects are delayed while we pay overseas suppliers for equipment that is used on other projects that, unfortunately, often serve no real purpose. There's no need to cite the examples that we're all aware of. What is important is that there be sufficient discipline not to burden the Ministry of Construction with a single project that is not in the plan, unless it commits to doing it without affecting the projects already in the plan (other than, of course, in the case of a genuine emergency). And let's not forget, too, that people need houses to live in and we're building fewer and fewer houses; we're spending less and less on houses, but the unit cost of houses is going up, so our indices are being continually revised downwards. This state of affairs must change.

I want to turn now to explaining to you, as briefly and succinctly as I can, my ideas on the Budgetary Finance System. These ideas were borne of experience and were later given theoretical form. I will begin with some historical considerations in order to elaborate on my conception.

Marx spoke of two periods on the path to communism: the period of transition, also referred to as socialism or the first stage of communism; and communism, or fully developed communism. He began from the idea that capitalism as a whole was doomed to a total rupture after having reached a level of development in which the productive forces would clash with the relations of production, etc. Although he provided glimpses of this first period called socialism, he didn't dedicate much time to it. But in his *Critique of the Gotha Program*, Marx described it as a system wherein various categories of commodities are suppressed because the level of development indicates that society has reached a new stage. Then came Lenin, with his theory of uneven [and combined] development, his theory of the weakest link in the chain, and the application of this theory to the Soviet Union. With this came a new period Marx had not foreseen: the first transition period or the period of the construction of socialism, which then becomes a socialist society before passing over definitively to a communist society. The Soviets and the Czechs thought they had surpassed this first period; but I believe objectively that this was not the case because some elements of private property continued to exist in the Soviet Union and also in Czechoslovakia.

But that is not the important point here, which is that no one has come up with an anaysis of the political economy of this whole period or studied it. After many years of developing its economy in a certain direction, [the Soviets] rationalized a number of features of Soviet reality and converted them into presumed laws that regulate the functioning of a socialist society. I believe this is where we find one of [the Soviets'] greatest errors. The most important of these, in my view, was when Lenin, pressured by the immense dangers and difficulties confronting the Soviet Union, along with the failure of an economic policy that was extremely difficult to implement, backtracked and established the New Economic Policy (NEP),[47] opening the door once again to former capitalist relations of production. Lenin based his argument on the existence of five aspects of tsarist society inherited by the new state. It is necessary to point out that there were at least two (perhaps three) completely different Lenins: the first, whose story ends precisely at the moment he wrote the last paragraph of *The State and Revolution*, wherein he says that it is far more important to act than to talk; and the later Lenin, who had to confront the real problems [of the revolution in the Soviet Union]. We could say that Lenin had a middle period when he had not yet retracted all the theoretical conceptions that had guided his actions up to the moment of the revolution. In any case, from 1921 onwards, and until shortly before his death, Lenin sets out along the path that led him to the NEP and to moving the whole country in the direction of establishing relations of production that represent what Lenin called state capitalism, but which, in reality, could be described as pre-monopoly capitalism in terms of the nature of economic relations.

In the last period of Lenin's life, if one reads him carefully, a great tension can be observed; there is a most interesting letter [he wrote] to the president of the [state] bank, in which he ridicules its supposed profits and criticizes payments and profits transferred between enterprises (i.e. paperwork simply being passed from one institution to another). This Lenin, who is also overwhelmed by the divisions he can see within the Party, is not confident about the future. Although this is something completely subjective, I get the impression that if Lenin had lived [and been able] to continue

---

47   The Soviet government under Lenin introduced the New Economic Policy in 1921 to assist the country's recovery from the economic devastation caused by the civil war that followed the 1917 revolution.

leading the [revolutionary] process, of which he was a principal actor and over which he had complete authority, he would have rapidly introduced changes to the relations established by the New Economic Policy. In this last period [of Lenin's life], there was often talk about copying some aspects of the capitalism of that era, certain types of exploitation, such as Taylorism, which don't exist today. In reality, Taylorism is nothing more than Stakhanovism: simply piecework, or rather, piecework dressed up with tinsel. This type of payment system was proposed in the first Soviet plan as a supposed creation of Soviet society.

The reality is that the entire legal-economic scaffolding of Soviet society today originated with the New Economic Policy, which maintained old capitalist relations and all the old categories of capitalism, including commodities, bank interest and profit (to a certain extent). Moreover, the direct material interest of workers continues to [be used]. In my view, this entire scaffolding belongs to what we could call, as I have already said, pre-monopoly capitalism. [Modern] management techniques and the concentration of capital were not yet extensive enough in tsarist Russia to allow for the development of big trusts. This was the period of isolated factories, independent units, something that is practically impossible to find in US industry today, for example. Today in the United States, there are only three firms that manufacture automobiles: Ford, General Motors, and a group that includes all the small companies — small in terms of the United States — that have united to try to survive. None of this was happening in Russia back then. But what was the main defect of the whole system? That it limited the possibility of development via capitalist competition but didn't eliminate its categories or impose new, higher categories. Individual material interest is the capitalist weapon *par excellence*, and today the idea is elevated as a lever of development, even though its effectiveness is limited in a society in which the exploitation [of labor] has been abolished. In such conditions, workers do not develop their full productive potential or develop themselves as conscious builders of a new society.

Furthermore, as a consequence of this [reliance on] material interest, it is extended to unproductive sectors and the service industry. This is how the grand marshals with their grand marshal salaries, the bureaucrats, the dachas and the chiefs' cars with their little curtains came about. This is perhaps the justification for the material privileges of the leaders, the beginning of corruption; but in any case, it is consistent with the whole development strategy in which individual incentive is the driving force because it is there, in the individual, where, using direct material interest, the attempt is made to increase production and efficiency.

Moreover, this system encounters serious obstacles that prevent it from becoming automatic; the law of value cannot operate freely because there is no free market where profitable and non-profitable, efficient and inefficient producers compete, and where the inefficient ones die out. It is necessary to provide certain products to the population at affordable prices etc. But when a decision is made to generalize profitability across all units of production, the system of prices changes and new relations are established; the concept of value that exists under capitalism is lost, which, even in its monopoly stage, is fundamentally guided by the market and becomes like a Roman circus where the strongest prevail. In this case, the strongest are those with the most advanced technology. All this led to the rapid development of capitalism and new technology, which is totally alien to the old methods of production. The Soviet Union compares its advances with the United States and shows how they produce more steel, but in the United States development has not been paralyzed.

So what is happening? Steel is simply no longer the

fundamental factor for measuring the efficiency of a country because of the existence of other factors such as chemistry, automation, non-ferrous metals; moreover, we have to look at the quality of the steel being produced. The United States produces less, but produces a large amount of superior quality steel. In the vast majority of sectors of the Soviet economy, technological advances have stalled, relatively speaking. Why? Because they had to invent a mechanism that would operate automatically, establishing a new order in which the market no longer acts implacably as it does in capitalism. But the new mechanisms they came up with to replace [the market] are fossilized mechanisms, and that is where the technological mess begins. Without the ingredient of competition — which has not been substituted by something else following the brilliant successes the new society obtained thanks to the revolutionary spirit that existed in its initial years — technology is no longer the driving force of development.

This does not occur in the branch of defense. Why? Because defense is a sector where the norm of profitability does not operate and where structurally, everything functions in the service of society in order to produce what is required by humans for their survival and the survival of the new society in formation. But here again the mechanism fails; capitalism maintains a strong unity between the defense apparatus and the productive apparatus, it often involves the same companies — in fact, they are twin businesses — and all the big advances obtained in the science of war are immediately passed on as technologies of peace, and consumer goods take truly gigantic steps forward in terms of quality. In the Soviet Union, however, this does not happen; these are two discrete compartments and the military scientific developments have little application to peace.

These errors, excusable in Soviet society, the first to initiate this experiment [with socialism], were transplanted to much more developed, and quite different, societies, leading them down a dead end and provoking reactions from those other states. The first to revolt was Yugoslavia, then came Poland and, in this sense, it is now the turn of Germany and Czechoslovakia, putting to one side Romania, due to its special characteristics. What is happening now? They are rebelling against the system but no one has sought out the root of the problem, which is attributed to the curse of bureaucracy, the excessive centralization of the apparatus. There is resistance against the centralization of the apparatus and enterprises have achieved a certain level of autonomy in their struggle for a free market.

Who is pushing for this? Putting aside ideologues and the technocrats, who analyze the problem from their [theoretical] point of view, the most effective clamor for autonomy comes from the actual units of production. This seems remarkably similar to the struggle capitalists wage against the bourgeois state that controls certain activities. Capitalists agree that the state should have control over some things, such as those services that are not profitable or that benefit the whole country. But the rest should be in private hands. The spirit is the same: the state, objectively, begins to convert itself into a state that manages relations between capitalists. Of course, the law of value is increasingly used to measure efficiency, as the fundamental law of capitalism, a law intimately tied to commodities, the economic cell of capitalism. When commodities and the law of value acquire their full attributes, a readjustment occurs in the economy in accordance with the efficiency of the different sectors and units, and those sectors or units that are not efficient enough disappear.

Factories close and Yugoslav (and now Polish) workers emigrate to those countries in Western Europe experiencing a full economic expansion. They are the slaves that the socialist countries send as an offering to the technological development of the European Common Market.

We want our system to advance along two fundamental lines in order to reach communism. Communism is a phenomenon of consciousness: you cannot get there by leaping into the void, changing the quality of production or through a simple clash between productive forces and the relations of production. Communism is a phenomenon of consciousness and we must develop this consciousness among the people, which is why individual and collective education is an essential part of communism. Economically speaking, we cannot talk in quantitative terms. Perhaps we may be in a position to reach communism within a few years, before the United States moves away from capitalism. We cannot measure the possibility of attaining communism in terms of per capita income; there is no complete correlation between income and the communist society. China will take hundreds of years to reach the per capita income of the United States. Despite this, we believe that per capita income is an abstraction; measuring the median salary of the United States worker, even if we include the unemployed, even if we include Blacks, even then this level of lifestyle is so high that it will cost the majority of our countries a great deal to reach that level. Yet, we are advancing toward communism.

The other aspect is that of technology; consciousness plus production of material goods is communism. Fine, but what is production if not the increasing use of technology, and what is the increasing use of technology if not the product of an increasingly fabulous concentration of capital, that is, the ever greater concentration of fixed capital or dead labor in relation to variable capital or living labor. This phenomenon is occurring in developed capitalism, imperialism. Imperialism has not succumbed thanks to its capacity to extract profits and resources from dependent countries and by exporting conflicts and contradictions to them, due to its alliance with its working class against the rest of the dependent countries. In developed capitalism, we find the technological seeds of socialism much more than in the old system of Economic Calculus[48] that is, in turn, the heir of a form of capitalism that has already been surpassed but which, nevertheless, has been taken as a model for socialist development. We should, therefore, take a look in the mirror, where we will see reflected a series of correct methods of production that still don't clash with the relations of production. Some might argue that this is due to the existence of the imperialism on a world scale; but nevertheless, this would allow for some corrections to our system and we are only speaking here in general terms. To give you an idea of the extraordinary practical difference that exists today between capitalism and socialism, just look at the case of automation: while in capitalist countries automation is advancing at an extremely rapid pace, the socialist countries are lagging a long way behind. We could argue about various problems that the capitalists will have to confront in the near future due to workers' struggles against unemployment, something that is very real; but it is also true that, today, capitalism is developing much more rapidly along that path [of automation] than socialism.

If, for example, Standard Oil needs to remodel a factory, it will halt production and provide compensation to its workers. The factory is closed for a year, the new equipment is installed and production begins again with greater efficiency. What happens in the Soviet Union? The Academy of Science has hundreds and perhaps thousands of projects for automation that cannot be put into practice because factory directors cannot allow themselves the luxury of failing to meet their annual plan. And because this is a problem related to fulfilling plans, if a factory is automated,

---

48   The Economic Calculus (or Auto-Financing) system was the economic management system adopted in the Soviet Union and the socialist camp of Eastern Europe.

it will be asked to produce more, which fundamentally works against increasing productivity. Of course, this could be solved, from a practical point of view, by giving automated factories greater incentives; this is Libermann's system and it is the system they are starting to implement in the Democratic Republic of [East] Germany; but all this shows the level of subjectivism into which one can fall and the lack of technical precision when it comes to managing the economy. The harsh blows of reality need to be felt before we begin to change; and we always prefer to change the form, that which is most clearly visible as being negative, rather than tackle the real essence of all the difficulties that exist today, which is this false conception of the communist human being based on a long-established economic practice that tends, and will always tend, to convert humans into little more than numbers in the production process through the lever of material interest.

On the technical side of things, our system tries to adopt the most advanced aspects of capitalism and therefore tends towards centralization. This centralization is not absolute; to implement it intelligently it should be applied in accordance with what is possible. We could say: centralize as far as possibilities allow; this is what should guide our actions. This allows for savings when it comes to administration, labor; it allows for a better utilization of equipment based on existing technology. We cannot build a shoe factory in Havana that will distribute this product to the whole republic if there is a problem with transportation. The utilization of a factory, its optimum size, will be determined by an analysis of technical-economic factors.

We are trying to eliminate capitalist categories as far as possible. As such, we don't consider the transportation of a product between socialist factories as an act of commerce. For this to be efficient, we have to restructure prices. I have written about this, and I don't have anything more to add to the little I have written, except to say that more research should be done on this issue.[49]

In summary, our goal is to eliminate capitalist categories — commodity exchange between enterprises, bank interest, direct material interest as a motivating force, etc. — and adopt the latest administrative and technological advances of capitalism.

You might say that all our aspirations equate to wanting to have an Empire State Building here because the United States has one. Of course, we cannot have an Empire State Building but, nevertheless, we can have many of the advances that created US skyscrapers and the technology used to build those skyscrapers, even if ours are smaller. We cannot have a General Motors that has more employees than all the workers in the Ministry of Industry combined, but we can have an organization and, in fact, we have one, that is similar to General Motors. Technology plays a role in the matter of administrative methods: technology and administrative methods have constantly changed. Although intimately linked throughout the whole process of the development of capitalism, under socialism [technology and administration] have become totally divorced from each other, and one of them has remained completely static. And when gross technical errors in administration were eventually identified, the solution discovered was capitalism.

To reiterate: the two main problems challenging us, in terms of our Budgetary System, are the creation of the communist human being and the creation of a communist material milieu, two pillars united by the edifice they support.

There's a big gap in our system: how do we get people to

---

49   See the following articles "Sobre la concepción del valor," "Sobre el Sistema Presupuesto de Financiamiento," "La banca, el crédito y el socialismo" and "La planificación socialista" published in *Nuestra Industria económica y Cuba Socialista* in 1963-1964 and in *El Gran Debate* (Ocean Sur, new edition, 2017).

identify with their work so that it's no longer necessary to use what I myself call material disincentives? How to make every worker feel the vital necessity to aid their revolution and, at the same time, how to make work a pleasure? How to make them feel as all of us in the leadership feel?

If the people cannot grasp the bigger picture and we can only ever get the person in charge, the one capable of running a project, to take an interest in the work they do, then we will never be able to get a lathe operator or a secretary to work with enthusiasm. If the solution were to lie in that same worker being offered material incentives, then we would be going about things the wrong way.

It's true that as things stand people do not fully identify with their work, and I think there's some truth to the criticism levelled at us, although not the ideological content of that criticism. That is, we are criticized because the workers don't participate in drafting the plans, in the administration of the state enterprises, etc. This is true. But [our critics] conclude that this is because the workers have no material interest [in what they produce] and therefore shun responsibility for production. The remedy is seen as having the workers run the factories and take financial responsibility for them, by making their incentives and disincentives dependent on their managerial performance. To me, this is the crux of the matter. I think it's a mistake to expect the workers to run the enterprises. Someone has to run the enterprise, someone representating all the others, if you like, but as a representative of everyone in terms of their designated role, in terms of the responsibility or honor bestowed on them, but not as a representative of the whole enterprise against the larger enterprise — the State — in an antagonistic way. When planning is centralized, as it should be, the rational utilization of each of the various elements of production is very important, and what is produced cannot depend on a workers' council or on the opinion of one worker. Clearly, the less well-informed the top and intermediate levels of the planning apparatus are, the more useful is the workers' initiative from a practical point of view.

This is the reality, but we have also learned two things from experience that I regard as axiomatic: a well-placed technical cadre can do far more than all the workers in a factory; and a managerial cadre in a factory can make it function completely differently in many ways. There are countless examples of this and we know of such cases in every sector of the economy, not just in the Ministry of Industry. The problem can be posed in another way: how is it that a managerial cadre can change everything? Why is it that they do work of a technical nature, that is, administrative work, better than all their employees as a group, or how is it that they can get all the employees to participate in such a way that they feel differently about their work, with a new enthusiasm, or with a combination of these two things? I still haven't found the answers and I think we need to study this further. The answer must be inseparably linked to the political economy of this period, and these questions must be grappled with in a holistic way that is consistent with political economy.

How to get the workers to participate? This is a question I haven't been able to answer. I consider this as my greatest stumbling block and my greatest failure, and it's one of the things we need to think about because it's bound up with the problem of the Party and the State, with the relationship between the Party and the State.

Now to the third point I wanted to address: the role of the [Cuban Communist] Party and the State.[50]

So far our poor party has been like one of those wind-up Soviet

---

50   A process was initiated after the 1959 revolution to unite all revolutionary parties (the July 26 Movement, the Revolutionary Directorate and the Popular Socialist Party) in a single organization as the Cuban Communist Party, which was formally created in October 1965.

soldier dolls with a cord you pull. It started walking Soviet-style: like a good doll, it began to strut about of its own accord until it crashed into the crockery and we solved the problem by removing the cord. Now it's stuck in a corner but we're trying to reanimate this doll by moving one leg and then another. I dare say that at any moment now it will break another piece of porcelain, because there are deep-seated problems which have not been adequately addressed and which hinder its development.

In my conception, the Party is an apparatus with a dual nature. It is both the ideological engine of the Revolution and its most efficient oversight mechanism. It is the ideological engine by virtue of the fact that the Party and its members must take the government's key guidelines and transform them, at every level, into directives for the relevant bodies and individuals. The Party [must act as] an oversight apparatus in the sense that its grassroots committees and its leadership bodies, to a greater degree at each successive level, are able to tell the government what is really going on about everything that isn't conveyed in statistics or economic analyses, such as morale, discipline, leadership methods, public opinion, etc.

To play its role as an ideological engine, the Party and every member must act as the vanguard, and this means that their conduct must approximate that of the communist ideal. Their standard of living — the standard of living of the Party member, whether they are party functionaries or workplace cadres — should never exceed that of their colleagues. A communist's morality is their most prized possession, their true weapon, so it must be cherished, even in their private life. The practical aspect of this, namely how the Party should uphold individual morality, is one of the thorniest problems. But naturally, there is no place for thieves, opportunists or Pharisees in the Party, regardless of past merit.

In this period the revolutionary cadre, with their moral virtues as their calling card, must apply themselves to the vital task of consciousness-raising in the three most important spheres: education, both technical and cultural, that is, a deepening of consciousness; the country's defense, both military and ideological; and all aspects of production. In defending these three essential spheres and leading by example, they must participate in all national plans, aligning their own priorities with those of the government.

All this must be in the context of a ceaseless struggle against the tendency to bureaucratize the Party, turning it into yet another governmental mechanism of statistical oversight or an organ of executive power or a parliamentary body, with lots of people on the payroll and lots of driving around in jeeps, lots of meetings, etc., etc.

The Party cadres must be trained to carry out their oversight role. Naturally, the Party must have its own organization, separate from the State, even when there is occasionally a number of positions that combine Party and State functions.

Our immediate tasks are selecting the mid-level cadres extracted from the Party base by methods similar to those employed in the selection of the lower-level cadres and restructuring the national leadership, making changes in line with our current thinking.

One of the first tasks of the Party must be to analyze is its own relations with Administration at all levels. What kind of relationship will it have with the [national] Government? How will the provincial party leaderships relate to the provincial governments or to the Coordination, Execution and Inspection Council (JUCEI), and how will the regional party bodies and base committees relate to their respective governmental counterparts? This is probably the fundamental task, the key point of the discussion, and if we can clear this up we will have already laid the foundation for the entire apparatus to move forward.

So far I've made a number of observations of a general nature, positive and negative, but which contribute nothing toward solving the problem. I think we must implement a series of concrete measures that enable the Party to play its role. One of the key points, it seems to me, is to proceed with the selection of the mid-level cadres and with the restructuring of the Organizational Secretariat to give it real executive power over all professional cadres in relation to all the tasks involved in organizing the Party. This can be done quickly and we can come up with a system to propose to the secretariat, transferring all mid-level cadres who don't measure up to jobs in production. At the same time, we have to give some thought to cadre development; and for cadre to develop they must have an understanding of the Party's central role. If we accept my conception of a communist [cadre], then we must establish strict systems of discipline, oversight and self-criticism that enable us to remove the dead wood from the Party.

The key tasks of the nation should be prioritized, along with the key tasks of the administrative entities. The Party should assume responsibility for a range of these tasks. In the industrial sector, I'm talking about vanguard groups, vanguard workers who go to the most backward factories. The communists should be paid their regular wage or the average wage, not a wage bonus.

All communists, regardless of their role in the Party, should be willing to relocate to any part of Cuba at the Party's request. This means, for example, that a communist who is a Havana-based accountant is duty-bound to relocate to Nicaro [in eastern Cuba] at the Party's request, making it clear that this is their obligation as a Party member, not as a functionary. We should establish a continual review process of Party members in regular assemblies to accept new candidates as members and to get rid of any old ones who don't come up to scratch. In cases where their deficiencies are not so serious, they should be made candidate members of the Party.

The Organizational Secretariat should draft an organizational plan for the Party as a whole, but divided into two parts, one of which covers the provincial leadership level down, so that, if we are unable to proceed with the proposed restructure under current conditions, we can begin to do some serious work from the provincial leadership level down. We should set up a commission for this work, headed by the Organizational Secretary and with the participation of members from the provinces, either one member from each province or someone chosen by the provinces to represent them all.

The Party should appoint a small group of compañeros to draft some provisional Party statutes, to regulate its functioning until the convening of a congress that will make a final decision on the Party program. The relationship between the Party and the Union of Young Communists needs to be formalized. We should also set up a joint commission comprising either Party members who are also administrators, or Party members and members of the Administration. This commission would define relationships between the Party and Administration from the ministerial level down.

Some of these proposals could be discussed by the base committees first, while others could go straight to the higher levels.

I think the most important tasks are the following:

- Adopt the conception of what a communist [cadre] should be, whatever that conception may be or whatever parameters are established.

- Launch the discussion on Party-Administration relations.

- Determine the Party's functions — whether they are what I propose, namely an ideological engine and an oversight apparatus, or others that might be decided on — and adopt a methodology that allows us to divide the work into two parts.

Even if the Party remains chaotic in some ways, it can establish a firm foundation at the grass-roots level.

That is pretty much all I have to say about the Party, which is little more than an appeal for investigation, always in the framework of my overriding concern: the creation of the new human being.

I have even less to say about the State. I think this is the biggest mess of all, but I also think we have to make a systematic effort to tackle it. I think the system we have set up for the administrative restructure, the struggle against bureaucratism, etc., is fundamentally flawed. We are once again falling into the trap of sketching someone by starting with the nose, without seeing the bigger picture. If the [Central Planning] Board is the body tasked with compiling statistics and the administrative entities are also assigned this role, then a regional commission cannot change the models decided on centrally. We have been unable to rationalize further because we come up against either a series of bureaucratic limitations or demands made by the Board, or indiscipline. It would be better to involve the Party in this and work systematically from the top down. The Party's base committees can, if they wish, analyze all the necessary measures. The analysis should then proceed to the top levels of the Party making a final recommendation at the end, rather than taking action at the outset.

The proposal to restructure the Board makes sense to me logically, but I don't know whether it's correct conceptually, from the standpoint of the character of the State during the first period of the [socialist] transition. This begs the question of what the communist human being will be like and, therefore, how that person should be developed and, on the other hand, the political economy of this period, and thus the character of the structure that is based on that political economy. We need to establish a serious research base capable of coming up with answers to these very complex questions, and we need to begin to build up a new Socialist State that is nothing like the existing ones. But that's all I know about this topic: I'll leave it here with this degree of vagueness.

I'll try to be concrete now in this section on general recommendations.

Political Economy: I think a small group should devote itself to studying the political economy of this [transition] period, but we cannot wait for them or imagine that it will be an easy conundrum for them to solve. There are probably very few people in Cuba, if any, who are capable of doing this work, because historically only a few people have ever studied it, and Marx was perhaps the only one who did so comprehensively.

It can be shown, however, that there are various concepts in political economy regarding the urgent tasks, on which we can focus. The most important of these is to "globalize," in the positive sense of the word, our aspirations. I think that if enthusiasm is tempered a little by reality and we do a comparative analysis with other countries, and if we don't succumb to another attempt to achieve annual growth rates of 15 or 20 percent, then we can think about what we want to achieve by 1980. On this basis, we can work out what we will need to produce, what we'll need to import, how much we'll have to spend on productive and non-productive investments respectively, and we can answer the biggest question of them all: can we do it with our current methods and with the degree of economic development we have today? Yes or no?

There are some analyses, done by compañeros in [the Ministry of] Industry, that suggest we can't do it. These are preliminary analyses, I'm not sure if you'll want to read them. They suggest we can't achieve an adequate development by 1980 solely on the basis of cattle ranching and sugar cane, that we will have to do something else as well. That something is industry.

How much can we spend on industry and which industries? How much on services, transportation, etc.? This is not the place to put numbers on these things, all I want to do is advocate methods. This should take no more than a day to give us an overall picture. We can then analyze the obvious things, such as the fact that there are not as many markets for meat products as has been suggested; various capitalist countries have protectionist laws that prevent the unlimited sale of products and the prices of some processed beef products are not forecast to rise significantly over the next few years; moreover, this requires huge investments, and investments in this area come at the expense of investments elsewhere.

In other words, we must make an elementary assessment of our needs and our desires. If we were able to do this just once and stick to a plan of action that does not have to be minutely detailed, we could then adopt long-term development guidelines for the domestic economy with five-year plans that can be far more detailed. The first five-year plan, for 1966–1970 doesn't really exist, but is based on a number of contractual commitments and will be largely agricultural. We will have to make the big shift [to an industry-oriented plan] after 1970. I say this most sincerely (for what it's worth): if we focus solely on agriculture and agro-industry then we're doomed when it comes to the real possibilities of achieving balanced development and becoming a rich country.

We must invest in industry, including the most advanced industries. We must have a mechanical industry base that is sufficently solid, and at least a rudimentary metallurgical industry. We have to do this. We must devote ourselves to petrochemicals, sugar, basic chemical industries, including fertilizers. We must apply chemistry to everything we possibly can. We must automate, which is the only way to compete. We must address the disturbing lack of preventive maintenance.

By doing all these things, plus laying the basis for effective geological exploration, developing agricultural machinery wherever possible, mechanical industries such as ship building — on a shoestring budget, and with education that is accelerated, ongoing and linked to these objectives — we can go a long way. If we do nothing along these lines, then from 1970 Cuba will once again have unemployment problems.

There are urgent tasks that must be carried out. Perhaps one of the most important is to establish guidelines for the [Central Planning] Board once and for all, to give it some real and indisputable authority, at least in terms of the annual plans. Let nobody go beyond strict limits without considering special plans. We need to gradually extend the Budgetary Finance System to agriculture; this would be the ideal way to resolve a great many of the problems that we face, as long as the cadres are honest and the workers are aware of what needs to be done. We must reexamine the problems we're having with prices and, along with prices, wages. This is going to explode at some point if we don't watch out. It's not an explosive situation right now, but discontent is brewing in certain industrial regions where wages have been frozen while rural wages are rising. We must adhere to a policy of extreme caution regarding investments, a single well-thought-out policy based on a single plan of a single entity, overseen by the Board.

[Commander] Osmany [Cienfuegos] said something very sensible the other day: we delay public works in order to send people to cut sugar cane, yet the entity responsible for cane cutting keeps its own workforce busy with its own construction projects. These things continue to happen.

At the very least, we need to restructure all administrative entities on the basis of a single plan led by the Board. We then need to adopt certain general guidelines so that we can clean up a whole series of murky relations between entities, horizontal and vertical relations, etc. It's important, as I said, that the Party's role be clearly defined: if it cannot be involved in everything, then it should at least play a major role at certain lower levels, more or less consistently throughout the country. [We must] start educating party cadres in philosophy in a broader sense, including more advanced Marxist humanism. This is not a matter of labelling a position in a debate as either correct or incorrect, but rather of participating in study circles or at least studying compilations of documents, trying to analyze what the debate is about. [Let's] turn the Party cadres into thinking beings, not only in terms of our country's reality but also in relation to Marxist theory, which is not an ornament but an outstanding guide to action. (The cadres aren't familiar with Trosky [sic] or Stalin but they have already dogmatically decided both are "bad.") [We should] put an end to dogmatism and apologetics and abide by one and the same Party discipline in all Party bodies (I'm thinking of *Hoy* here).[51]

Develop a coherent education policy in line with everything we want to achieve, coherent at every level and consistent with our goals.

The same principle should apply in foreign affairs.

I think these are the most important things. I also believe I've said nothing new. I get the feeling this is a bit of a waste of time for everyone, since I have copies of other letters I have written along these lines and nothing much has really changed, certainly nothing of importance. However, some big administrative advances have now been made, and some leadership changes may improve the apparatus and create more confidence in it. […]

We can make a great deal of progress in this way. Maybe we didn't correct mistakes in a timely fashion, but it's sometimes best to slow things down a bit and not correct them immediately

---

51   *Hoy* was the newspaper of the former communist party in Cuba, the Popular Socialist Party.

without considering the possibility that we might be committing a new error.

My criticisms here are grounded in our long-standing friendship and in my appreciation and admiration for you, and in my unconditional loyalty to you.

This is such a long letter that I'm not sure you'll get this far.

Homeland or Death.

[Unsigned]

LETTERS FROM AFAR:
THE CONGO AND BOLIVIA
(1965-1967)

Introduction

"Once again, I feel the ribs of Rocinante[1] beneath my heals," Che writes to his parents in 1965. As had been his intention from the moment he signed on to join the 1956 *Granma* expedition to Cuba and throw in his lot with the Cuban people in their struggle against the Batista dictatorship, Che had his eyes set on extending the revolutionary movement to continental Latin America, beginning in Bolivia.[2] But first, he would lead a Cuban contingent to aid the revolutionary movement in the Congo, Africa, in 1965.[3]

After writing up his Congo diary in Tanzania, where his partner Aleida joined him for a few weeks, Che returns clandestinely to Cuba in March 1966 in order to train the group of guerrilla combatants who will accompany him to Bolivia. He leaves Cuba in November 1966.

This new period of Che's life sees a revival of his youthful peripatetic spirit, but now as a committed revolutionary leader. He is driven to share everything he has learned from his experiences

---

1   Rocinante was Don Quixote's horse.
2   See Ernesto Che Guevara, *The Bolivian Diary* (Seven Stories Press, 2021)
3   See Ernesto Che Guevara, *Congo Diary: Episodes of the Revolutionary War in the Congo* (Seven Stories Press, 2021).

as a leader of the Cuban Revolution and his constant study of everything from political economy to philosophy, expressed in letters to some of his closest revolutionary collaborators, such as Fidel Castro and Armando Hart, which are published here for the first time.

In these last letters, aware he has not always been able to adequately express his affection or emotions, Che feels a need to convey his deepest thoughts, his hopes and dreams, his love and admiration for his partner Aleida and their young children, his parents, Fidel and other Cuban compañeros. Che writes to Aleida from Bolivia in 1967, saying he desperately misses his "only one" and that the "star-filled sky" reminds him of "how little [he] had taken from life in a personal sense."

These letters sometimes surprisingly echo the yearnings and personal anxieties of his youth, while, at the same time, expressing his satisfaction that he has lived his life true to his convictions.

To Aleida March
[No date]

My darling,

This might be my last letter for some time. I'm thinking of you and the little pieces of my flesh I left behind. This situation gives me a lot of time for reflection, in spite of everything.

I won't send you the ring because I don't think it's appropriate to spend money on that, now that we need it so much.

I will send you something from my next stop. For the moment, I'm sending you passionate kisses capable of melting your cold heart, and you can divide one kiss into little pieces for the children. Give the in-laws and the rest of the family more modest ones. To the newlyweds [my niece], a hug and the recommendation that they name their first child Ramón.

In the tropical nights I'll be returning to my old and poorly executed trade as a poet (maybe not in composition but at least in my mind), and you will be the only protagonist.

Don't give up your studies. Work hard and remember me now and then.

A final, passionate kiss, with no rhetoric, from your

Ramón[4]

---

4   Che used a passport in the name of Ramón Benítez to travel undercover to Africa in 1965.

To my children

My dearest Hildita, Aleidita, Camilo, Celia and Ernesto,

If you ever have to read this letter, it will be because I am no longer with you. You will hardly remember me, and the littlest ones will not remember me at all.

Your papa has been a man who acted on his beliefs and has certainly been loyal to his convictions. Grow up as good revolutionaries. Study hard so that you can master technology, which allows us to master nature. Remember that the Revolution is what is important, and each one of us, alone, is worth nothing.

Above all, always be capable of feeling deeply any injustice committed against anyone, anywhere in the world. This is the most beautiful quality in a revolutionary.

Until forever, my children. I still hope to see you. A great big kiss and a great big hug from

Papa

To my parents

Dear *Viejos* [old folks],

Once again, I feel the ribs of Rocinante beneath my heels and I'm back on the road with my shield on my arm.

Almost 10 years ago, I wrote you another farewell letter. As I recall, I lamented not being a better soldier and a better doctor. The latter no longer interests me and I'm not such a bad soldier.

Nothing has changed in essence, except that now I am much more conscious, my Marxism has taken root and become purified. I believe in armed struggle as the only solution for those peoples who fight for their liberation, and I act according to my beliefs. Many will call me an adventurer, and that I am — only one of a different type: one who risks his neck to prove his truths.

It's possible that this may be the end. I don't seek it, but it's within the logical realm of probabilities. If it should be so, here's a final embrace.

I have loved you very much, only I haven't known how to express my affection. I am extremely rigid in my actions, and I think that sometimes you didn't understand me. It was not easy to understand me, but nevertheless, please believe me today.

Now a willpower I have polished with an artist's delight will sustain some shaky legs and some weary lungs. I'll do it.

Give a thought once in a while to this little soldier of fortune of the 20th century.

A kiss to Celia, to Roberto, Ana María and Patotín [Juan

Martín], to Beatriz, to everyone. For you, a big embrace from your prodigal and recalcitrant son,

Ernesto

To Carlos Rafael Rodríguez[5]

[1965]

Carlos,

I sit in Rocinante's stirrups to send you greetings.

Other souls will illuminate my theories and make them accessible, but I have the impression that they will feel as if something is missing when there's no one to discuss them with.

I bid you farewell as always: If I am right, we can win a war like this one (and we will win).

I embrace you,

Che

---

5   At the time of the polemic about political economy that took place in Cuba and internationally in the 1960s, Carlos Rafael Rodríguez was president of INRA (the National Institute of Agrarian Reform). See also footnote 29, p. 250.

To Fidel Castro[6]

Havana, April 1, 1965

Fidel,

At this moment I remember many things — when I met you in María Antonia's house [in Mexico], when you proposed I come along, all the tensions involved in the preparations.[7]

One day, they came by to ask who should be notified in case of death, and the real possibility of that fact struck us all. Later we knew that it was indeed the case, that in a revolution (if it is a genuine revolution) one either wins or dies.

Many compañeros fell along the way to victory. Today everything has a less dramatic tone because we are more mature, but the situation is repeated now. I feel that I have fulfilled the part of my duty that tied me to the Cuban Revolution in its territory, and I now take my leave of you, the compañeros, your people, who now are mine.

I formally resign my responsibilities in the leadership of the

---

6　This letter was read by Fidel Castro at a public ceremony presenting the Central Committee of the newly created Cuban Communist Party on October 3, 1965. In the presence of Che's partner Aleida, Fidel announced he was "going to read a letter, handwritten and later typed, from Ernesto Guevara, which is self-explanatory…. The letter is undated because it was to have been read at the most opportune moment, but it was actually sent on April 1 of this year." The reading of this letter was the first public explanation of the circumstances of Che's absence from Cuba, which at the time was the subject of much speculation.

7　A reference to the preparations for the expedition from Mexico on board the cabin cruiser *Granma* to launch the armed struggle against the Batista dictatorship in Cuba.

Party, my post as minister, my rank of commander, and my Cuban citizenship. Nothing legally binds me to Cuba, only ties of another kind — those that cannot be broken as can an appointment to a post.

Recalling my past life, I believe I have worked with sufficient honesty and dedication to consolidate the revolutionary triumph

My only serious failing was not having had more confidence in you from the first moments in the Sierra Maestra, and not having understood quickly enough your qualities as a leader and a revolutionary.

I have lived magnificent days, and at your side I have felt the pride of belonging to our people in the brilliant yet sad days of the Caribbean [October Missile] crisis. Seldom has a statesman been more brilliant than you in those days. I am also proud of having followed you without hesitation, identified with your way of thinking and of seeing and appraising dangers and principles.

Other nations of the world call for my modest efforts. I can do that which is denied you because of your responsibility at the helm of Cuba, and the time has come for us to part.

I want it known that I do so with a mixture of joy and sorrow. I leave here the dearest of my loved ones and the purest of my hopes as someone seeking to build a new society. And I leave a people who received me as a son. That lacerates a part of my spirit. I carry to new battlefronts the faith that you taught me, the revolutionary spirit of my people, the feeling of fulfilling the most sacred of duties: to fight against imperialism wherever it may be. This gives comfort and heals the deepest wounds.

I state once more that I free Cuba from any responsibility, except that which stems from its example. If my final hour finds me under other skies, my last thought will be of this people and especially of you. I'm thankful for your teaching, your example, and I will try to be faithful up to the final consequences of my acts.

I have always been identified with the foreign policy of our Revolution, and I continue to be. Wherever I am, I will feel the responsibility of being a Cuban revolutionary, and I shall behave as such. I am not sorry that I leave nothing material to my children and my wife; I am happy it is that way. I ask nothing for them, as the state will provide them with enough to live on and educate them.

I would have many things to say to you and to our people, but I feel they are unnecessary. Words cannot express what I would want them to, and I don't think it's worthwhile to keep scribbling pages.

¡*Hasta la victoria siempre*! [Until victory always!]

Homeland or Death!

I embrace you with all my revolutionary fervor.

Che

To Fidel Castro[8]

Congo, October 5, 1965

Dear Fidel,

I received your letter, which has stirred contradictory feelings in me, because in the name of proletarian internationalism, we are committing errors that may prove very costly. I am also personally worried that, either because I have failed to write with sufficient seriousness or because you don't fully understand me, it may be thought that I am suffering from the terrible disease of unwarranted pessimism.

When your Greek gift [Tembo][9] arrived here, he told me that one of my letters had given the impression of a condemned gladiator, and the minister, in conveying your optimistic message, confirmed the opinion that you were forming. You will be able to speak at length with the bearer of this letter, who will give you his first-hand impressions after visiting much of the front; for this reason, I'll dispense with anecdotes. I'll just tell you that, according to those close to me here, I have lost my reputation for objectivity by maintaining an unfounded optimism in the face of the actual situation. I can assure you that were it not for me this beautiful dream would have catastrophically collapsed in a heap.

---

8   For a full account of the 1965 Cuban mission in Africa, see Guevara, *Congo Diary*, op.cit.

9   "Tembo" (Swahili for elephant) was the pseudonym of Emilio Aragones, a member of the Central Committee of the Cuban Communist Party. José Ramón Machado Ventura (1930–) was Minister of Public Health in Cuba (1960–1968) and today is a member of the Political Bureau of the Cuban Communist Party. He had met with Che in the Congo the day before (October 4).

In my previous letters, I asked that not so many people should be sent but only cadres; there is no real lack of weapons here, except for a few special ones; on the contrary, there are too many armed men; what we lack are soldiers. I particularly warned that no more money should be handed out unless it was with an eyedropper and after many requests.

None of these things have been taken into consideration, and incredible plans have been made that threaten to discredit us internationally and may put me in a very difficult position.

I will now explain:

Soumialot and his compañeros have been leading you all down the garden path. It would be tedious to list the huge number of lies they have spun, and it is preferable to explain the present situation by the attached map. There are two zones where something like an organized revolution exists: the area where we are based and part of Kasai province where Mulele is based — a great unknown. In the rest of the country there are disparate bands living in the forest; they lost everything without a fight, just as they lost Stanleyville without a fight. More serious, however, is the way in which the groups in this area — the only one with contacts on the outside — relate to one another. The differences between Kabila and Soumialot are becoming more serious all the time and are used as a pretext to keep handing over towns without a fight. I know Kabila well enough not to have any illusions in him. I cannot say the same about Soumialot, but I have some indications such as the string of lies he has been spinning, the fact that he doesn't bother to come to these godforsaken parts, his frequent drunken sprees in Dar es-Salaam, where he lives in the best hotels, and the kind of allies he has chosen to unite with against the other group. Recently a group from the Tshombist army landed in the Baraka area, where a major-general loyal to Soumialot has no fewer than 1,000 armed men, and they captured this strategically important point almost without a fight. Now they are arguing about who was to blame: those who failed to put up a fight, or those at the Lake [Base] who didn't send enough ammunition. The fact is that they shamelessly ran away, ditching in the swamp a 75 mm. recoilless cannon and two 82 mm. mortars; all the men assigned to these weapons have disappeared, and now they are asking me for Cubans to get them back from wherever they are — no one knows quite where — and to use them in battle. Moreover, they are doing nothing to defend Fizi, 36 kilometers from here; they don't want to dig trenches on the only access road through the mountains. This will give you some idea of the situation. As for the need for a careful selection of men rather than sending me large numbers, you and the commissar assure me that the men here are good and I'm sure most of them are, otherwise they would have quit long ago. But the fact is one has to be really easy going to put up with the way things are here. It's not good men but supermen that are required...

And I still have my 200; believe me, right now they would do more harm than good, unless we make a definitive decision to fight alone, in which case we'll need a division and we'll have to see how many divisions the enemy puts up against us. Maybe that's a bit of an exaggeration; maybe a battalion would be enough to get back to the frontiers we had when we arrived here in order to threaten Albertville. But numbers are not what counts; we can't by ourselves liberate a country that does not want to fight; you have to create a fighting spirit and find soldiers with the torch of Diogenes and the patience of Job — a task that becomes more difficult, the more fools there are messing everything up along the way.

The question of the launches deserves a separate mention. For some time, I have been requesting a couple of mechanics to prevent the dock at Kigoma from becoming even more of a cemetery for broken-down boats. Of the three brand-new Soviet launches that

arrived a little over a month ago, two are already out of service
and the third, in which the emissary crossed the lake, is in bad
shape. The three Italian launches will go the same way unless they
have a Cuban crew. But this and the artillery business require the
acquiescence of Tanzania, which will not be easy to obtain. These
countries, unlike Cuba, are not going to stake everything on a
single card, however big, and the card being played right now is
feeble. I have given the emissary the task of clarifying how much
support the friendly government is prepared to offer. You should
know that almost everything that came on the ship has been
impounded in Tanzania, and the emissary will also have to talk to
them about that.

The business with the money is what pains me most because
of the repeated warnings I have given. At the height of my
"spending spree" and only after they had made a big fuss, I
committed to supply one front (the most important one) on
condition that I would lead the struggle and form a special
mixed column under my direct command, in accordance with
the strategy that I had outlined and communicated to them. With
a very heavy heart, I calculated it would need $5,000 a month. I
now learn that 20 times that sum is given to people who are just
passing through, so that they can live it up in all the capitals of
Africa, with no acknowledgment of the fact that they receive free
board and lodging and often also their travel costs from the main
progressive countries. Not a cent will reach the wretched front
where the peasants suffer every imaginable misery, including
the rapaciousness of their own protectors; nor will anything get
through to the poor devils stuck in Sudan. (Whiskey and women
are not expenses covered by friendly governments, and they cost a
lot if you want quality.)

Finally, 50 doctors would give the liberated area of the Congo
an enviable ratio of one per 1,000 inhabitants, a level surpassed

only by the Soviet Union, the United States and two or three of the most advanced countries in the world. But they are distributed according to political allegiance without the least consideration given to the organization of public health. Instead of this gigantism, it would be better to send a contingent of revolutionary doctors augmented as I requested by some very experienced nurses of a similar caliber.

The attached map summarizes the military situation, so I'll limit myself to a few recommendations that I ask you all to consider objectively: forget all the men in charge of phantom groups; train up to 100 cadres (not necessarily all Black [Afro-] Cubans) and choose from Osmany [Cienfuegos]'s list plus whoever stands out most over there. As for weapons: the new bazooka, percussion caps with their own power supply, a bit of R-4 and nothing else for the moment; forget about the rifles, which won't solve anything unless they are automatic. Our mortars must be in Tanzania, and with those — plus a new complement of men to operate them — we would have more than enough for now. Forget about Burundi and tactfully discuss the question of the launches (not forgetting that Tanzania is an independent country and we must play fair there, leaving aside the little problem I caused). Send the mechanics as soon as possible, along with someone who can navigate across the lake reasonably safely; this has been discussed and Tanzania has agreed. Let me handle the problem of the doctors by giving some to Tanzania. Don't make the mistake again of handing out money in such a manner, for they cling to me when they feel hard up and definitely ignore me if the money is flowing freely. Trust my judgment a little and don't go by appearances. Shake up those in charge of providing truthful information because they are not capable of untangling this mess and paint utopian pictures which have nothing to do with reality.

I have tried to be explicit and objective, precise and truthful. Do you believe me?

A hug.

To Armando Hart
December 4, 1965

To Armando Hart[10]
[Africa]
December 4, 1965

My dear secretary,

My congratulations for the opportunity they have given you to be God: you have six days for it. Before you finish and sit down to rest (unless you choose the wise road of the God before you, who rested earlier), I want to suggest a few small ideas about [developing] the culture of our vanguard and of our people in general.

In this long vacation period, I have had my nose buried in philosophy, something I've wanted to do for some time. I came across the first problem: nothing is published in Cuba, if we exclude the Soviet bricks that have the drawback of not letting you think because the party has already done it for you, and all you have to do is digest it. In terms of methodology, it is as anti-Marxist as can be and, moreover, the books tend to be very bad. Second, and no less important, was my ignorance of philosophical language (I fought hard with maestro Hegel and in the first round I twice bit the dust). So, I made a study plan for myself, which I think could be considered and improved a lot, but it might constitute

---

10   At the time this letter was written Armando Hart had just been appointed Organizational Secretary of the newly formed Cuban Communist Party.

the basis for a real school of thought. We've achieved a lot but someday we'll have to think. My idea is a reading plan, naturally, but it could be expanded to bringing out a series of publications by Editora Política [the party publishing house].

If you take a look at your publications, you'll see the profusion of Soviet and French writers. This is because of the ease of obtaining translations and also ideological parrotry. This is not how to offer a Marxist culture to the people, or teach Marxism, which is necessary if the presentation is good (not the case), but it is insufficient.

My [study] plan is this:

I.   Philosophical classics

II. Great dialecticians and materialists

III. Modern philosophers

IV. Classics in economics and their precursors

V.   Marx and Marxist thought

VI   Socialist construction

VII. Unorthodox thinkers and capitalists

VIII. Polemics

Each series would be independent of the others and the program could be as follows:

I. Take the well-known classics that are already translated into Spanish, adding a serious introduction by a philosopher, a Marxist if possible, and a full explanatory vocabulary. A dictionary of philosophical terms would be published simultaneously, along with some history of philosophy. This could be Dennyk's [Dynnik] and also Hegel's. Publication could be in a certain selective chronological order; in other words, start with one or two books of the greatest thinkers and continue the series through to the modern period, then go back to the past with other less important philosophers, and build on this with the tomes of the more representative ones, etc.

II. The same general model could be followed here, with compilations of some of the ancients (some time ago I read a study published in Argentina that included Democritus, Heraclitus and Leucippus).

III. The most representative modern philosophers could be published here, accompanied by serious and detailed studies by the experts (not necessarily Cuban) with the corresponding criticism of the perspective of idealism.

IV. This is being done now, but unsystematically and lacking the basic works of Marx. Here it would be necessary to publish the complete works of Marx and Engels, Lenin, Stalin and other great Marxists. For example, nobody has read anything of Rosa Luxemburg, who may have made some errors in her criticism of Marx (Volume III) before she was assassinated, but her instincts regarding imperialism are better than ours in some respects. There is also a notable absence of Marxist thinkers who later went off the rails, like Kautsky and Hilfering (not spelled like that [Hilferding]) who did make a contribution, and many contemporary Marxists, who are not exactly scholars.

V. Socialist construction. Books that deal with specific problems, not just of present leaders, but also of the past, with a serious scrutiny of the contributions of philosophers, and especially of economists and statisticians.

VI. Here would come the great revisionists (you can have Khrushchev here if you want), properly analyzed and, you should also have, in more depth than any other, your friend Trotsky, who, it seems, did exist and did write. Also, the great theorists of capitalism, like Marshall, Keynes, Schumpeter, etc. These should also be carefully analyzed with explanations of the whys.

VII. As the heading suggests, this is the most polemical part, but that's how Marxist thought has advanced. Proudhon wrote *The Philosophy of Poverty* and we know it exists because of [Marx's] *Poverty of Philosophy*. A critical edition might shed some light on the period and Marx's own development, which was not yet complete. Robertus and Dühring belong to this period, and then came the revisionists and the big controversies of 1920 in the Soviet Union, which are perhaps the most important for us.

Now I can see that I skipped one section so the order's changed (my pen is flying here).

It would be Series IV, the classics on economics and their precursors, which would include Adam Smith, the physiocrats, etc.

It's a gigantic job but Cuba deserves it and I think it can be attempted. I won't bother you anymore with this chatter. I've written to you because I don't know much about the people who are presently responsible for ideological orientation and it may not be prudent to write to them for other reasons (not just ideological parrotry, which also counts).

So, my illustrious colleague (in the philosophical sense), I wish you success. I hope we can meet on the seventh day. A hug to the huggables, including one from me to your dear and feisty better half [Haydée Santamaría].

R[amón]

To Aleida March
[from the Congo, 1965]

To my only one in the world (I've borrowed this phrase from old Hikmet),[11]

What miracle have you performed with my poor old shell that I no longer want a real hug and just dream of the concave space in which you comfort me, your smell and your rough rural caresses?

This is another Sierra Maestra, but without the same sense of constructing something or the satisfaction of making it my own. Everything happens very slowly here, as if war was something to be done the day after next. For now, your fear of me being killed is as unfounded as your feelings of jealousy.

My work involves teaching several classes of French every day, learning Swahili and providing medical care. Within a few days, I'll begin the serious work of training. A sort of Minas del Frio[12] from the war, not the one we visited together.

Give a tender kiss to each child (including Hildita).

Take a photo with all of them and send it to me. Not too big and another little one. Study French in preference to nursing and love me.

A long kiss, like our kiss when we are reunited.

I love you,

Tatu[13]

---

11   The Turkish poet Nazim Hikmet was one of Che's favorite poets.
12   Minas del Frio was the guerrilla training camp set up during the revolutionary war in Cuba.
13   "Tatu" (meaning "three" in Swahili) was Che Guevara's *nom de guerre* in the Congo.

To Hilda Beatriz Guevara Gadea[14]
February 15, 1966

Hildita darling,

I am writing you now, although you'll receive this letter much later. But I want you to know I am thinking about you and I hope you're having a very happy birthday. You are almost a woman now, and I cannot write to you the way I do to the little ones, telling them silly things or little fibs. You must know I am still far away and will be gone for quite some time, doing what I can to fight against our enemies. Not that it is such a big thing, but I am doing something, and I think you will always be able to be proud of your papa, as I am of you.

Remember, there are still many years of struggle ahead, and even when you are a woman, you will have to play your part in the struggle. Meanwhile, you have to prepare yourself, and always be ready to support just causes. Furthermore, obey your mother and don't think you know it all too soon. That will come with time.

You should fight to be among the best in school. The best in every sense, and you already know what that means as far as study and revolutionary attitude are concerned. In other words: good conduct, seriousness, love for the Revolution, comradeship, etc. I was not that way at your age, but I lived in a different society, where man was an enemy of man. Now you have the privilege of living in another era and you must be worthy of it.

---

14   This letter was sent to Che's eldest daughter, the child of his first marriage to Hilda Gadea, on her 10th birthday.

Don't forget to go by the house to keep an eye on the other kids and advise them to study and behave themselves. Especially Aleidita, who pays a lot of attention to you as her older sister.

So, *Vieja* [old lady], again, I hope you are very happy on your birthday. Give a hug to your mother and to Gina and receive a great big strong one to last for as long as it is until we see each other, from your

Papa

To Haydée Santamaría[15]

[Approximately July-November 1966]

Dear Yeyé,

Armando and Guillermo have told me about your tribulations. I respect and understand your decision, but I would have liked to have hugged you personally instead of writing this letter. The security precautions here have been very strict, and this has made it impossible for me to see many of the people I love (I am not as cold as I sometimes seem).[16] I'm now seeing Cuba almost as if I'm a foreigner coming to visit, seeing everything from a different angle. And despite my isolation, this makes me understand the impression that visitors come away with.

Thank you for the medical-literary parcels. I see you've become a woman of letters with the power of creation, but I confess that the way I like to think of you best is that one day, early in the new year, with all your fuses blown, firing volleys for miles around. This image and those from [the days in] the Sierra (even our battles of those days are dear in my memory) are the ones of you I will

---

15   Haydée Santamaría (1922–1980) had participated in the attack on the Moncada barracks in July 1953 and later was a combatant in the Rebel Army. After the revolution, she became head of the important cultural institution, Casa de las Américas.

16   Che returned to Cuba clandestinely in July 1966 to begin training the group of Cuban guerrilla fighters who would be going to Bolivia. The training camp was established at San Andrés, in Pinar del Rio (in the western part of the island). Haydée had evidently asked to come and see Che at the camp before he left for Bolivia

privately treasure. The affection and determination of all of you will help us in the difficult times that are approaching.

Your colleague, who loves you

To Aleida March[17]

Bolivia, December 1966

My only one,

I'm taking advantage of a friend's trip to send you these words. Of course, this could be posted, but it is more intimate to use the "unofficial" route. I could say that I miss you to the point where I can no longer sleep, but I know you wouldn't believe me, so I won't tell you that. There are days when I feel so homesick, it takes a complete hold over me. Especially at Christmas and New Year, you can't imagine how much I miss your ritual tears, under a star-filled sky that reminds me how little I have taken from life in a personal sense […].

I can say nothing interesting about my life here. I like the work, but it is tiring and excludes all else. I study when I have time, and occasionally I dream. I play chess with no serious opponents and I walk a great deal. I am losing weight, partly from longing, and partly from the work. Give a kiss to the little pieces of my flesh and blood and to the others. For you, a kiss filled with sighs and sorrow from your poor, bald

Husband

---

17   This was the last letter Aleida received from Che in Bolivia. It was delivered by Juan Pablo Chang ("El Chino") after he visited the guerrilla camp in Ñancahuazú on December 2, 1966, before he too joined the guerrilla column in Bolivia.

To my children

[From somewhere in Bolivia, 1966]

My dearest Aliusha, Camilo, Celita and Tatico,

I write to you from far away and in great haste, which means I can't tell you about my latest adventures. It's a pity, because they've been very interesting, and Pepe the Crocodile has introduced me to many new friends.[18] I'll tell you all about this another time.

Right now I want to tell you that I love you all very much and I think about you all the time, along with mama, although I really only know the littlest ones through photos, as you were very tiny when I left. I'm going to get a photo taken soon so that you can see what I look like these days — a little older and uglier.

This letter should arrive about the time Aliusha has her sixth birthday, so let it serve to congratulate her and hope that she has a very happy birthday.

Aliusha, you should study hard and help your mother in every way you can. Remember, you are the oldest.

Camilo, you should swear less because you shouldn't speak like that in school and you must learn what is appropriate.

Celita, help your grandmother around the house as much as you can and continue being as sweet as when we said goodbye — do you remember? How could you not?

Tatico, you should grow and become a man so that later we'll see what you make of yourself. If imperialism still exists, we'll set

---

18 Che used to entertain his children with stories about an imaginary character, Pepe el Caimán [Pepe the Crocodile].

out to fight it. If it is finished, you, Camilo and I will take a vacation on the moon.

Give a kiss from me to your grandparents, to Myriam and her baby, to Estela and Carmita, and here's an elephant-sized kiss from

Papa

PS To Hildita, another elephant-sized kiss and tell her I'll write to her.

APPENDICES:
LETTERS WRITTEN TO CHE GUEVARA

From Juan Almeida[1]

Sierra Maestra, December 20, 1957

Che

As Ramirito has probably already told you, the commander has not been able to personally write to you as he is currently writing the manifesto, which will be released as soon as possible, responding to the pact that you know about.[2] I can tell you that it is formidable; it has filled those of us on this side with happiness, so you can imagine how the other side will take it. In my very modest opinion, it will feel to them like a total bombardment. Armando [Hart] has been here the whole time. But he also has been hit by some shrapnel, or rather, some fragments from the bomb.

You will already know by now that we ordered an attack on Veguita. We were unsuccessful due to negligence on the part of

---

1   Juan Almeida (1927-2009) participated in the 1953 attack on the Moncada barracks and was captured and imprisoned. He joined the *Granma* expedition in 1956 and attained the rank of commander as head of Column Three in the revolutionary war. He became a central leader of the revolutionary government after 1959.

2   The pact referred to in this letter, and the following letters to Che from Celia Sánchez and Armando Hart, was the Miami Pact was signed on October 15, 1957, by former President Carlos Prío and other Authentic Party politicians opposed to the Batista dictatorship, establishing a Liberation Junta in exile. It supposedly included the leadership of the July 26 Movement but this was vociferously repudiated by Fidel Castro on December 14, 1957.

those responsible for throwing the grenades and Molotov cocktails. I don't know if what they say is true, but nevertheless they didn't use them and that was enough for everything to turn out bad. Guerrita was injured on the ankle when the shots began. In the end, everything turned out badly. I believe that we didn't have full control over the personnel. There are still five men missing from that attack.

We are sending the Mexican[3] back to you. I hope he is not the great charlatan that I think he is. He has brought a mess with him from which even he doesn't know how to extricate himself. We gave him $200 peso to get rid of him; it seems he wanted to live the good life in Mexico with our money. He takes advantage of others, he wants so many things that you have to send him back down the same path he came. I am telling you about the money so that he doesn't try to give you the traditional "backhander," as he already tried that with us.

Well Che, that is more or less the report for the day.

With nothing more to say,

Your brother,
Almeida

---

3   Francisco Rodríguez ("the Mexican") was a captain in the Rebel Army who later betrayed the revolution.

From Celia Sánchez[4]

Sierra Maestra

December 13, 1957

Dear Che,

Some three weeks ago we received the painful news that the revolution had been handed over to Prío [Carlos Prío Socarrás] and his gang of politicians.[5] Today we heard the bad news about your foot injury. All of this means we have to get our strength back and fight the National Guard and our National Directorate [of the July 26 Movement urban underground]. I've written them three strong letters stressing that all of us in the Sierra disagree with them. I can't wait for the letter from Fidel to the Unit putting on record his and our position. For the time being we have to forget about them and continue killing soldiers and burning cane. In spite of your wounded foot, we are confident you will recover soon from all this pain and carry on your brave struggle as usual.

On the news from the interior [central Cuba] about burning cane, it appears a lot has been burnt, but…the National Directorate, especially René [Ramos Latour], is responsible for not carrying out the slogan, "No sugar harvest with Batista." When he left here, we agreed that the date would be November 12. This wouldn't

---

4   Celia Sánchez (1920–1980) led the amnesty campaign for the Moncada prisoners and was a key leader of the July 26 Movement in Oriente province. She ultimately joined the guerrillas in the Sierra Maestra and became a member of Fidel Castro's general staff.

5   Cuban President Carlos Prío Socarrás went into exile in the United States after he was overthrown in Batista's coup on March 10, 1952.

have allowed time to get the sugar mills running. So, the National Guard would have spread their forces to the mills and wouldn't have focused on the Sierra. And this is what led to the loss of Ciro [Redondo García] and Juanito. All we can do is to accept all this and continue the struggle.

A big hug for your troops and one for you. With all our admiration.

[Signature illegible]

From Armando Hart[6]

Sierra Maestra, December 25, 1957

My most admired Che,

I write this second note after receiving the one that you sent Daniel [René Ramos Latour] and his response. I regret even more not having gone to see you days ago, but believe me, we've had to deal with a thousand things and my presence outside is becoming indispensable.

I am sure that a conversation between us would solve a thousand problems, even your proper and legitimate doctrinal concerns in relation to us.

But I must say to you that, in addition to being insulting, you have been unjust. That you think that we are rightists or from the native petit bourgeoisie or, more accurately, that we represent that class, is logical and doesn't surprise me because it is in keeping with your interpretation of the historical process of the Russian Revolution. But in the end we've had no option but to undertake this small national revolution, because the guides of the world proletariat transformed the powerful explosion of 1917 into a nationalist revolution that took up first of all — something very

---

6   This draft letter was published in January 1958, in a Cuban newspaper after it was found on Armando Hart, a leader of the urban underground of the July 26 Movement, when he was captured. Hart explained years later that the letter had been written in the context of an intense exchange of ideas and opinions between two revolutionaries about tactics rather than strategy. See Hart's foreword to Ernesto Che Guevara, *Diary of a Combatant*, op. cit.

legitimate for the Russians — a liberation movement against tsarist feudalism. But they left the people situated outside that country without the opportunity of unleashing a universal revolution that perhaps will now arrive by an unexpected route.

The worst thing about this is that Stalin wasn't French, English or German, and therefore he did not go beyond the limits of being a Russian ruler. Had he been born in Paris perhaps he would not have viewed the world so narrowly.

I repeat, none of this is our fault, but is due to the political incapacity to evaluate this situation on the part of the real geniuses of the October Revolution.

What does make me a little angry is your lack of understanding in relation to our attitude to a pact that we were always going to reject. As soon as I reach Santiago, I will send you all the documents about this. I want to say, dear Che, that if there might be differences in the international aspect of revolutionary policy, I am to be found among the most radical in terms of the political outlook of our Revolution.

We rejected the [Miami] Pact and insisted that they comply with our points. We did not make this public because at that time it would have created confusion among the people, so we waited to exhaust the possibility that they might accept our points and then to discuss with Fidel the need for a public rejection. And we felt great satisfaction when we saw that Fidel was publicly adopting positions that were identical to ours. We also felt satisfied when in Miami one of the signers of the Sierra Manifesto,[7] Raúl Chibás, said that what we were raising encompassed his points also. We felt further satisfaction in seeing that there was complete agreement

---

7   Sierra Manifesto had been released on July 12, 1957, outlining a revolutionary program for the struggle against Batista. For further reading, see Guevara, *Reminiscences of the Cuban Revolutionary War*, op. cit.

between "the leftist leader of the petit bourgeoisie" and the petit bourgeoisie that you say we embody.

I do want to tell you that I am happy to be considered petit bourgeois because my conscience is clear and such jibes don't affect me. [This is because] I have been the one person within the Movement who has most devoted himself to organizing workers, so that they can become the determining force in our revolution. If we have gone down the wrong path, I ask that you point out to me the correct one. But never identify me with people who for 25 years dominated the CTC [Federation of Cuban Workers] and were not able to unleash the great social revolution for which I'll struggle to the very end.

Yours, with respect,

Jacinto

From Camilo Cienfuegos
April 24, 1958

Che, soul brother,

I received your note. I see that Fidel has made you head of the military school.[8] I'm happy with this because it means we are guaranteed top-class soldiers in the future. When they told me that you were coming to "grace us with your presence," I wasn't very pleased. You've played the leading role in this struggle. While we need you in this stage of the insurrection, Cuba will need you even more when the war is over. So, the Giant [Fidel] is doing the right thing to look after you.

I would love to be always by your side. For a long time you were my commander, and will always continue to be. Thanks to you I have the chance to be more useful. I'll do whatever it takes not to let you down.

Your eternal *chicharrón,*[9]

Camilo

---

8   This was the guerrilla training school established in Minas del Frío during the revolutionary war.

9   Literally, curly or pork crackling, a Cuban delicacy.

From Fidel Castro "To the Rebels of Las Villas"[10]
Sierra Maestra, October 2, 1958

We have received with great joy the news that a group of Cubans is also fighting in this province.

Whatever the revolutionary militancy of this group, we have given instructions to the [July 26] Movement to provide them with any help they can.

We would like to know what condition you find yourselves in. There is little we can directly do for you from so far away, but we hope to express to you our most sincere solidarity.

We consider it to be of value to the struggle against the dictatorship to maintain this battle front at all cost. We can imagine the initial obstacles you are facing. If the topography of the areas makes it impossible to resist or the tree cover runs out, we would suggest moving in this direction, hiking at night and hiding during the day in places where planes cannot see you, traveling along a zig-zag route.

After the enemy has fallen into your trap once or twice, it will stop hounding you, and you will be able to advance some 20 to 30 kilometers each night. We have placed a patrol between Bayamo and Victoria de las Tunas that could provide you with a point of contact with us. We will try to intensify our campaign with the aim of alleviating pressure on you.

The messenger can provide you with details and experiences

---

10   Che Guevara was leading the "invasion" of Las Villas province from the Sierra Maestra.

of interest. We will wait for news. We hope for the success of this front and send a fraternal embrace to its brave combatants.

Fidel Castro

From Lidia Doce to Che[11]

[No date]

My dear Commander,

How are you? Do you still remember me? Well I haven't been able to stop thinking of you for one moment, always waiting for the mail to see if you've written to me. I think you've already received the camera and are pleased with me. I want to remind you of something, perhaps you've forgotten. In Las Vegas [de Jibacoa] you offered me a pistol, and I think you forgot. I need it now here in Havana because I don't have one. When are you going to send for me?

I'm waiting for you, my dear commander. I hope you get the uniforms as I didn't know where to send them. I'm still fighting, although I'm unhappy because I don't have my commander here to give me orders, or to know what to do. So I am organizing women. It's called the July 26 Women's Group. What do you think? I have a lot of work. It's too much for me on my own because, since [Delio Gómez] Ochoa left [for the mountains], I've been very much on my own. Tell me if you received what I requested in Bayamo, that is, plates, pots and everything you need in your command post.

But for God's sake, send for me soon! Because I want to see you and give you a big hug just as you deserve, even if I don't.

---

11   Lidia Doce Sánchez (1912–1958) was a courier for the guerrillas during the revolutionary war. Just days after she wrote this letter on September 12, 1958, Lidia was captured, tortured and killed, along with Clodomira Acosta Ferrals (1937–1958), while they were on a mission to Havana. Che dedicated a story to both women in his *Reminiscences of the Cuban Revolutionary War*, op. cit.

Send my warm regards to Guile [Israel Pardo Guerra] and Miguel [Álvarez]. I've got a ferocious German puppy for you. Its parents are champions from New York. Would you like it? I hope so.

As always, with respect and the strongest embrace.

Yours always,

Lidia

Letter from Raúl Roa[12]

Havana, December 19, 1963

Che,

Although greatly delayed, I am sending you a copy of the [recently published] English version of your book *Guerrilla Warfare*.

If you like, I could use my good relations with Mao to ask them to publish 600 million copies in the language of Lao Tzu.[13]

An embrace from

Raúl Roa

---

12   Raúl Roa [1907–1982] was an intellectual and politician, who served as Cuba's Foreign Minister from 1959 to 1979.

13   Lao Tzu was an ancient Chinese philosopher.

ERNESTO GUEVARA DE LA SERNA was born in Rosario, Argentina, on June 14, 1928. During his medical studies in Buenos Aires, he took a trip with his friend Alberto Granado on an old Norton motorcycle through all of Latin America, the basis for *The Motorcycle Diaries*. After he completed his medical degree, he took a second trip throughout the continent. Living in Guatemala in 1954 — then under the elected government of Jacobo Árbenz — he became involved in political activity there and was an eyewitness to the overthrow of that government in a CIA-organized military operation. Forced to leave Guatemala, Guevara went to Mexico City and linked up with exiled Cuban revolutionaries and met Fidel Castro in 1955. Guevara joined an expedition to Cuba that began in the Sierra Maestra mountains. He was originally the troop doctor and became Rebel Army commander in July 1957. Following the rebels' victory on January 1, 1959, Guevara became a key leader of the new revolutionary government. In September 1959 he began serving as head of the Department of Industry of the National Institute of Agrarian Reform; in November 1959 he became president of the National Bank; and in February 1961 he became minister of industry. He was also a central leader of the political organization that in 1965 became the Communist Party of Cuba.

ALEIDA GUEVARA is the eldest of Che Guevara's four children with Aleida March. Like her father before her, she is a physician and a champion of human rights. She specializes in pediatrics and lives in Havana, Cuba.

MARÍA DEL CARMEN ARIET GARCÍA has a doctorate in history and is a world-renown scholar of the works of Ernesto Che Guevara. She played a leading role in the research that led to the discovery of Che's remains in Bolivia in 1997. She now coordinates the work of the Che Guevara Studies Center in Havana. Her other published books include *El Pensamiento Político de Ernesto Che Guevara, Che Guevara: Fases integradoras du su proyecto de cambio social* and *Resonancias de futuro: Para leer al Che*.

DISAMIS ARCIA MUÑOZ (editor) is a researcher with the Che Guevara Studies Center in Havana.

The Motorcycle Diaries: Notes on a Latin American Journey
Introductions by Walter Salles and Cintio Vitier
Foreword by Aleida Guevara
"The enormity of our endeavor escaped us in those moments; all we could see was the dust on the road ahead and ourselves on the bike, devouring kilometers in our flight northward," wrote a young Ernesto Guevara as he and his buddy Alberto Granado hit the road on a vintage Norton motorcycle to discover Latin America.

This is his lively and highly entertaining diary of that adventure, featuring exclusive, unpublished photos taken by the 23-year-old Argentine medical student on his journey across a continent, and a tender foreword by Aleida Guevara offering an insightful perspective on her father—the man and the icon. (July 2021). ISBN: 978-1-64421-068-0

The Bolivian Diary
Introduction by Fidel Castro
Foreword by Camilo Guevara
Che's account of the fateful Bolivia mission that attempted to spark a continent-wide revolution. This is Che Guevara's last diary, compiled from the notebooks discovered when he was captured and executed by the Bolivian army in October 1967. It became an instant bestseller. This newly revised edition has an insightful preface by Che's eldest son Camilo, a chronology, maps, and 32 pages of rare or unpublished photos. (December 2021). ISBN: 978-1-64421-074-1

Congo Diary: Episodes of the Revolutionary War in the Congo
Foreword by Aleida Guevara
Introductions by Gabriel García Márquez and Roberto Saviano
Che Guevara's intriguing account of the revolutionary war in the Congo, filling in the missing chapter in his life. Prior to his fateful mission to Bolivia, in 1965 Che led a secret Cuban force that went to aid the African national liberation movement against the Belgian colonialists, after the assassination of Patrice Lumumba by the CIA. (October 2021). ISBN: 978-1-64421-072-7

I Embrace You with All My Revolutionary Fervor: Letters 1947–1967

Foreword by Aleida Guevara

Ernesto Che Guevara was a voyager—and thus a letter writer—for his entire adult life. The letters collected here range from letters home during his *Motorcycle Diaries* trip, to the long letter to Fidel after the success of the Cuban revolution in early 1959, from the most personal to the intensely political, revealing someone who not only thought deeply about everything he encountered, but for whom the process of social transformation was a constant companion from his youth until shortly before his death. His letters give us Che the son, the friend, the lover, the guerrilla fighter, the political leader, the philosopher, the poet. Che in these letters is often playful, funny, sometimes sarcastic, and deeply affectionate. His life was short, and these twenty years, from when he was nineteen until days before his death, show it was also incredibly rich and full. (October 2021). ISBN: 978-1-64421-095-6

Latin America Diaries:
The Sequel to *The Motorcycle Diaries*

This sequel to *The Motorcycle Diaries* includes letters, poetry, and journalism that document young Ernesto Guevara's second Latin American journey following his graduation from medical school in 1953. It reveals how the young Argentine is transformed into a militant revolutionary, ready to commit himself to the guerrilla struggle Fidel Castro and his compañeros are about to launch in Cuba against the dictatorship of General Fulgencio Batista. (August 2023). ISBN: 978-1-64421-100-7

Reminiscences of the Cuban Revolutionary War

Foreword by Aleida Guevara

Originally published a series of articles for Cuban papers, this thoroughly revised edition includes for the first time corrections made by Che himself to his diary on which he based the essays. This book also includes a foreword by Che's daughter Aleidita about how her parents met during the revolutionary war and 32 pages of photos and maps of the guerrilla campaign. (August 2023). ISBN: 978-1-64421-107-6

Che Guevara Reader:
Writings on Politics & Revolution

Edited by David Deutschmann and María del Carmen Ariet García

Recognized as one of *Time*'s "icons of the 20th century," Che Guevara became a legend in his own time and has now reemerged as a symbol of a new generation of political activists. Far more than a guerrilla strategist, Che Guevara made a profound and lasting contribution to revolutionary theory and Marxist humanism as demonstrated in this bestselling book. (February 2022). ISBN: 978-1-64421-112-0

Global Justice: Three Essays on Liberation and Socialism
Introduction by María del Carmen Ariet García
Is there an alternative to the corporate globalization and militarism that is ravaging our planet? These classic works by Ernesto Che Guevara present a revolutionary view of a different world in which human solidarity and understanding replace imperialist aggression and exploitation. (October 2023). ISBN: 978-1-64421-156-4

Guerrilla Warfare: Authoritative, Revised New Edition
Foreword by Harry "Pombo" Villegas
A bestselling classic for decades, this is Che Guevara's own incisive analysis of the Cuban revolution—a text studied by his admirers and adversaries alike. Although often regarded as a "manual" for guerrilla warfare, this book is primarily a political account of what happened in Cuba and why, explaining how a small group of dedicated fighters grew in strength with the support of the Cuban people, overcoming their limitations to defeat the US-backed dictator's army. He also analyzes why the Cuban revolution attained a "continental and international transcendence." (October 2023). ISBN: 978-1-64421-146-5

The Awakening of Latin America
Edited by María del Carmen Ariet García
In a letter to his mother in 1954, a young Ernesto Guevara wrote, "The Americas will be the theater of my adventures in a way that is much more significant than I would have believed." In *The Awakening of Latin America* we have the story of those adventures, charting Che's evolution from an impressionable young medical student to the "heroic guerrilla," assassinated in cold blood in Bolivia. Spanning seventeen years, this anthology draws on from his family's personal archives and offers the best of Che's writing: examples of his journalism, essays, speeches, letters, and even poems. As Che documents his early travels through Latin America, his involvement in the Guatemalan and Cuban revolutions, and his rise to international prominence under Fidel Castro, we see how his fervent commitment to social justice shaped and was shaped by the continent he called home.

Nearly half of this book is published for the first time and pre-dates Che's arrival in Cuba with Fidel Castro's guerrilla expedition in 1956. Also included are his notes for his unfinished book, *The Social Role of Doctors in Latin America*. (August 2023). ISBN: 978-1-64421-164-9